WITHIN REACH?

Managing Chemical Risks in Small Enterprises

David Walters

Professor of Work Environment
Cardiff Work Environment Research Centre
Cardiff University

Work, Health, and Environment Series
***Series Editors*: Charles Levenstein, Robert Forrant, and John Wooding**

Routledge
Taylor & Francis Group

LONDON AND NEW YORK

First published 2008 by Baywood Publishing Company, Inc.

2 Park Square, Milton Park, Abingdon, Oxon OX14 4RN
711 Third Avenue, New York, NY 10017, USA

First issued in paperback 2017

Routledge is an imprint of the Taylor & Francis Group, an informa business

Copyright © 2008 Taylor & Francis

Library of Congress Catalog Number: 2007040997
ISBN 13: 978-0-89503-347-5 (hbk)

Library of Congress Cataloging-in-Publication Data

Walters, David, 1950-
   Within REACH? : managing chemical risks in small enterprises / David Walters.
      p. ; cm. -- (Work, health and environment series)
   Includes bibliographical references and index.
   ISBN 978-0-89503-347-5 (cloth : alk. paper) 1. Industrial safety--European Union countries. 2. Hazardous substances--Risk assessment--European Union countries. 3. Hazardous substances--Safety regulations--European Union countries. I. Title. II. Series.
   [DNLM: 1. REACH (System) 2. European Union. 3. Hazardous Substances--Europe. 4. Occupational Health--Europe. 5. Occupational Diseases--prevention & control--Europe. 6. Occupational Exposure--prevention & control--Europe. 7. Risk Management--Europe. 8. Workplace--Europe. WA 465 W231w 2008]

   T55.3.H3W366 2008
   363.17094--dc22   2007040997

ISBN 978-0-89503-347-5 (hbk)
ISBN 978-0-415-78440-5 (pbk)

Table of Contents

List of Tables

List of Boxes and Figures

Acknowledgments

This book is based on the findings of a study that was made possible by the financial support of the Long Range Research Initiative (LRI) of the European Chemical Industry (CEFIC). The study was undertaken by a team of researchers from six EU countries. I would like to acknowledge the considerable contribution made to the original research project by my colleagues in Austria, Germany, the Netherlands, Spain, Sweden and the UK. In particular I would like to thank Ann-Beth Antonsson for information on Sweden, Howard Fidderman for the UK, Mat Jongen for the Netherlands, Günther Kittel for Austria, and Henning Wriedt for Germany. I would also like to thank all these colleagues for their continuing help and advice during the course of writing this volume and for their constructive comments on early drafts.

Each national research group or individual produced a country report on which I have drawn extensively for the material included in the following pages. Some of these reports have been published separately and are available on the Web sites of the national research organizations. Their details are included in the References section. A previously published article based on the same study, "The Efficacy of Strategies for Chemical Risk Management in Small Enterprises in Europe: Evidence for Success?" in *Policy and Practice in Health and Safety*, Vol. 4, No. 1, pp. 81-116, has also been used in the following pages.

This book also draws some of its material from an earlier study financed by the UK Health and Safety Executive (HSE). A full report of this previous study entitled "The Role of Occupational Exposure Limits in the Health and Safety Systems of EU Member States," HSE Research Report 172, was published by the HSE in 2003. The book *Beyond Limits? Dealing with Chemical Risks at Work in Europe*, which was based on this earlier study, is also referred to in the following pages.

I am grateful to Louise Deeley for her help in producing some of the figures in the present volume and to Hazel Slavin for many stylistic corrections and helpful editorial suggestions.

While acknowledging the help of all these sources, the responsibility for the content and views expressed in the following pages and any inaccuracies or misrepresentations therein remain my own.

INTRODUCTION

The Relevance of Approaches to Controlling Workplace Chemical Risks

Controlling the risks of working with chemical substances is widely recognized as one of the major elements of preventive occupational health and safety. Not surprisingly, therefore, control strategies for chemicals used at the workplace feature prominently in both regulatory and voluntary approaches to improvement in the working environment. Partly because of the scientific, medical, and technical elements involved, a considerable body of knowledge has developed, to which disciplines like occupational medicine, hygiene, toxicology, and epidemiology contribute. There is consequently a wide range of understandings concerning chemical hazards and the risks they pose, as well as a variety of control methods and systems intended to minimize risks of harm to workers.

This has led to a substantial regulatory profile for managing chemical risk coupled with considerable technical attention to the development of instruments for its implementation in workplaces. However, their impact on the majority of workplaces in which chemicals are used remains problematic; these are the small enterprises across the range of economic sectors and work activity in which there is demonstrably poor understanding among owner/managers concerning their responsibility for chemical risk management. Despite the proliferation of regulatory and technical interest in the safe use of hazardous substances, there is an accumulation of evidence that indicates its failure to reach these workplaces. Why this is so, how it is addressed and with what results are the subjects of this book.

Currently in Europe the regulatory profile governing the management of chemical risks at work is in the process of major restructuring, as implementation of the REACH (Registration, Evaluation and Authorisation of Chemicals) reforms in European legislation takes place. REACH is not limited to the workplace; it also has implications for controlling the environmental and consumer aspects of chemical production and use, as well as being concerned with systematizing the authorization of the supply of chemical products and refocusing the responsibility of suppliers in this process. The impact of its provisions and their means of achievement on the future regulation of occupational exposures to chemical substances will be substantial and significant. This is claimed to be especially so in relation to downstream use in smaller enterprises, because the new regulations will aim to improve risk communication within the supply chain—identified as a particular weakness of previous approaches. This book examines the evidence for this problem and the extent to which it is likely to be addressed by the new regulatory framework.

The plethora of institutionalized technical and regulatory provisions on safety in the supply and use of chemical substances at work notwithstanding, the most effective ways of evaluating and controlling the risks of hazardous substances in the majority of work situations remain the subject of debate. This is especially so for small enterprises, many of which are at some degree of remoteness from both the regulatory scrutiny and the technical sophistication necessary to support the approaches to chemical risk management that have traditionally dominated both regulatory and technical thinking. The following chapters, therefore, examine the strategies and tools used to support chemical risk management in small enterprises. They seek to discover the extent to which these approaches have been successful and what are the principal supports and constraints to their application.

This book is based on a European study to examine the evidence of the effectiveness of current strategies for chemical risk management in small enterprises. With the changing regulatory context in mind, the aims of the study were to:

- review and compare strategic approaches to achieving effective and sustainable risk management in the use of chemical substances in small enterprises, including the approaches of regulators, industry and other stakeholders to the provision of exposure/risk management advice;
- identify the main factors that determine the effectiveness of such approaches; and
- explore the implications for their support.

The research focused on six countries in the European Union (EU): Austria, Germany, the Netherlands, Spain, Sweden and the UK. The research was undertaken between 2004 and 2005. Based on a review of published and unpublished documentary sources in each country and at the level of the EU,[1] as well as on interviews with key players it:

---

[1] Effort has been made to update sources to 2006, however, continuing political and administrative changes mean that in some cases sources cited will no longer be current. This is especially true in relation to state institutions where reorganization has redistributed roles at federal and regional levels in several countries.

- examined the extent of current knowledge on the use of chemical products in small enterprises and the consequences of this use for health and safety;
- reviewed the nature of the risks of working with chemical substances in small enterprises and the extent to which such risks are related to workplace size;
- identified significant actors and processes—including manufacturers and suppliers, regulatory agencies, insurance organizations, occupational health services and trade unions and employers' organizations and trade bodies— and explored evidence of their role in determining best practice in managing the risks of using chemical substances in small enterprises;
- identified the main tools used in the implementation of strategies for chemical risk management in small workplaces in each country and the evidence for their success; and
- considered the implications of this evidence for the application of new regulatory strategies such as those envisaged under REACH.

The study was especially concerned with accounting for the social and economic contexts in which the management of chemical risks takes place in small enterprises. Experiences reported in countries other than the six that were examined in detail have been included where relevant. The study attempted to understand the success, sustainability and transferability of support for chemical risk management strategies and the small business environment in these terms, since previous work on health and safety management more generally in small enterprises suggests that this approach helps to explain why some initiatives to improve health and safety lend themselves to application in small enterprises more than others (Walters, 2001). Following the same theoretical approach to understanding the sociology of health and safety at work as developed previously by Nichols (1997) and Walters (2001), particular attention is paid to the so called structures of vulnerability and the multifaceted absence of resources that are characteristic features of work in these establishments and which need to be taken into account if initiatives to support workers' health and safety in these enterprises are to be successful and sustainable.

This book details the findings of the study in the above sequence. It begins with a consideration of the scale of the problem of chemical risks in small enterprises. Chapter 1 outlines what is known of the extent of the use of chemicals at work in the EU. It looks at the role of small enterprises in the economies of the countries studied and reviews the available information on exposure to chemical substances in these workplaces. It points out that as a consequence of the reorganization of work and the increased fragmentation of its structure and management in recent times, current work undertaken in small enterprises often includes outsourced activities formerly undertaken by employees of larger enterprises. Many such activities are hazardous and many involve chemical exposures. The chapter reviews the evidence of occupational mortality and morbidity that can be linked to chemical exposure and discusses some of the controversies surrounding the data.

It draws attention to the considerable gaps in knowledge and concludes with some reflections on the implications of these uncertainties for regulatory policies.

Chapters 2 and 3 deal with regulatory approaches. Chapter 2 outlines the development of chemical regulation at the level of the EU. While dealing with chemicals policy overall, it is particularly concerned with policy application to workplace situations and especially to small enterprises. It therefore reviews regulatory measures such as those on chemical, biological and carcinogenic agents that have been aimed at occupational exposures and discusses these approaches in the wider contexts of EU chemicals policies, before concentrating on REACH and its implications. The chapter examines the antecedents of REACH, including the EU White Paper "Strategy for a Future Chemicals Policy" and outlines its main themes in relation to regulating the occupational risks of chemical substances through attention to the supply chain and downstream users.

Chapter 3 focuses on regulatory strategies at the national level and considers the position in each of the countries studied. It identifies the features of the hierarchy of controls on chemical risk management, noting similarities, such as the focus on substitution, suppliers' information, risk assessment and information for employees and further noting the influence of the EU on the convergence of regulatory approaches. As well as the requirements themselves, the chapter reviews the evidence of their application in practice in each country and concludes with a discussion of the continuing problems of compliance in small firms.

Chapter 4 turns to the institutional infrastructures that support chemical risk management in small workplaces in each country. The chapter starts from the premise, derived from evidence presented earlier, that whatever the national regulatory strategy, successful chemical risk management in small firms requires some degree of institutional mediation. This is because the multifaceted lack of resources in small firms implies they will be unlikely to support, unaided, the effective application of requirements concerning chemical risk management. The level of infrastructural support available in each country is therefore likely to be a major influence on successful chemical risk management in these firms. The review embraces state support, the extent and role of prevention services and occupational health and safety (OHS) practitioners, support from statutory and voluntary organizations of business and employees as well as the role of statutory accident insurance organizations. It finds considerable variation in the infrastructures in place in different countries—a variation that is related to the different approaches to the development of the health and safety systems in the countries studied and also to differences in approaches to the regulation of their economies more generally.

The extent to which these variations give rise to differences in experiences of support for chemical risk management in small firms is examined in Chapter 5. It presents a review of tools to aid improvement of chemical risk management that are especially relevant to small enterprises in each country. A typology of the instruments is presented, identifying those with strong relationships to regulatory strategies as well as those that have evolved through support structures in place at sectoral and regional levels. Infrastructural support for chemical risk management is highly developed in Germany, as a consequence of regulatory style and the role of the statutory accident insurance associations. This is examined in depth; the chapter also considers structural aspects of the role of the supply chain in supporting chemical risk management among small-enterprise downstream users.

Findings emerging from these chapters include evidence of convergent strategic approaches to improving chemical risk management across the EU, variations in the levels of infrastructural supports in place to do so in different countries, and the existence of a large number of instruments of potential usefulness as aids to achieving outcomes desired by policymakers at national and European levels. However, evidence of the effectiveness of these strategies and instruments is less clear. In Chapter 6 this evidence is subject to a systematic review. The chapter is concerned with identifying properly conducted evaluations of chemical risk management strategies and tools applied to small firms. While it confirms that present-day regulatory approaches have been derived from reasonably robust research, it is less able to find similarly convincing documentation of the extent to which these approaches are successful. Indeed it shows that there is a paucity of properly conducted evaluative study to underpin current strategies.

One of the main arguments consistent throughout this book is that success with supporting chemical risk management in small firms is conditional upon wider support from the institutional frameworks and economic contexts in which such strategies are developed and deployed. In Chapter 6 elements of these frameworks identified in previous chapters are considered in terms of how critical they are to success or to what extent they represent constraints to effectiveness. These wider contexts are shown to be especially important when attempting to answer questions of coverage and sustainability. In light of the centrality of the supply chain to the business of production and use of chemical substances in advanced market economies, Chapter 6 undertakes a detailed consideration of the elements of its role as a basis of support for chemical risk management in advanced market economies. It argues that while dependent economic relationships within supply chains have come to be regarded as a potential way of achieving desired outcomes through the leverage they provide, even in the most neoliberal of market-based economies, suppliers and supply chains do not operate entirely in isolation from regulatory requirements or public interest. Influences derived from less directly economic dependencies are therefore also important. The chapter also shows that influences on supply chains do not operate singly and outcomes are likely to be the products of the interactive effects of constellations of such factors acting on and within the supply chain. It points to the implications of these arguments for current strategies to support chemical risk management in small firms, a topic that is again taken up in the final chapter.

Chapter 7 summarizes the main conclusions that can be drawn from the findings of the previous chapters and then presents a discussion of their implications for the successful implementation of REACH. Picking up the argument concerning the need for a wider understanding of the nature and usefulness of supply chains, it considers the evidence of what works in chemical risk management in small firms, identifies the considerable knowledge gaps and discusses their implications both for policy implementation and for future research.

Overall the aims of this book are to identify what is known, what is not known, and what more needs to be known concerning support for chemical risk management in small firms and to consider the usefulness of this understanding for the application of strategies to achieve improved work environments for the considerable number of people working with hazardous chemicals in these firms. In addition, it considers further issues underlying the support for chemical risk management in small firms. It identifies the shifts in the orientation of regulatory policies on chemical risks away from a reliance on the achievement of technical compliance with exposure limits and the demand for exposure monitoring, toward more generic approaches to estimating exposures and the provision of equally generic guidance to support practices that are predicted to limit exposures to acceptable levels. Some of the reasons for these shifts are evident in the clear failure of previous systems to convey their requirements to the owner/managers of small firms. Others are found in the failure to appreciate the extent of the lack of resources in small firms that prevent them from either acting on the requirements directly or gaining the support necessary to enable them to do so. Moreover, they reflect the failure of the regulatory system to convince suppliers of the need for adequate provision of information to enable users in small firms to work safely with hazardous substances as well as failure to more generally enforce the requirements effectively.

All this raises questions concerning the effectiveness of the new approaches in the light of previous regulatory failure and in particular, of the continued focus on risk assessment and management of hazardous substances. It is questionable that merely changing the style of what is required of small firms in terms of risk assessment and control from technically difficult and resource-intensive requirements to simpler and cheaper options entirely addresses the reasons for regulatory failure. The final chapter of this book gives some additional thought to the feasibility of more radical approaches, including consideration of whether there is a need to reassess the extent to which the principle of substitution has been promulgated and whether more emphasis needs to be placed on a broader meaning of this concept within regulatory frameworks.

These are all questions that can be asked in the context of the application of REACH. However, they are more universal than this and can be applied to the impact of chemical risk regulation on the work environment in small enterprises in all market economies. REACH is regarded internationally as a major regulatory reform for chemical risk management. Its application in the countries of the EU will be observed with considerable interest elsewhere. The issues covered in this book concerning the frameworks for the support of the implementation of strategies to improve chemical risk management, such as those based around enhanced risk communication in supply chains, are therefore of international relevance. The economic dependencies on which they are based, and the roles of institutional actors and of supporting instruments in their operation are all universal in market economies, as are the wider influences of the market, social interest groups and public opinion. This book demonstrates that the effects of the interaction of all these factors for chemical risk management in small firms are far from certain and it shows the importance of multifactorial analysis in understanding "what works" in these situations. Since these workplaces are both increasingly common features of the structure of advanced market economies and increasingly beyond the reach of conventional regulatory approaches, these are issues that transcend national boundaries and ones that should be of widespread concern, regardless of the character of particular regulatory regimes.

CHAPTER 1

Chemicals, Health and Small Enterprises in the European Union

> There are known knowns. These are things we know that we know. There are known unknowns. That is to say, there are things that we know we don't know. But there are also unknown unknowns. There are things we don't know we don't know.
>
> Donald Rumsfeld
> Former U.S. Secretary of Defense

It is not difficult to establish that there is a problem of death and disease that is related to the occupational use of chemical substances and that its dimensions are considerable. However, as policymakers at the EU level and elsewhere have discovered, it is considerably harder to demonstrate with any exactitude the extent of its component parts, their occurrence and their relative contribution to outcomes in terms of measures of mortality, morbidity and associated economic loss. It is therefore an area in which the celebrated opinion of the former U.S. Secretary of Defense, on the nature and extent of knowledge, is particularly apposite.

There is a host of reasons why this is so, including problems associated with reporting ill health, problems with measurement of exposure, collection of data and most significantly, establishing links between exposures and health consequences for which there may be a long time lag. As with other indices of work-related injury and ill health, many of these difficulties are especially evident when dealing with small enterprises and related forms of employment; yet the extent of employment in such workplaces and their estimated use of chemical substances is substantial. Moreover, the dimensions of risk become even more significant when it is borne in mind that the hazards of by-products of the use of chemical products also need to be taken into account when considering the exposure of workers.

What is known about the incidence of serious occupational injuries and fatalities more generally suggests a size-related occurrence in which work in smaller workplaces may present greater risks of injuries and fatalities than in larger ones. This is widely thought to indicate that failures of management of health and safety create greater risks in small enterprises, rather than the presence of a greater hazard. There is little reason to suppose that such failure would be any less in relation to chemical hazards than it is for occupational safety more generally and therefore it might be anticipated that work with chemical hazards in these enterprises may pose greater risks to health than similar work in larger enterprises.

To explore these issues further, this chapter outlines something of the extent of the known use of chemical substances in small enterprises and related forms of work in Europe. This involves considering the dimensions of the European chemical industry, the distribution and use of chemical products, an overview of the importance of small enterprises in the countries studied and an exploration of data on exposure to chemical hazards in these enterprises as well as in related work scenarios. The known and anticipated health effects of such exposure are then considered before this information is integrated in the discussion of implications for strategic approaches to improving chemical risk management in small enterprises that concludes the chapter.

THE USE OF CHEMICALS AT WORK IN THE EU

The Chemical Industry

During the 20th century the global production of chemicals increased from 1 million tonnes in 1930 to 400 million tonnes by the time the EC White Paper was published in 2001 (European Commission, 2001, p. 4). There is little sign of this production trend diminishing in the early part of the 21st century. The EU chemical industry is responsible for about one-third of the total international output and as such is the largest chemical industry in the world. It has a 65% share of world exports, a 53% share of imports and contributes 2.4% to the EU economy. In 2003 its estimated turnover in the EU-25 countries was €556 billion (CEFIC, 2004a). It is Europe's third-largest manufacturing industry, employing 1.7 million people directly with a further 3 million jobs dependent on it. Between 1999 and 2004 overall chemical production grew by 3.3% (1.1% if pharmaceuticals are excluded). This compares with an all-industry growth of 1.5%. The greatest growth in chemical production by sector was in pharmaceuticals (6.4%), followed by plastics and synthetic rubber (1.8%), petrochemicals (1.2%), speciality and fine chemicals (1.1%), consumer chemicals (1%) and basic inorganics (0.8%). Employment in the chemicals sector in the EU fell by 1.2% between 1999 and 2004 (against an all-industry fall of 1.4%).

Although large multinational corporations are prominent in the industry, in Europe there are also 36,000 small and medium sized enterprises (SMEs), accounting for over 95% of the total number of chemical firms in Europe, between them responsible for 28% of chemical production (European Commission, 2007). Table 1.1 shows the importance of SMEs in the industry. Firms with up to 500 workers employ half of the total workforce in the industry, account for 98% of the enterprises, and almost half of the sales. As with patterns of employment in small enterprises generally, these proportions vary between countries. In Spain for example, nearly 90% of employees in the chemical industry work in enterprises of fewer than 100 and over half in enterprises with fewer than 10 employees.

The chemical industry itself is mainly concentrated in Germany, France, Italy and the UK. The largest share is in Germany, with 26% of total EU production, followed by France (17%), the UK (14%) and Italy (12%). Aside from chemical production, the European Union is also the single largest market for the chemicals industry.

In addition to the original manufacturers and importers of chemical products, there are formulators that use chemicals supplied by their original manufacturers or importers in various combinations in their own products before marketing them to further users. There are also distributors of these products as well as those of the original manufacturers and importers.

The Wider Use of Chemicals at Work

Chemicals are used in a huge number of workplaces across the spectrum of economic sectors, both private and public. This means that the workers who may be at risk of exposure to hazardous chemicals will be found throughout the economy and not just among the employees of the chemical industry and its dependents. Table 1.2 shows the percentage of chemical consumption within the EU and how widespread chemical use is in Europe.

The role of intermediaries in the downstream supply chain from manufacture to use contributes to the remoteness of some users from the original suppliers of the substances they are using. Many users may be working in small companies that are subcontractors for larger ones and providing services to these larger organizations on their premises, such as is frequently the case in construction and also in many cleaning and maintenance operations. This may complicate,

Table 1.1 EU Chemical Sector by Size (Percent):
Enterprises, Employees, and Sales (Excluding Pharmaceuticals)

	Small (1–49)	Medium (50–499)	Large (500+)
Employees	14%	37%	59%
No. enterprises	86%	12%	2%
Sales	9%	39%	52%

Source: Adapted from CEFIC (2004b) and Eurostat (2004).

Table 1.2 EU Chemical Consumption

Textile and clothing	6.3%
Agriculture	6.4%
Electrical goods	3.9%
Office machines	0.7%
Industrial machinery	1.9%
Metal products	2.5%
Services	16.4%
Rest of manufacturing	6.1%
Construction	5.4%
Automotive	5.3%
Paper and printing products	4.5%
Consumer products	30.3%
Rest of industry	10.3%

Source: Adapted from CEFIC (2004a) and Eurostat (2004).

alter, or obstruct the quality of information flow concerning safe use of chemical substances from supplier to end user. Such potential effects on the consequent ability to use hazardous substances safely pose challenges for the chemical industry to fulfill its statutory obligations to the users of its products effectively and at the same time present problems for appropriate regulation. Users in small enterprises at the end of complex supply chains are especially vulnerable. They use substances in relatively small quantities in comparison with larger firms and lack both the economic power to exert influence on suppliers, as well as sufficient profile to be conspicuous to regulatory inspectors or command support from the health and safety infrastructure. It is in such firms, which make up the vast majority of workplaces in the European Union, that regulating the management of chemical risks is problematic.

THE GROWTH OF SMALL FIRMS

Small firms are a characteristic feature of modern economic life in all advanced market economies. Once of little interest to economic and social policymakers and analysts alike, their growth in number and significance in recent years has made them a focus of attention for business and regulatory policies. Despite this attention, the number, diversity and relative inaccessibility of many small firms means that they remain a challenge for the implementation of regulatory policy.

Before exploring the dimensions of this problem more fully in relation to chemical risks, it is important to be clear what is meant by the term "small enterprises," since definitions vary. The European Commission (EC), for example, uses three types of criteria in defining what constitutes small- and medium-sized enterprises, related to the number of employees, the size of the business in financial terms, and its independence. It distinguishes three types of SME:

- the micro-enterprise (employing fewer than 10 people);
- the small enterprise (employing fewer than 50); and
- the medium-sized (employing fewer than 250).

The way the terms small, medium and large are used in practice varies according to country and the nature of the industry concerned. For example, a small firm in petrochemicals will have a higher level of capitalization, sales and employment than a small firm in car repairs.

Steady growth in the number of small firms in EU-15 countries began in the 1980s. During the 1990s both the number of small firms and the number of persons employed in them continued to increase, so that by the end of the 1990s there were as many people working in micro-enterprises of fewer than 10 employees as in large enterprises of over 250 employees.

Detailed analysis shows that in EU-15 countries (Walters, 2001):

- the highest growth was among small and micro-enterprises (fewer than 50 employees);
- medium-sized companies declined in absolute number and also in proportion of total employment; and
- although the number of large companies increased, their relative contribution to total employment decreased.

However these generalizations mask some significant national differences. For example, two predominant patterns are evident in the developing role of small enterprises in the economies of EU member states. In some countries change in economic structure has resulted in unprecedented growth of the proportion of the labor force employed in small enterprises. While in others, small enterprises already formed the backbone of the economy, and while the restructuring processes of the end of the last century increased their dominant position, it did not alter the essential features of the productive system.

Table 1.3 shows the dominance by different enterprise sizes in relation to total employment in the countries on which this book is focused. It is apparent that in 2003, in Germany, the Netherlands, and the UK, large enterprises still had the biggest share of total employment, although employment in small and micro-enterprises has grown substantially in these countries. In the UK for example, large enterprises account for the biggest share of employment (46%), and the number of large and multinational companies remains higher in Britain than in other European countries except Germany. However, economic restructuring over

Table 1.3 Dominant Form of Employment in 2003 in the
Countries in the Study

	No enterprises 1000s	Occupied persons per enterprise	Size-class dominance
Austria	270	11	Micro-firms
Germany	3,020	10	Large-sized enterprises (LSE)
Netherlands	570	12	LSE
Spain	2,680	6	Micro-firms
Sweden	490	7	Micro-firms
United Kingdom	2,230	11	LSE

Note: Micro-firm = employing fewer than 10 persons; LSE = 250 or more.
Source: Observatory of European SMEs, European Commission (2004).

the last two decades has reduced the average size of the workplace and encouraged the growth of small firms in manufacturing and services. Two main categories of enterprises have contributed to creating jobs: the very small (fewer than 10 employees) and the very large. The overall effect has been that while large enterprises became bigger, the average workplace size reduced more in the UK than elsewhere in the EU during the 1990s (Walters, 2001, p. 43).

There was a major economic restructuring in Sweden during the 1990s as many large enterprises downsized. Externalizing and outsourcing their activities prompted growth in new small enterprises. In the other countries in the study, small enterprises already formed the backbone of their economies before the restructuring of the past 20 years. By the end of 2003 in Austria, 84% of firms employed fewer than 10 people, with a further 14% employing between 10 to 99 persons; 54% of employees worked in enterprises with fewer than 100 employees and nearly 21% in micro-enterprises with fewer than 10 workers. In Spain substantial growth of large companies has actually contributed to an increase in average workplace size in recent years; nevertheless, employment overall remains dominated by work in small enterprises.

EXPOSURE TO CHEMICAL SUBSTANCES IN SMALL FIRMS

Surveys conducted by the European Foundation for the Improvement of Living and Working Conditions found that 22% of respondents throughout the EU thought themselves to be exposed to dangerous substances for at least a quarter of their working time, while 16% thought they handled dangerous substances daily (European Foundation, 2001). Based on 1998 data, it has been estimated that in EU countries 32 million workers were exposed to occupational carcinogens (Kauppinen et al., 2000). There is further information from national surveys supporting this thesis; for example, analysis of the French 2003 SUMER survey indicated that 13.5% of the French workforce were exposed to one or more of 28 carcinogenic substances at their place of work (DARES, 2005). How much of this, and exposure to chemical substances generally, occurs in small firms is not systematically documented. Nevertheless, there are sufficient indications to suggest that exposure to chemical risks is likely to be extensive in all countries.

In the Netherlands for example, quantitative information on chemical risks in relation to company size can be derived from national monitoring systems. Three surveys, one based on information from employers (the *Arbomonitor*), and the other two, the *Nationale Enquête Arbeidsomstandigheden* (*NEA*) and the *Arbobalans*, with information from employees, give indications of chemical exposures in relation to workplace size. Table 1.4 shows *Arbomonitor* data from 2002 and 2003. It indicates that almost 40% of Dutch employers report their employees to be regularly working with dangerous substances. This percentage is higher (53%) for companies with more than 100 workers and varies for SMEs: 37% for companies with fewer than 10 workers and 47% for companies with 10–100 workers. The same survey also shows that cleaning agents and organic solvents are among the most widespread dangerous substances regularly used

Table 1.4 Chemical Risks and Control Measures in Companies in Which Workers Use Hazardous Chemicals Regularly

Item	Arbomonitor 2002: % of companies (N = 1735)	Arbomonitor 2003: % of companies (N = 1741)
Company size:		
< 10 workers	36	37
10–100 workers	42	47
> 100 workers	53	53
Total[a]	38	39

[a]This percentage has fluctuated over the previous years: 19% (1999), 37% (2000), 30% (2001). To put this in perspective, other percentage exposures in the survey include companies in which workers are regularly exposed to dangerous noise: 25%; to psychological work loads: 18%; to RSI-related activities: 54%; and to carrying or lifting loads over 25 kg: 6% (*Arbomonitor*, 2003).

Source: *Arbomonitor* 2002 and *Arbomonitor* 2003, Dutch Labour Inspectorate, The Hague.

(12% and 10% of companies respectively). In 9% of the companies, employees regularly work with "other substances," including paints and oil.

A somewhat different picture is derived from the employee-based surveys *Arbobalans* and the *NEA*. These both show that there are greater percentages of workers in small enterprises regularly exposed to chemical agents than in larger workplaces (Table 1.5).

Table 1.6 shows an overview based on secondary analysis of data from the 2003 *NEA* survey (Kremer, 2005). It demonstrates a strong inverse relationship between exposure and company size.

Analysis of exposure by sector has also been undertaken in the Netherlands. Qualitative analysis based on literature and interviews with sectoral organizations identified a number of high-risk sectors, the majority of which were dominated by small firms such as bakeries, car trade and repair, cleaning, furniture production, hairdressing, hotels and catering, and paint and ink production. (Nossent et al., 2003a). There is also quantitative data in which sectors where the majority of workers were regularly exposed to dangerous substances included agriculture, construction, manufacturing industry, hotels, catering and repair and trade; these are all, in the main, sectors in which work in small enterprises is predominant (Dutch Labour Inspectorate, 2003, 2004; Dutch Ministry of Social Affairs and Employment, 2004). This information has led the Dutch authorities to the conclusion that exposure of workers in small enterprises in the Netherlands is a serious cause for concern and has resulted in a reorientation of prevention strategies.

There were no systematic national surveys of exposure to chemical substances by company size available in any of the other countries studied, although for most of these countries the data that exists, when analyzed by sector, shows a similar pattern of exposure to that identified for the Netherlands. Agriculture, manufacturing, construction, cleaning, vehicle repair, hotels and catering, health care and hairdressing feature as sectors in which employees regularly work with chemical substances. These are mostly sectors in which small firms predominate

Table 1.5 Exposure to Chemical Agents—Quantitative
Information from *NEA* and *ArboBalans*, 2004

Regularly exposed to chemical agents	% of workers in general (AB, 2003)	% of workers in SMEs (AB, 2003)
Gases/vapors	15	< 10 workers: 28
Inhalable dust	13	10–100 workers: 25
Skin irritating agents	10	> 100 workers: 23

Source: Dutch Ministry of Social Affairs and Employment.

Table 1.6 Relationship between Exposure to Hazardous
Substances and Company Size

	Company size						
	1–9 n = 1516	10–49 n = 2782	50–99 n = 1525	100–499 n = 2278	500–999 n = 623	1000+ n = 1262	Total n = 9986
Frequency							
Skin exposure							
Daily/weekly	45.3	33.5	33.6	27.4	28.4	23.7	32.4
Only monthly	11.3	9.5	7.3	8.3	4.2	5.4	8.3
Never	43.4	57.0	59.0	64.3	67.4	70.9	59.3
Respiratory exposure							
Daily/weekly	50.0	43.5	43.0	36.1	33.1	29.4	40.3
Only monthly	10.0	9.7	8.1	9.4	8.8	9.0	9.3
Never	40.0	46.8	49.0	54.5	58.1	61.6	50.5
Total exposure							
Daily/weekly	58.4	50.0	48.8	41.5	39.8	33.6	46.4
Only monthly	9.6	8.8	7.7	9.0	8.2	8.0	8.7
Never	31.9	41.2	43.5	49.5	52.0	58.4	44.9

Source: Kremer, 2005.

or where a substantial proportion of work is undertaken within increasingly fragmented organizational and management structures, such as are found on multi-employer worksites, in outsourced and contracted work and in the use of agency labor.

Conversely, in Sweden, there was some limited data on work-related exposure to chemical substances analyzed according to workplace size. However, while it showed significant differences between the exposures of men and women to various generic groups of chemicals (caustics, oil or cutting fluids, organic and inorganic dusts), it did not demonstrate significant differences that could be consistently attributed to company size. In the UK, while there is no systematic collection of national information on chemical usage in small firms, the HSE (Health and Safety Executive) has maintained records of detailed measurements of exposure to hazardous substances on a National Exposure Database since 1986, which records size of workplace and type of industry. However, in a study that looked at the use of three substances in over 400 organizations, it was concluded that the vast majority of SMEs do not measure their employees' exposure to chemicals (Cherrie et al., 1999).

OTHER RELATED HARD-TO-REACH
EXPOSURE SCENARIOS

Restructuring of economic activity in advanced market economies means that there is an increase not only in work in small enterprises but also in a variety of "contingent" and "peripheral" forms of work that are embraced within the notion of "work in small enterprises" and sometimes existing separately. For example, outsourcing, multi-employer/contractor worksites, agency work and self-employment are all forms of work in which small enterprises and especially micro-enterprises predominate. Moreover, work in small enterprises is frequently temporary or casual, peripheral to and contingent upon the core activities of larger organizations. It is work in small enterprises and self-employment that characterizes the shadow economy in most countries. Although the obscurity of much of this work means there is very limited systematic information concerning exposure to chemical risks, there are sufficient reported incidents in which failures of risk management have led to exposures with catastrophic consequences to suggest that the limitations of approaches to chemical risk management for such work may be especially extreme.

Additionally, other measures of the health and safety conditions in these forms of work make them relevant by analogy to a discussion of chemical risk management in small enterprises. Subcontracting arrangements, for example, frequently result in complex matrices of control, leading to poor communication and confusion over health and safety management, in turn creating an environment in which accidental injuries are more frequent (see for example Hillage et al., 1998; Birchall & Finlayson, 1996; Rebitzer, 1995). The organization of work in the construction industry is typical of this pattern, and its poor accident record, including accidental exposures of workers to hazardous substances, is well known.

Mayhew and Quinlan (1998) found that outsourced garment workers reported three times as many injuries in all categories than their factory-based counterparts. In Sweden Blank et al. (1995) found that contract workers in mining experienced more frequent and more severe injuries. Similar findings have been reported in the United States (Rousseau & Libuser, 1997). In the U.S. chemical industry, Rebitzer (1995) found that main employers avoided directing and training contract workers for fear of being implicated in potentially expensive legal liabilities; yet the outsourcing of maintenance in the industry led to several major occupational health and safety problems, including several catastrophic chemical explosions. In France similar findings are well documented in relation to employment practices in the nuclear industry in which trade union surveys and those of occupational physicians showed how risks had been transferred to contract workers and as a result they experienced considerably greater exposure to hazardous conditions than the permanent workforce (Walters, 2001, pp. 313-318; Hery et al., 1996; Thebaud-Mony et al., 1992).

There is a close relationship between temporary and casual work and work in small enterprises. Here again, although there is little systematic evidence of damage caused by exposure to hazardous substances for these workers, there have been several studies that suggest problems are not uncommon, such as for example that shown by Hery et al. (1996). Moreover, other indices of poor health and safety outcomes give cause to believe that chemical risk management is also likely to be weak in relation to these forms of work. In 1998 in Spain, 60% of the workers who had a work-related accident were employed on a temporary contract (temporary workers form 33% of the Spanish labor force). Research on trends in workplace injuries in the UK shows that workers are most likely to suffer a workplace accident during the first 12 months of their employment and especially during the first six months, suggesting that the growth of the use of temporary workers on short-term contracts may therefore expose a greater proportion of workers to accidents (McKnight et al., 1999). Short-term work is closely associated with work in small enterprises. Young workers are also disproportionately engaged in temporary or casual work in small enterprises; their propensity for sustaining more injuries is well known (see for example Castillo et al., 1994; Kinney, 1993; Laflamme, 1997).

Reviewing the evidence in over a 100 separate studies of the health and safety effects of the various contingent and peripheral work practices such as those just stated, Quinlan et al., (2001) argue that they serve to redefine the relations of employment in ways that adversely affect health and safety. They point out that although there is growing evidence of damaging health and safety effects, there is little systematic information concerning their interrelationships and the potential synergy that results from these forms of work and the way they are managed or, as in the case of health and safety, not managed.

Given the known requirements for effective chemical risk management, and their likely absence from the above forms of work, it seems that the vulnerability of workers using chemicals in these situations will be especially significant. In addition to this vulnerability, another disturbing feature is the remoteness of many of these forms of work from both management and monitoring of health and safety. For the workers concerned, not only is there a likelihood of them experiencing greater risks to their health and safety because they are distanced from approaches to systematic risk management, but the consequences of this remoteness for their health and safety may well go unrecognized by monitoring and reporting systems that are geared to the needs of main employers; Thebaud-Mony (1999) showed this in her analysis of exposures experienced by contractors and subcontractors in the French nuclear power industry (see also Walters, 2001). Although not all these situations are encountered while working for small enterprises, the association is a close one. It clearly contributes to challenges facing the regulation and management of preventive health and safety generally in the small business sector and specifically in relation to effective chemical risk management.

HEALTH AND SAFETY OUTCOMES OF WORKING WITH
HAZARDOUS CHEMICALS IN THE EU

Injuries, diseases and fatalities are prominent outcomes of working with chemicals. Accidental injuries resulting from exposure to harmful chemicals are a significant feature of statistics on serious injuries at work in many industrial sectors in EU countries, and such exposures also lead to a substantial proportion of occupational fatalities.

It has been estimated from EU aggregate data[1] that nearly one-third of all occupational diseases recognized annually in the EU are related to exposure to chemical substances (Musu, 2004).[2] It is also acknowledged that this is only a partial measure of the full extent of the health effects of working with chemical products. A major problem with measurement is that because the hazards of many of the chemical products marketed in Europe are not themselves adequately researched, quantification of the risks to health from working with them is largely based on estimates extrapolated from limited and uncertain data.

There are several main sources of data on occupational health outcomes related to exposure to chemicals at work, and they include both routine data collection systems and specific surveys and studies. Information is available from:

- national statutory reporting requirements for occupational diseases, injuries, and fatalities;
- registries of specific conditions such as cancer and skin or respiratory diseases associated with occupational exposure;
- household surveys of self-reported sickness absence;
- epidemiological studies in relation to specific forms of ill health and their occupational causes;
- other ad hoc studies in relation to specific substances, incidents, or diseases.

The limited scope of the officially reported data from these sources is well documented (Walters, 2001). Reporting requirements are often defined by laws that were put in place for reasons that are at odds with the collection of comprehensive data on occupational disease.[3] Such data in some systems is also known to underreport the occurrence of the conditions it records because of failure to report them on the part of management. There are national variations in the nature of what is required to be reported and in the administrative systems for recording it. These lead to further variation in the quality and comprehensiveness of the

---

[1] Available from Eurostat No. 15 (2004) (Occupational Diseases in Europe in 2001, Statistics in Focus).

[2] A substantial proportion of these are caused by chemical dusts such as asbestos.

[3] Such as in the UK, for example, where historically the rationale for such requirements is not primarily concerned with documenting the incidence and prevalence of disease but more to do with limiting the number of claimants eligible for social welfare benefits, and thus often excludes cases that would be counted under different reporting criteria.

national data and make aggregation and consistency of such material problematic at the European level. There is a time lag between the exposure and onset of disease, which in some cases may be considerable and means that current information about health effects may, in fact, refer to exposures that took place at times in the past when such exposure may have been of a different character to that experienced later.

In some reporting systems the extent of the experience of ill health is derived from workers' own self-reporting (such as in the UK Labour Force Survey for example). These approaches usually result in substantially larger estimations of the extent of work-related ill health than found under legal reporting requirements, as is evident from Table 1.7. However, while such estimations may be useful in calculating time lost to economic production and burdens on the health care and social welfare systems, as measures of the nature and extent of ill health, they also need to be treated with some caution since they rely on respondents' self-diagnosis and memory of their work experiences.

Estimations of mortality and morbidity, whether based on routine sources or on specific studies, are themselves controversial. The uncertainty of risk estimation has therefore been a central feature of the strategic development of regulatory approaches to risk management of hazardous substances. This is well documented with regard to the development of appropriate exposure standards.[4] It is further evident in the development of more systematic regulation of chemical substances at the EU level. Thus, one of the most significant challenges that REACH is attempting to address concerns reducing the burden of mortality and morbidity associated with occupational exposure to chemicals with little-known health effects and with situations in which exposure is unknown or unspecific.

An illustration of the difficulties encountered with estimation is provided in the case of cancer. Probably the best-known and most widely used approach to estimating the extent of mortality from cancer that is due to occupational causes is that of Doll and Peto (1981). The authors of a recent review identified nearly 450 scientific articles citing their 1981 paper (Clapp et al., 2005). Doll and Peto's calculations, undertaken in a study for the U.S. Congress, estimated that 4% of the overall proportion of cancer in the United States was attributable to occupational causes (with a range of uncertainty between 2% and 8%). Their methods have been followed in a variety of subsequent estimations and have informed national and European strategies for dealing with occupational cancer (see for example Kauppinen et al., 2000; Morrell et al., 1998; also, more generally see Greenberg et al., 2001; Leigh et al., 1999). In the UK for example, the HSE based its calculation that cancer from occupational causes is responsible for an estimated 6000 deaths annually on the Doll and Peto study and set its occupational health strategy accordingly. In a review to inform the European Commission in its deliberations

---

[4] See Walters and Grodzki (2006, pp. 15-35) for a more detailed discussion of this point.

Table 1.7 Comparison of the Burden of Ill Health Estimated from
Legal Reporting Systems and Self-Reported Surveys

Type of occupational disease	Number of self-reported cases	Number of recognized cases
Skin diseases	200,000	8,000
Disorders of the respiratory tract (including cancers)	600,000	10,000

Source: Musu (2004).

on the introduction of REACH, Postle et al., (2003) used the same basis to estimate that 3.5% of the total cancer mortality in the EU was associated with occupational exposure.

Yet the Doll and Peto estimates are not without their critics. For example, Landrigan and Baker (1995) identified several limitations to their data and the calculations they used. They pointed out that Doll and Peto relied on epidemiological studies of workers in large industries or broad categories of employment, but failed to consider exposures in smaller workplaces or from indirect contact with carcinogenic substances such as asbestos in maintenance operations. In other contributions, Landrigan et al., (1995) and Davis (1990) also noted that Doll and Peto (1981) limited their analyses to deaths of those under age 65. In doing this, they missed effects that are seen in older people whose cancers may have been caused by exposures while working. These authors suggest that an estimate of 10% for the proportion of cancer attributable to occupational exposures would be more plausible, based on their review of the literature and clinical experience. Others have also drawn attention to perceived weaknesses in the Doll and Peto approach, pointing out that it mostly ignored cancer risks faced by women (Zahm & Blair, 2003) and African Americans (Epstein, 2005). The review by Clapp et al. (2005) argues that the Doll and Peto (1981) calculation "probably underestimates the occupational exposure contribution by a factor of two to four in both the US and the UK," and therefore agrees with others that a more realistic estimate of the proportion of cancer attributable to occupational causes is within the range of between 8% and 16%.

A further important point of particular relevance to small enterprises and related work situations is that estimations of the incidence of occupationally caused cancer, whatever the proportion of total cancer they suggest is linked to occupation, do not mean that risks are evenly spread throughout all workplaces and among all workers. They are a consequence of exposure and therefore will be considerably greater in some work situations than in others. Since the evidence on chemical risk management generally points to the likelihood of fewer controls being in place in smaller enterprises than in their larger counterparts, it is also likely that many workers in these enterprises will experience greater risks of contracting occupationally related cancer when working with the same hazards as those encountered in larger and better controlled workplaces.

Of course, there is another side to this discussion. The chemicals industry is at pains to point to improving control of exposure to known carcinogens in the industry. Based on evidence from large German chemical companies, for example, CEFIC has argued that there is evidence to show that, in fact, measured exposure to carcinogens in large plants in the industry has declined (CEFIC, 2003). On this basis they suggest that exposure to chemicals in similar plants in the industry is also likely to have declined and argue that this indicates the success of OHS management measures in the industry. However, at the same time it should be remembered that, as pointed out previously, a substantial proportion of the chemical industry is not based in large enterprises but in small ones.

There is further support in the occupational hygiene literature for the general thesis that "things are getting better." Kromhout and Vermeulen (2000) for example, discuss long-term trends in occupational exposure to hazardous substances that indicate the improvement of exposure scenarios over time. However, while these observations may be accurate reflections on what has been achieved in large and well-managed enterprises, they do not negate the wider evidence of the relationship between known hazardous substances and the extent of deaths from cancer, nor do they contradict the proposition that a substantial, though unknown, proportion of deaths also result from exposure to hazardous substances that are not yet identified as carcinogens and, most significantly for our purposes, they do not apply to exposures to hazardous substances in the small enterprises and related forms of work that are the focus of our attention.

Cancer is not the only disease associated with occupational exposure to chemical substances. By far the most prevalent health effects of working with chemicals are diseases of the respiratory system and the skin, of which asthma and chronic obstructive pulmonary disease (COPD) in the case of the respiratory system and contact dermatitis in the case of the skin are the most common. Diseases of the central nervous system are also associated with such exposures, as are allergies and reproductive, developmental and endocrine disorders. However, here again, there are no reliable data concerning the full occurrence of such conditions on a European scale. Nor is there anything like complete data on exposure in any individual country—although there are specific cases of very good exposure databases at sectoral level.[5]

---

[5] Such as the database DOK-MEGA run by the BGIA and the BGen in Germany for example (see Chapter 5).

Some indications of the extent of the toll of these conditions can be gained from individual estimates. For example, calculations carried out by trade union organizations using European Occupational Disease Statistics (EODS) compensation statistics that are shown in Table 1.8 suggest that 88% of occupational skin disease cases and 36% of occupational respiratory disease cases are related to chemical exposure (Musu, 2004).

Recent estimates of the most prevalent of these diseases—respiratory and skin diseases—suggest that for example there is an approximate incidence rate of occupational asthma of 200–400 per million per year, equivalent to 40,000–80,000 new cases per year in the EU-25 countries (Pickvance et al., 2005).[6] In the case of skin diseases, the same authors suggest a figure of 200 cases per million per year for an EU-25 workforce of 200 million for the incidence of occupational skin disorders they believe attributable to substances that would be covered by the proposed REACH regulations. It is not known how much of such ill health would be the result of exposure in small workplaces, but as with occupationally related cancers, the assumption must be that it is a considerable proportion.

Detailed information from the countries included in the present study supports these broad estimations. For example in Sweden, as Figure 1.1 shows, skin conditions and asthma are the most commonly experienced health effects related to chemical exposure.

In Germany information on the extent of work-related diseases caused by chemicals is limited to overall figures, which may be roughly separated for industrial sectors, but not differentiated according to size of enterprise. They are based on the annual statistics of the insurance associations (*Bgen*) on compensation claims for occupational diseases and on their decisions on these claims. Again, obstructive respiratory diseases and severe or repeatedly occurring skin diseases are of particular interest because not only are they mainly of chemical origin but can also serve as indicators for recent or still existing deficits in occupational hygiene. In 2002 recorded claims in these categories were 4,998 and 19,189 respectively, filed with the 35 BGen for industrial sectors (HVBG, 2003). In the same year for the two categories, an occupational cause was confirmed for 1,338 and 7,933 cases, respectively (HVBG, 2003). Although information on the exact fraction of causes other than chemicals is not available, it can be assumed that the majority of these diseases were of chemical origin. For skin diseases, for example, Zober (2002) estimates 80% to be chemical related.

Expenses in compensation incurred by the BGen for the two diseases in 2002, both for new cases and for cases already acknowledged in previous years, are given by Rühl (2004) as €120 million and €160 million, respectively. They do not include direct and indirect costs for loss of production. For two sectors in which

---

[6]This is corroborated by separate national estimates such as that of the HSE in the UK, indicating incidence rates of occupational asthma of 5,000 per year (HSE, 2005a). The UK labor force is roughly one-tenth that of the EU-25.

Table 1.8 Estimated Percentage of Occupational Diseases Related
to Exposure to Chemical Substances

Occupational diseases	% linked to chemical exposure	% among all recognized diseases	% chemicals related among all recorded diseases
Cancers	4–90%[a]	5%	0.2–4.5%[a]
Neurological diseases	2%	8%	0.2%
Respiratory diseases	36–89%[a]	14%	5.0–12.5%[a]
Skin diseases	88%	14%	12.3%
Total			18% to 30%[a]

[a]Including chemical dust (asbestos, silica dusts, wood dusts).
Source: Musu (2004).

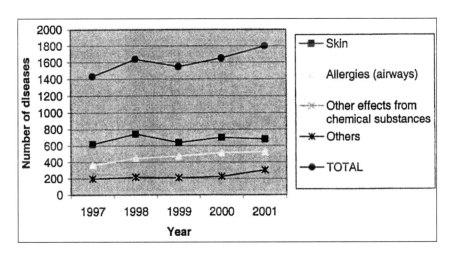

Figure 1.1 Statistics on work-related diseases caused by
chemical exposure in Sweden 1997–2001.
Source: www.prevent.se/kemiguiden—Based on statistics compiled
by Swedish ISA for the KemiGuiden.

skin diseases have a particular high incidence, namely the health services and the metal industry, an estimate of these costs for occupational skin diseases was calculated disregarding whether or not they were compensated. For 2002 the figures range from €240 to €500 million in the former, and from €307 to €638 million in the latter sector (Batzdorfer & Schwanitz, 2004). Such costs were an important stimulus for the insurance associations to develop new chemical control strategies that especially targeted SMEs (see Chapter 5).

A similar prevalence is seen in Austria in relation to occupational respiratory and skin diseases recorded in routine statistics. As Table 1.9 shows, on the basis of data from 2002 to 2004, skin diseases were in second place, respiratory diseases such as asthma in fourth place and respiratory and lung diseases caused by irritant and toxic substances in fifth place for occupational diseases overall.

As is generally known, because of the dependence on the legal definition and the high rates of underreporting that are experienced, these official statistics of occupational diseases represent only a small proportion of work-related conditions (Leleu, 2003), rendering them unhelpful in identifying many of the associations between workload and ill health (Heider, 2003). As in other countries, surveys based on self-reporting of respondents' own perceptions of these associations show considerably greater experience of ill health; this is shown in Austria by the results of the Microcensus survey of working conditions summarized in Table 1.10.

Table 1.9 Ranking of the Most Common Recognized
Occupational Diseases in Austria

Rank	Most common occupational diseases	Percentage of all occupational diseases		
		2004	2003	2002
1.	Hardness of hearing caused by noise	36.1	34.7	36.2
2.	Skin diseases	22.0	22.4	26.7
3.	Infectious diseases	8.2	10.4	12.5
4.	Bronchial asthma caused by allergens	10.0	9.9	8.3
5.	Respiratory and lung diseases caused by irritant and/or toxic substances	5.8	5.8	5.8

Source: AUVA (Allgemeine Unfallversicherungsanstalt) (2003a, 2004a, 2005a).

Table 1.10 Some of the Ill Effects Reported by Workers in the 1999
Microcensus Survey Concerning Working Conditions
Compared with the Previous 1994 Survey

Workers reporting ill effects	1999	Compared to 1994
Solid/liquid dangerous or toxic chemicals	14.8%	About the same
Dusts, vapors, fumes	14.4%	About 10% less
Risk of accidents and injuries	35.2%	About 10% higher
Uncomfortable work clothes/protective equipment/protective devices	9.4%	About 75% higher

Source: AK Wien (2001).

As already noted, in the UK the HSE, using the Doll and Peto model, estimated annual deaths from occupational cancer at around 6,000. Critics have pointed out that this methodology seriously underestimates the problem and suggest that the true number may be twice this figure (O'Neill, 2005). There are indications that the HSE is in the process of revising its estimates. On the other conditions commonly associated with exposure to chemicals, the pattern is similar to that found in other countries. Surveillance schemes indicate up to 7,000 new cases of work-caused or related asthma (of which specialist physicians see 1,500); and 66,000 new or existing occupationally related cases of skin disease every year (two-thirds are dermatitis or eczema), with around 30,000 further cases exacerbated by the working environment. Dermatologists and occupational physicians see 4,000–5,000 new cases each year (Brown & Rushton, 2003).

Table 1.11 shows the estimated prevalence and rates for 2001–2002 of illness for breathing/lung and skin problems caused or exacerbated by work for people employed in the UK. The figures put the prevalence for breathing and lung problems at 168,000 and skin problems at 39,000 (out of a total of 2.3 million for all ill health). Although they encompass exposures that are not limited to chemicals, they nevertheless provide a useful indication of the situation in the UK. These figures are drawn mainly from the most recent self-reporting survey on work-related illness (Jones et al., 2004), backed up by voluntary reporting of occupational diseases by specialist doctors in the Occupational Disease Intelligence Network (ODIN), which includes the data-gathering schemes EPIDERM (Occupational skin disease surveillance by dermatologists) and SWORD (Surveillance of Work-Related and Occupational Respiratory Disease).

In addition, other estimations show that occupational asthma is the most frequently diagnosed respiratory disease in Great Britain, with an estimated 1,500 to 3,000 people developing it each year. Common causes are associated with

Table 1.11 Ill Health Caused or Exacerbated by Work
Prevalence in the UK

	Type of complaint	Sample cases (no.)	Estimated prevalence (thousands)			Rate per 100 ever employed		
				95% confidence limits			95% confidence limits	
			Central	Lower	Upper	Central	Lower	Upper
All persons	Breathing or lung problem	380	**168**	151	185	**0.39**	0.35	0.42
	Skin problems	82	**39**	30	48	**0.09**	0.07	0.11
	Total	5,015	**2,328**	2,261	2,394	**5.3**	5.2	5.5

Source: HSE. www.hse.gov.uk/statistics/causdis/swi0102.pdf

exposure to sensitizing chemicals such as in spray painting with isocyanates in the car industry for example. In early 2001 the HSE estimated that 63,000 people suffered from a skin disease caused by work with chemicals. It put the cost to industry at between £24 and £59 million and stated that industries and occupations particularly at risk included catering, food processing, engineering, agriculture, hairdressing, cleaning, printing, health care, construction, rubber manufacturing/processing, and offshore work. It estimated that 4 million working days were lost in all industries each year as a result of work-related skin problems. In the printing industry alone, 41% of workers who took part in HSE-funded research had suffered from a skin complaint at some time (Livesley & Rushton, 2000).

DEALING WITH "KNOWN UNKNOWNS"

The Limits of Information

The evidence presented in the preceding pages, from that on the extent of chemical usage at the workplace to that on its known health effects, confirms that the mortality and morbidity linked to the use of chemical products in the economy are substantial. There are sufficient general data available to support broad conclusions about relationships between the type and extent of chemical usage and the extent and seriousness of unwanted health effects such as cancer, respiratory diseases, and skin disease as well as that of other conditions such as neurological disorders. They indicate a serious cause for concern, both in terms of the degree of suffering caused and in relation to the economic cost.

At the same time, this evidence is patchy and incomplete. As such, it is probably an underestimation of the dimensions of the problem in a number of important respects. It is clear that there is incomplete basic information on the hazards of many chemical products that are currently marketed in the European Union. There are also major gaps in knowledge concerning how these and other substances are used in workplaces. Given these limitations, it is hardly surprising that there is a further information deficit on the link between using chemical products at work and the consequent health effects.

At one end of the spectrum of working with chemical products is the large enterprise, in which there is considerable expertise in systematic approaches to managing health and safety, including that of managing chemical risks. Such firms frequently have access to specialist expertise that can be deployed in advising on the purchase of chemical products, on the requirements necessary to ensure their safe use, and in monitoring to ensure that control strategies, designed to protect employees at the workplace level, work effectively. These enterprises, because of their size and because of the nature of the processes with which they are engaged, are likely to have a high profile with regulatory agencies. Their management therefore often has a close relationship with inspectors of these agencies, which further supports attention paid to systematic approaches to chemical risk management. Moreover it is in these firms that worker representation and its trade union support are most likely to be found, providing further checks and balances to ensure serious consideration is given to chemical risk management. It is also these firms that, for all these reasons, provide the most reliable data on exposure, its health outcomes, and the means of its prevention and control.

At the other end of the same spectrum is the small firm and related work scenarios in which, through a combination of facets of the underresourcing and remoteness of their economic activity, exposure of workers to risk from the use of chemical substances is likely to be both significant and, at the same time, incompletely documented. Although the data is far from complete, it indicates that firm size is not a barrier to using hazardous substances. This chapter has demonstrated that they are used as often by small firms across a range of economic sectors as they are by larger firms. Indeed, sectors in which chemical risks are notably high, such as in agriculture, construction and private services such as cleaning and hairdressing, as well as in manufacturing, are made up of substantial proportions of small firms. Recent restructuring of the organization of economic activity in many of such sectors has resulted in the growth, not only of small firms but also of the peripheral and contingent employment. In all cases, chemical substances continue to be used, but the situations in which they are used are increasingly remote from the influence of both systematic risk management and regulatory surveillance. As a result, not only is it likely that exposures to risk will take place, but that it and its consequences may go unrecorded. Thus, poorly controlled exposure to chemical hazards in small firms and related work situations becomes one of Rumsfeld's "known unknowns" for which contingencies need to be made.

The information outlined in this chapter demonstrates that while current estimates make it clear that the burden of ill health associated with exposures to chemical substances is substantial, both its dimensions and those of its component parts are difficult to quantify reliably. This is especially the case in relation to exposure at work in small enterprises. It is therefore another known unknown, and there is no systematic national data that presents a complete overview in any of the countries studied.

The Failure of Regulation

All this is a major challenge for regulatory strategies aimed at controlling workplace chemical risks and one that has exercised policymakers at national and European levels in recent years. As we showed in a recent review, regulatory policy on controlling the exposure of workers to risks to their health from hazardous substances used or produced at work has passed through several transformations in recent decades (Walters & Grodzki, 2006, pp. 19-36). Beginning with the prescriptive specification standards traditionally found in employers' duties in most national legislation, regulatory strategies took increasing account of the quantification of exposure and exposure standard setting. For example, by requiring employers to ensure adequate and appropriate ventilation, measures controlling dust and fumes were supplemented by requirements to restrict the airborne contamination of workplace atmospheres to levels well below those that could be scientifically deemed to pose unacceptable risks to health. At the same time wider regulatory thinking about the work environment increasingly emphasized regulatory means to influence the processes with which more systematic risk management could be achieved.

The results of these approaches were regulatory requirements emerging at EU and national levels in which good occupational hygiene practices were emphasized as a framework for systematic chemical risk management. Thus, where safer substances or processes could not be introduced, concepts of controlling exposure were advocated in which monitoring and evaluation became important elements. Standards were required against which exposures could be monitored and the risks to workers controlled. The levels at which these standards were set and the balance of economic and scientific influence on the process had been subject to debate from the outset. However, the transformation of the role of these standards—from being tools for specialist practitioners in occupational hygiene to being an important cornerstone of regulatory strategies—intensified such debate and gradually unforeseen weaknesses in this approach were highlighted.

It became increasingly apparent, for example, that the effective implementation of systematic approaches to chemical risks management was dependent on several preconditions. They included good quality information concerning the hazards of substances; clear criteria on which exposure standards could be determined; good systems for communicating this information to those responsible, sufficient technical capacity to monitor, evaluate and control risks in workplace scenarios; sufficient grasp of what was required and how it should be achieved; as well as adequate inspection and control. Yet the reality was that information on the hazards of the vast majority of substances used in European workplaces was far from complete, exposure standards were set for comparatively few substances, and the criteria used were subject to variation and debate. The quality of communication of hazard information to management as well as that between management and their employees was in many cases reported to be poor. Technical capacity was limited to large enterprises or external services that met the requirements of large enterprises; there was also growing evidence that a substantial proportion of management neither understood what was required of them, nor possessed the capacity to deliver the systematic approaches framed by regulation. Further, it became evident that regulatory inspectorates also lacked the capacity to check compliance adequately across the range of those subject to the regulation.

It was in short, a situation in which there was mounting evidence of regulatory failure. This was hardly surprising, given that the model on which the regulatory approach had been based was that which applied in large workplaces that were themselves a small and diminishing proportion of the situations to which such regulation was meant to apply.

Strategies for Reform

It was to address this regulatory failure that recent approaches to chemicals regulation discussed in the following two chapters developed. In parallel with the refocusing of regulatory approaches however, wider concern about the effects of the manufactured uncertainties inherent in the growth and diversity of the chemical industry and use of chemical substances in society at-large has led to the development of two additional related ideas. The first is the desirability of applying a precautionary principle in strategic rationales for regulating the management of chemical risks. The second is the concept of substitution, which when widely applied not only to chemical substances but to their applications and processes, provides a further strategy to reduce risks and uncertainties concerning the effects of chemical exposures.

Precautionary principles in disease prevention and public health are not new; they have been advocated in relation to disease prevention for centuries. John Snow's recommendation to remove the handle of the Broad Street water pump in London in the nineteenth century to prevent the spread of cholera, despite the incomplete evidence of its cause, is a textbook example. But these principles are notable for being exceptions to the rule of "innocent until proven guilty," which has applied more widely in the case of chemical exposure. In the history of occupational diseases resulting from exposures to chemical hazards, there have been many instances wherein economic interest has ensured that pre-cautionary principles were resisted and their lessons not applied in time to prevent substantial death and disease. Asbestos, benzene, polyvinyl chloride monomer, and aromatic amines, to name but a few, are all substances for which controversy has raged for many years concerning the details of their health effects, allowing continued exposure to take place, along with the accumulation of associated deaths and disease, until sufficient evidence has combined with public concern to result in regulatory action.

One of the consequences of the growth of risk awareness in modern post-industrial society is greater public and political unwillingness to tolerate consumer and environmental risks and it is here that the application of the precautionary principle has been more pronounced in the policy debates of recent years. Originating in Europe with the work of German scientists and policymakers in the 1970s, who generated a general rule of public policy (*Vorsorgeprinzip*) in relation to environmental protection where, in the case of serious or irreversible threats to health or the environment, recognition was given to the need to reduce potential hazards before there was strong proof of harm, it has been increasingly applied in national and international strategies to protect the environment. At the level of the EU, the significance of the adoption of a precautionary principle in public policy emerged with the EC Communication on the Precautionary Principle (EC, 2000) and also in the Nice decision of the Council of Ministers in 2000 (European Environment Agency, 2001). As discussed in the following chapter, there are strong links between these wider policy statements and the development of policy on controlling chemical risks. However, it also needs to be borne in mind that the application of the precautionary principle remains widely debated and, as the evidence of the foregoing pages suggests, its impact to date on the use of chemical substances in small enterprises has been limited.

Similar thinking lies behind the prioritization of substitution in regulatory approaches to chemical risk management. As outlined in the next two chapters, such an approach has been evident for a number of years at both European and national levels. It is, for example, ideally the first principle in the hierarchy of measures on the control of chemical risks at work, and it is found not only in occupational health and safety regulation on hazardous substances, but also in that on chemicals more widely and on environmental protection. Indeed, since the emergence of the principle, for both regulatory and market-based reasons, quite a number of known hazardous substances have either disappeared from markets or have a much reduced presence (for example substances such as asbestos, pesticides such as DDT, chlorinated fluorocarbons (CFCs), and poly-chlorinated biphenyls [PCBs] have been banned; others such as chlorinated solvents and toxic heavy metals are subject to tight controls). Despite these developments however, problems have also emerged in relation to the concept of the substitution of hazardous substances with safer ones. As Ahrens et al., (2006, p. 2) note, such problems are of two kinds. First there is the question of the fundamental ability and willingness to substitute hazardous substances, and second there is the question of whether the substitute is in fact any less dangerous. Combined they lead to a degree of inertia and resistance to change that present considerable barriers to substitution. In common with Ahrens et al., it is argued in subsequent chapters that the real potential of substitution in relation to chemical risk management in small enterprise lies not so much in the replacement of specific chemical products with safer ones, but in a wider application to processes, equipment and tasks and in its role in the stimulation of innovation in the production and supply of chemicals and related technology. There are signs of the recognition of this potential in the discussion surrounding REACH, but it remains to be seen whether there are sufficient infrastructural supports in place for its implementation.

The Challenge of Neoliberalism

At the same time it needs to be remembered that the course of all this development has largely taken place against an increasingly neoliberal political and economic background in the EU in which governance has generally favored nonregulatory approaches to risk management. The effects of this influence on the trajectory and orientation of regulation are unmistakable and will also be considered in the following chapters. A related consideration is the capacity of the health and safety system and its infrastructure to support regulatory strategies. As has been demonstrated, this is clearly problematic in the case of small enterprises. In several countries in the study there are indications that policymakers have tried to take these challenges into account in developing regulatory strategies, by mixing a neoliberal policy orientation with pragmatism over available resources for inspection and control. However, the resulting approaches are not without their critics. In the UK for example, the recent changes to the regulatory framework for chemical risk management (outlined in Chapter 3) have occasioned debate as to the extent to which they are in fact a missed opportunity to strengthen the support required to operate chemical risk management effectively. As representatives of the professional body for occupational hygienists have argued, in relation to what they view as an oversimplified and underfunded regulatory approach embraced by the revised measures (Allen, 2004, p. 9),

> Getting it right isn't always simple and easy, especially for small and medium sized enterprises. The best way to do this is to provide an effective occupational health and hygiene service to SMEs and for HSE to rigorously enforce the law where necessary.

That this is not simply a protectionist view from the occupational hygiene profession is borne out by similar comments from the Engineering Employers Federation that argue (Allen, 2004, p. 9):

> . . . the failure of COSHH (Control of Substances Hazardous to Health) is basically down to a lack of knowledge within companies and a lack of proper enforcement.

CHAPTER 2

The Regulatory Approach of the European Union to Chemical Risk Management in Small Enterprises

Regulatory strategies for the management of chemical risks at work are much in evidence in current political debate at the level of the European Union. While this might be anticipated given the scale of the use of chemical substances and the extent of the associated health and safety problems already discussed, in fact such debate is of relatively recent origin. It has been occasioned by attempts by the European Commission to address the perceived failure of previous legislative efforts to produce a workable framework for chemical regulation and, in particular, by the Commission's efforts to shift responsibility for risk assessment and control of chemical hazards from the state to industry.

This chapter outlines the development of these approaches and considers the extent to which they address, or are relevant to, the use of hazardous substances in small enterprises and related forms of work. It does so in the context of the historical development of chemical regulation overall at the level of the European Union. It reviews regulatory measures such as those on chemical, biological, and carcinogenic agents that have been aimed at occupational chemical exposures and discusses these approaches in the wider contexts of EU chemicals policies more generally before concentrating on development of the proposal for a "Regulation of the European Parliament and of the Council concerning the Registration, Evaluation, Authorisation and Restriction of Chemicals"—otherwise known as REACH.

It examines the antecedents of REACH, including the EU White Paper "Strategy for a Future Chemicals Policy" and outlines its main themes, especially in relation to regulating the occupational risks of chemical substances through attention to the supply chain and downstream users.

Although the working environment is the main focus of this book, it is of course only one kind of environment in which the risk of exposure to hazardous chemicals may occur. Perhaps more than most occupational hazards, those associated with the supply of chemical products affect not just workers, but also consumers, society and the environment. They further include risks such as fire and explosion. One consequence of this is that regulatory strategies at the EU level have evolved a collection of instruments with measures that embrace the workplace but are not limited to it. It is not the purpose of this study to present a comprehensive account of these wider elements of the European Union approach to chemicals regulation. However, in as far as they are intertwined with the development of regulatory strategies that are aimed specifically at workplace risks, it becomes necessary to address some of their elements in this chapter.

Similarly, an important consideration in the workplace application of regulatory approaches to chemical risk management concerns its wider relationship to the regulation of occupational risk management. In all of the countries studied, measures seeking to implement the EU Framework Directive 89/391 provide generic regulatory strategies for a systematic approach to risk management of health and safety at work, including managing chemical risks. The extent to which specific requirements are integrated into these more generic demands—and the significant problems in relation to the capacity of small businesses to respond to them—need to be taken into account. Discussion of the regulatory interaction of these elements is therefore included in this chapter.

THE DEVELOPMENT OF REGULATORY STRATEGIES AT EUROPEAN LEVEL

EU measures intended to protect workers from harm arising from exposure to hazardous substances are listed in Table 2.1, where they are separated into two groups: those placing requirements on the producers of chemicals and those related to the workplace. They illustrate three main European methods for dealing with chemical risks—through hazard identification, risk assessment and in a final step, risk reduction.

The directives that place requirements on the producers of chemicals are principally concerned with trade and the functioning of the internal market. They are made under the provisions of Articles 94 and 95 of the EC treaties. As such they are concerned with laying down rules for the marketing of substances in the EU and aim to establish a harmonization of national legislations. Those directives concerned with worker protection however are made under Articles 137 of the EC treaties and are concerned with establishing minimum standards for the protection of workers.

However this legal separation fails to convey the important fact that the requirements of the worker-protection directives rely for their operation on many of the provisions contained in the directives that regulate the marketing of

Table 2.1 Principal EU Instruments Regulating the Management
of Chemical Risks

Directives principally concerned with trade	Directives principally concerned with protection of workers
Council Directive 67/548/EEC of June 27, 1967, on the approximation of laws, regulations and administrative provisions relating to the classification, packaging and labeling of dangerous substances. Official Journal No. P 196, 08/16/1967, pp. 0001–0098.	Council Directives 98/24/EC of April 7, 1998, on the protection of the health and safety of workers from the risks related to chemical agents at work (fourteenth individual directive within the meaning of Article 16 (1) of Directive 89/391/EEC).
Council Regulation (EEC) No. 793/93 of March 23, 1993, on the evaluation and control of the risks of existing substances. Official Journal No. L 084, 04/05/1993, pp. 0001-0075.	Council Directive 90/394/EEC of June 28, 1990, on the protection of workers from the risks related to exposure to carcinogens at work (Sixth individual directive within the meaning of Article 16 (1) of Directive 89/391/EEC), Official Journal L 196, 07/26/1990, pp. 0001–0007.
Council Directive of July 27, 1976 on the approximation of the laws, regulations and administrative provisions of the member states relating to restrictions on the marketing and use of certain dangerous substances and preparations (76/769/EEC).	Council Directive 90/679/EEC of November 26, 1990, on the protection of workers from risks related to exposure to biological agents at work (seventh individual directive within the meaning of Article 16 (1) of Directive 89/391/EEC), Official Journal L 374, 12/31/1990, pp. 0001–0012. Amended and consolidated by Directive 2000/54/EC of the European Parliament and the Council of September 18, 2000, on the protection of workers from risks related to exposure to biological agents at work.

chemical substances. This means that in practice for example, worker protection requirements that give employers responsibilities for chemical risk management rely for their implementation on the provisions on the classification and labeling of chemical substances and the supply of information concerning their safe use that are found in the directives regulating the marketing of substances. The introduction of REACH, which essentially consolidates and develops the provisions of directives regulating chemical suppliers and is concerned with trade, for the same reasons will also have implications for the workplace. In this case, it explicitly addresses some of its requirements to users as well as to suppliers. Also, in terms of their operation at the workplace level, all these measures need to be understood in relation to the broad requirements of the EU Framework Directive 89/391.

Directives Principally Concerned with Trade

Two central elements are evident in these directives: requirements on hazard identification and risk assessment. These obligations are required of producers and place emphasis on their responsibilities to communicate information to users. There are also measures restricting the marketing and use of certain dangerous substances and preparations.

Their development began with Council Directive 67/548/EEC on the approximation of the laws, regulations, and administrative provisions relating to the classification, packaging and labeling of dangerous substances (known as the Dangerous Substances Directive or DSD). Its aim was to identify so-called intrinsic hazardous properties of substances either already on or intended to be on the European market. Although originally designed to cover hazards when handling substances at the workplace, additional hazards related to the environment and consumers were subsequently included. A parallel concern was to impose harmonized and legally binding obligations on manufacturers, producers and importers of hazardous chemicals and to classify and label the hazards of chemical products and in so doing, aid in the process of elimination of technical barriers to trade.

Substances identified as dangerous are listed in Annex I to the directive; their hazardous properties have to be communicated to the user via information provided on labels of the packaged chemical,[1] and in a more detailed form in so-called Safety Data Sheets. Under Directive 91/155/EEC as amended[2] (the Safety Data Sheet Directive) industrial and occupational users are entitled to receive additional information via Safety Data Sheets (SDSs). These provide basic information on the physical, chemical and toxicological properties of substances and preparations as well as information on how to handle, use, transport and dispose of them in safe ways. In addition, information on first-aid measures in case of fire, accidents, or other emergencies must also be provided. There are corresponding provisions for mixtures of substances (preparations) originally laid down

---

[1] In the form of pictograms, symbols and R(isk) and S(afety) phrases.
[2] Commission Directive 2001/58/EC of July 27, 2001, amending for the second time Directive 91/155/EEC defining and laying down the detailed arrangements for the system of specific information relating to dangerous preparations in implementation of Article 14 of European Parliament and Council Directive 1999/45/EC and relating to dangerous substances in implementation of Article 27 of Council Directive 67/548/EEC (safety data sheets) (Text with EEA relevance). Official Journal L 212, 08/07/2001, pp. 0024–0033.

in Directive 88/379/EEC, and more recently in Directive 1999/45/EC—the Dangerous Preparations Directive (DPD).

However while classification, labeling and SDSs may be the most important (and often the only) information sources for downstream users of dangerous substances and preparations, such information is far from universally correct or complete. A Europe-wide survey undertaken in the ECLIPS (European Classification and Labelling Inspections of Preparations, including Safety Data Sheets) project carried out by the Chemical Legislation European Enforcement Network (CLEEN) to assess the extent of compliance with the classification and labeling legislation in member states found that in practice such compliance was restricted (CLEEN, 2004). It focused on the DPD and on a restricted range of the more dangerous preparations in a limited number of product groups (such as paints and varnishes, cleaning agents [e.g., solvent based], detergents, preparations to be used in construction of buildings and photo-chemicals), in order to keep the results comparable. It found that not more than 40% of the preparations currently on the market in the EU and only 30% of SDSs complied with legal provisions. The labeling of about 60% of the preparations was incorrect and two-thirds of the SDSs were either incorrect or incomplete.

Classification under the DSD and the DPD also has a significant impact on the way substances are addressed in other community legislation, as well as in some national provisions and technical guidance, such as COSHH (Control of Substances Hazardous to Health) essentials and the similar recent German, Easy-to-use Workplace Control Scheme.

In more than 60 other pieces of community legislation, reference is made either to the criteria for hazard identification in the directives themselves or to their provisions for additional risk reduction for substances (listed in Annex I to the DSD). For example, substances and preparations classified as category one or two carcinogens or mutagens are subject to more stringent control and protective measures at the workplace than other (hazardous) substances and preparations. The classification also has implications for the marketing and use of a chemical that are addressed under Council Directive of July 27, 1976, on the approximation of the laws, regulations and administrative provisions of the member states relating to restrictions on the marketing and use of certain dangerous substances and preparations (76/769/EEC). They range from the prohibition of marketing to the general public to a complete ban of a substance.

The directives don't address substances existing prior to 1981. This led to the adoption of Regulation (EEC) 793/93 on the evaluation and control of the risks of existing substances (Existing Substances Regulation or ESR). This sets a framework for evaluation and control of existing substances (those listed in the European Inventory of Existing Commercial Chemical Substances [EINECS] as being on the market between 1971 and 1981). Because there are more than

100,000 of these, a prioritization took place at the European level that was primarily based on production volumes[3] and on the potential risk to man and the environment, resulting in four lists of about 140 substances of high concern. Requirements on risk assessment and control for these were addressed in further directives.[4,5,6]

Directives Principally Concerned with Protection of Workers

These measures have been made under the EU Framework Directive 89/39 and need to be seen within the aegis of its requirements. Article 6 of the Framework Directive lists the general principles of prevention. They include:

- avoiding risks;
- evaluating the risks that cannot be avoided;
- combating the risks at the source;
- adapting the work to the individual, especially with regard to the design of work places; the choice of work equipment and the choice of working and production methods;
- adapting to technical progress;
- replacing the dangerous with the nondangerous or the less dangerous;
- developing a coherent overall prevention policy that covers technology, organization of work, working conditions, social relationships and the influence of factors related to the working environment;
- giving collective protective measures priority over individual protective measures; and
- giving appropriate instructions to workers.

The directive therefore not only establishes a framework of general rules for workers' safety and health protection, but also implements Europe-wide the concept of a modern, comprehensive approach to occupational health and safety, which should be embedded in the overall management of a company. Individual directives adopted under Article 16 (1) of the Framework Directive are all based

---

[3] The regulation was initially concerned with so-called High Production Volume Chemicals (HPVCs), imported or produced in quantities exceeding 1000 tonnes per year, followed by those of lower volumes (between 10 and 1000 tonnes).

[4] Commission Regulation (EC) No. 1179/94 of May 25, 1994, concerning the first list of priority substances as foreseen under Council Regulation (EEC) No 793/93. Official Journal No. L 131, 05/26/1994, pp. 0003–0004.

[5] Commission Regulation (EC) No. 2268/95 of September 27, 1995, concerning the second list of priority substances as foreseen under Council Regulation (EEC) No 793/93. Official Journal No. L 231, 09/28/1995, pp. 0018–0019.

[6] Commission Regulation (EC) No. 143/97 of January 27, 1997, concerning the third list of priority substances as foreseen under Council Regulation (EEC) No. 793/93 (Text with EEA relevance). Official Journal No. L 025, 01/28/1997, pp. 0013–0014.

on the same main principles regulating OHS management. The two that are of most direct concern are Directive 98/24/EEC, which sets the frame for preventing the risks from chemical agents in general and Directive 90/394/EEC, which specifies requirements for dealing with carcinogens (there are further directives such as on biological agents, etc., but these will not concern us here).

The Chemical Agents Directive 98/24/EC attempts to provide a comprehensive framework for community legislation on chemicals in the workplace. Its principles (also found in the Carcinogens Directive; see below) are based on substitution, prevention, protection and control. The origins of this approach can be traced to Council Directive 80/1107/EEC[7] which set out measures for the control of risks due to chemical, physical and biological agents. It was amended in 1988 by the adoption of Directive 88/642/EEC which focuses on the mechanism for setting exposure limits for hazardous chemicals. This was repealed in 2001 with the adoption of the Chemical Agents Directive.

The Chemical Agents Directive 98/24/EEC contains minimum requirements for work with hazardous chemical agents. Links to DSD and the DPD exist, as the scope of both the Chemicals and Carcinogens Directives covers any chemical substance and preparation that either is already classified or meets the criteria to be classified as hazardous according to the meaning of the DSD and DPD. The Chemical Agents Directive also covers chemical substances that, although they do not meet these criteria, may present a risk to safety and health of workers owing to their physio-chemical, chemical, or toxicological properties, and it provides a framework for setting occupational exposure-limit values and biological-limit values at European levels. It requires that:

- risks arising from chemical agents are identified by employers through risk assessment;
- exposure be prevented or at least adequately controlled;
- exposure is monitored regularly;
- in those instances where a national OEL (Occupational Exposure Limit) is exceeded, the employer is to remedy the situation through preventative and protective measures;
- workers be informed and trained when handling dangerous substances;
- they are provided with regular health surveillance;
- individual exposure records are made and kept up-to-date; and
- employers draw up detailed procedures for dealing with accidents, incidents and emergencies that involve hazardous substances.

Directive 90/394/EEC on the protection of workers from the risks related to exposure to carcinogens at work is the sixth individual directive within the

---

[7] Council Directive 80/1107/EEC of November 27, 1980, on the protection of workers from the risks related to exposure to chemical, physical, and biological agents at work. Official Journal No. L 327, 12/03/1980, pp. 0008–0013.

meaning of Article 16 (1) of Framework Directive 89/391. Since its adoption, the directive has been amended twice,[8] and its scope extended to cover mutagens. A consolidated version of the Carcinogen Directive and its amendment was published in the Official Journal on April 30, 2004 (Directive 2004/37[9]). Its main objective is to protect workers' health and safety against risks specifically arising or likely to arise from exposure to carcinogens and mutagens at work; that is, those substances that meet the criteria for carcinogens and mutagens (category 1 and 2) under the DSD and the DPD. It lays down minimum requirements concerning these carcinogens and mutagens, including limit values.

It is the duty of the employer to minimize the use of a carcinogen or mutagen by replacing it with a substance, preparation, or process less dangerous or not dangerous. If it is not technically possible to carry out substitution, the employer must ensure that the carcinogen is manufactured and used in a closed system. Where neither of these precautions is possible, the employer must reduce the level of exposure to a carcinogen or mutagen to as low a level as is technically possible.

Furthermore, the Directive lists a number of measures to be followed when a carcinogen or mutagen is used including:

- limitation of the quantities of a carcinogen or mutagen at the place of work;
- keeping as low as possible the number of workers exposed or likely to be exposed;
- design of work processes and engineering control measures so as to avoid or minimize the release of carcinogens or mutagens into the place of work;
- evacuation of carcinogens and mutagens at the source, local extraction system, or general ventilation; all such methods to be appropriate and compatible with the need to protect public health and the environment;
- use of existing appropriate procedures for the measurement of carcinogens and mutagens, in particular for the early detection of abnormal exposures resulting from an unforeseeable event or an accident;
- application of suitable working procedures and methods;
- collective protection measures and, where exposure cannot be avoided by other means, individual protection measures;
- hygiene measures, in particular regular cleaning of floors, walls and other surfaces;
- information for workers;

[8] Council Directive 97/42/EC of June 27, 1997, Official Journal No. L 179, 07/08/1997, pp. 0004–0006. Council Directive 1999/38/EC of April 29, 1999. Official Journal No. L 138, 06/01/1999, pp. 0066-0069.

[9] Directive 2004/37/EC of the European Parliament and of the Council of April 29, 2004, on the protection of workers from the risks related to exposure to carcinogens or mutagens at work (Sixth individual directive within the meaning of Article 16 (1) of Council Directive 89/391/EEC) (codified version) (Text with EEA relevance) (Official Journal No. L 158, 04/30/2004, p. 50).

- demarcation of risk areas and use of adequate warning and safety signs including No Smoking signs in areas where workers are exposed or likely to be exposed to carcinogens and mutagens;
- drawing up plans to deal with emergencies likely to result in abnormally high exposure; and
- means for safe storage, handling and transportation, in particular by using sealed and clearly and visibly labeled containers.

In addition, the employers must, when requested, make available to the competent authority appropriate information on:

- activities and industrial processes carried out, including the reasons for which carcinogens and mutagens are used;
- quantities of substances or preparations manufactured or used that contain carcinogens or mutagens;
- number of workers exposed;
- preventive measures taken;
- type of protective equipment used;
- the nature and degree of exposure; and
- replacement.

The employer must also ensure that workers and their representatives receive sufficient and appropriate training on the basis of all available information concerning the potential risks to health and the precautions to be taken to prevent exposure. In particular, the employer shall inform workers of installations and related containers of carcinogens or mutagens, ensure that all containers, packages and installations containing carcinogens or mutagens are labeled clearly and legibly and display clearly visible warning and hazard signs.

Reinforced health surveillance is foreseen and the practical recommendations for health surveillance are given in Annex II of the directive. Annex III of the directive sets limit values on the basis of available information, including scientific and technical data.

THE EFFECTIVENESS OF THE EU APPROACH AND THE DEVELOPMENT OF REACH

By the end of the 1990s the Commission had reached the conclusion that the plethora of market instruments involved in the regulation of chemicals in the EU was failing to achieve desired effects. This understanding led a drive toward a new regulatory approach to chemicals regulation that was outlined in the EC Chemicals White Paper (EC, 2001). It became the focus for the development of the proposals embraced in REACH.

A Commission report on the operation of the main regulatory instruments for controlling chemical risks was published in 1998, causing some disquiet that the existing legal framework was not adequate (CEC, 1998). As a consequence, the Commission developed the White Paper "Strategy for a Future Chemicals Policy," adopted in 2001. The White Paper argued that at the European level:

- There was a lack of knowledge about the dangers of many chemicals on the EU market, making it difficult to assess their risks properly and to make informed decisions about controlling those risks.
- The current process of risk assessment was too slow, meaning that only a handful of chemical substances were assessed at the EU level each year.
- Resources were concentrated too much on the assessment of "new substances," which made up less than 1% of the total volume of substances on the market and not enough on "existing substances."

To remedy these and other perceived weaknesses, the White Paper proposed a dramatic reorientation of chemicals regulation so that it was more clearly based on a precautionary principle, with the chemicals industry being required to prove its products were safe, rather than the authorities having to show they were dangerous. It proposed to achieve this change through the creation of:

- a single efficient and coherent regulatory framework, providing equivalent knowledge about the hazards of both new and existing substances;
- shifting responsibility for testing and risk assessment of chemical products from the authorities to industry;
- promotion of innovation and competitiveness without compromising high levels of protection;
- introduction of an authorization system where stringent control is ensured for the most dangerous substances; and
- increased transparency of information.

The strategy as laid out in the White Paper had two objectives (Rogers, 2003): achieving a high level of protection for human health and the environment and promoting the efficient functioning of the EU internal market and the competitiveness of the chemicals industry.

In May 2003, after several impact studies and various discussions in the European Council and with different stakeholders, the Commission published the draft proposal "Regulation of the European Parliament and of the Council concerning the Registration, Evaluation, Authorisation and Restriction of Chemicals"—REACH. It was the subject of further widespread consultation and eventually resulted in the adoption of a revised version by the Commission in which several of the initial requirements were substantially modified in efforts to make what several commentators have seen as concessions to a powerful industrial lobby (Epstein, 2005). This legislative proposal was put before the European Parliament and the Council in 2005. Its main elements, as proposed by the Commission and subsequently modified in their passage through the EU legislature, consisted of several interlinked requirements on chemical producers concerning the registration, evaluation, and authorization of their chemical products. They were:

Registration

- Registration would be required for all chemicals manufactured in or imported into the EU in a volume of one tonne or more per year with the competent authority within a new European Chemicals Agency (ECA). The ECA will manage a central EU-wide database.
- Certain substances considered to be adequately regulated under other provisions, such as medicinal products or those presenting low risks (such as water, oxygen, etc.), occurring naturally and not chemically modified (such as minerals and mineral ores) are exempted.
- Manufacturers and importers of substances will need to obtain and submit basic information including a brief description of the uses of the substance and any uses that the manufacturer advises against.
  - A technical dossier, containing information on the properties, uses classification, and safe use of a substance, is required for substances in volumes of one tonne or more.
  - A chemical safety report is required for substances in volumes of 10 tonnes or more.
- Data requirements would therefore vary according to the production volume and suspected toxicity of the substance.
- Registration would be undertaken in several stages, with deadlines varying with production volumes.
  - Substances supplied in excess of 1,000 tonnes a year and some substances of so-called high concern (e.g., CMRs, PBTs, or vPvBs[10]) would be registered within 3 years of the law coming into force.
  - Those in excess of 100 tonnes are to be registered within 6 years.
  - Those in excess of 1 tonne and 10 tonnes to be registered within 11 years.
  - For chemicals that raise no particular concerns or annual production of which usually remains below a ceiling of 100 tonnes, registration will be sufficient. All substances produced or marketed in greater volumes, or which are more sensitive, will be subject to evaluation.

About 30,000 phase-in substances are expected to be registered over the first 11 years following REACH (Registration, Evaluation and Authorisation of Chemicals) coming into force, as well as a number of non-phase-in substances (that is, substances that were not produced or marketed before the entry into force of REACH).

---

[10]A CMR substance is one that is carcinogenic, mutagenic, or toxic to reproduction. PBTs are persistent biologically accumulative and toxic substances, while vPvBs are very persistent and biologically accumulative substances.

Evaluation

Two kinds of evaluation are proposed. The European Chemicals Agency will check registration dossiers for compliance with requirements (at least 5% of registrations will be checked). It will also check testing proposals to prevent unnecessary animal testing. The second kind of evaluation, is substance evaluation and this will be undertaken in cooperation with the competent authorities of the member states. Substance evaluation will be carried out if a competent authority suspects that a substance poses a risk to human health or the environment (for example because of its structural similarity to a known dangerous substance). This involves examining the dossiers of all registrations for a substance to clarify the risks and may result in the authority requesting further information from those registering the substance.

Authorization

Substances identified through registration and evaluation as being of high concern (such as CMRs, PBTs, vPvBs, or ones identified from scientific evidence as causing probable serious effects to humans or the environment, such as endocrine disrupters) cannot be used or placed on the market without authorization. The new European Chemicals Agency (ECA) will publish a list of such substances. The subsequent authorization procedure will be in two steps. In the first, a decision will be made as to which substances on the candidate list will be included and which uses of such included substances will be exempted from authorization requirements. In the second step, those using or making available substances on the list will need to apply for authorization for each use of the substance intended. Authorization (one for each use and user) will be granted to the producer and importer of a substance (or to users) only if they can demonstrate that they can control the risks posed by the chemical in an appropriate way. If not, it may be granted that the socioeconomic benefits of the substance outweigh the risks, and there are no suitable alternative substances or processes. This type of decision may take into account whether industry is actively researching to find an alternative substitute. Authorizations granted for socioeconomic reasons will be time limited and reviewed on a case-by-case basis. The use of other substances that pose unacceptable risks but are not classified as of high concern could be restricted if requested by a member state. Restriction may ban use in certain products, by consumers, or even any use at all.

Proposals for restrictions will be prepared by member states or by the Agency on behalf of the Commission in the form of a dossier that is required to demonstrate that there is risk to human health or the environment that needs to be addressed at the community level and to identify the most appropriate risk-reduction measures.

The final version of the regulation that was agreed upon in December 2006 reflects a range of compromises that were decided in the European Parliament and in negotiations between the Parliament, the Council, and the Commission, in which the chemical industry and its supporters achieved significant modifications to the original proposals.

Registration was the most controversial issue from the outset, because of the costs involved in gathering the health and safety data it required. Compromises agreed upon between the European Parliament and the Council meant that the 30,000 substances marketed or imported in volumes of less than 10 tonnes would need to be registered; but as much as two-thirds of them would be likely to be exempt from further testing. Instead, the new ECA would decide which of these substances should be tested. Other matters covered by the compromise deal included the "one substance, one registration" principle that had been actively sought by representations from the small enterprises among the chemical producers and that requires the sharing of registration data between chemical producers to reduce costs to industry (as well as reducing unnecessary animal testing). A waiver was agreed to for manufacturers and importers of substances produced in quantities of between 10 and 100 tonnes per year, whereby they could opt out of providing information if they provided adequate justification in their assessment of chemical safety. In its final form, the regulation requires that the Commission decide within 12 years whether or not to recommend extending the requirement for chemical safety reports for substances produced or imported in amounts of less than 10 tonnes per year. For cancerous or mutagenic substances or those toxic to reproduction, this deadline is shortened to seven years. The intellectual property provisions were also strengthened, with data protection extended from three to six years.

During the debate on approval, the European Parliament approved a "substitution principle," requiring companies to substitute dangerous chemicals with safer ones when available—a principle that was in turn rejected by national government ministers on the European Council. In its final form, the regulation contains an obligation for producers of the most dangerous substances to submit a substitution plan to replace them with safer alternatives. Where no alternative exists, producers will have to present a research and development plan aimed at finding one. Also agreed upon was a review clause requiring review after six years on the basis of the latest scientific data and the inclusion of endocrine disrupters among those substances that can be authorized only in the light of an analysis of the socioeconomic costs and benefits.

It is intended that the measures in REACH will increase the effectiveness of existing provisions to protect workers exposed to dangerous substances and combat risks of ill health caused by work-related exposure to chemicals by:

- providing information that is currently not available on the properties of chemical substances and ways of minimizing the risks associated with using them,
- improving the communication of such information throughout production and supply chains, and

• promoting substitution of the most harmful chemicals with less hazardous ones by means of its authorization and restriction provisions.

The extent to which this will actually occur depends on several issues for which the prognosis is at present unclear. This is one reason why REACH has generated considerable debate. For the social and economic interests involved, not surprisingly, much of the debate has polarized around issues of costs versus benefits. But the assumptions made by or on behalf of all the interest groups involved regarding these costs and benefits (as well as it being unclear what form the final implementation of the regulation would take or how it would work in practice), make it very difficult to predict such outcomes reliably. This has led to the entrenchment of widely differing views on their scale, typified for example by the contrasting perspectives of the trade unions (Musu, 2004), compared with those of the chemical industry (CEFIC, 2003).

The requirements of REACH will contribute to an increase in available information concerning the hazardous properties and safe use of more chemicals in Europe. The policy rhetoric behind REACH places considerable emphasis on not only how the measures will involve greater requirements on chemical producers to exercise responsible stewardship of their products, but also how such duties will extend through the supply chain with the result that formulators and users will also be bound to engage more actively in ensuring the safety of chemical substances than is currently the case.

Thus, substances manufactured or imported in quantities of 10 tonnes or more will require a chemicals safety report (CSR). This must document the hazards and classification of the substance and an assessment as to whether it is a PBT or vPvB. It will describe "exposure scenarios" for specific uses of substances that are classified as dangerous or are PBT/vPvB substances. Exposure scenarios have been defined as sets of conditions that describe how substances are manufactured or used during their life cycle and how their manufacturer or importer recommends that exposure of humans and the environment to them should be controlled (Christensen et al., 2003; EC, 2006; Karhu, 2006). They must include appropriate risk management measures and operational conditions that, when properly implemented, ensure risks from the use of a substance are adequately controlled. They should be developed to cover all identified uses. These embrace not only the manufacturer and importers' own uses but also other uses that are made known to the manufacturer or importer by downstream users. The exposure scenarios are required to be annexed to safety data sheets that are supplied to downstream users and distributors.

These requirements certainly imply the need for greater product stewardship for substances manufactured or imported in relevant quantities on the part of manufacturers and importers as well as greater risk communication within supply chains; but there remain major questions over how effective these requirements are likely to be in practice and what further supports might be required to ensure their effectiveness. Research demonstrates that although the supply of good quality information is obviously important in ensuring appropriate chemical risk management, the user's understanding and proper use of this information is the result of a more complex set of factors. Moreover, the new requirements on users to communicate their uses to manufacturers and importers, if they are different from those identified in the exposure scenarios, are made in the absence of evidence of the ability or willingness of downstream users to undertake such action. The construction of chemical-supply chains in combination with the known poor understanding of downstream users concerning the risks of chemical substances do not inspire confidence that these measure alone will necessarily result in the actions desired on the part of downstream users. They are based on a particularly optimistic (and untested) way of looking at how supply chains operate in relation to the health and safety of workers. They do not fully address what prevents users from either understanding or using the information on the safe use of chemicals that is currently available. Because of the quantities required before such measures apply (those manufactured or imported in quantities of 10 tonnes or more), they are unlikely to have a major impact on the quality of the classification and labeling of chemical products overall (Pickvance et al., 2005). These issues are discussed in the final chapter, where evidence is reviewed of the kind of support that downstream users—and especially those in small enterprises—may need in order to meet such legislative demands.

Concerns about the impact of REACH on small enterprises were present from the outset. They have been of two kinds. On the one hand, improved risk communication through better quality and more coordinated information transmission between suppliers and users was thought to be likely to benefit small enterprise users. Allied to this, the classification and labeling inventory requirements of REACH are intended to ensure that hazard classifications of all dangerous substances are available to all and to promote agreement on classifications. Under REACH, building on existing requirements, industry will be required to submit all its classifications to the European Chemicals Agency within three and a half years of the regulation coming into force. It is anticipated that this will support greater uniformity and harmonization of classification, especially through the removal of differing classifications of the same substances, thus helping to clarify problems of classification and labeling to the benefit of SME downstream users. In addition the Commission will issue a proposal for a further regulation to implement the Globally Harmonised System (GHS) for classification and labeling, which is intended to be consistent with the provisions of REACH.

On the other hand, efforts have been made to reduce the resource implications of REACH for small businesses. According to the official guidance on REACH, many of the revisions to REACH that were aimed at reducing its costs, such as reducing the testing and reporting requirements, simplifying the registration procedures for chemicals produced in lower volumes, restricting requirements

according to a tonnage threshold, and reductions in downstream-user requirements, were made with the intent of easing the regulatory and cost burden for
small enterprises. Similarly, data sharing in the registration of chemicals, the
proposed fee reductions for SMEs, and a proposed help desk arrangement for
them are further measures intended to reduce the burden on them (European
Commission, 2006).

While all these modifications may well achieve their intended purpose, they
also raise questions concerning the likely relevance of REACH in managing
the risks of using chemical substances in small workplaces, since the quantities
in which such chemicals are used in these workplaces will in many cases mean
that their control will fall outside the scope of the provisions of the REACH
regulation. They will nevertheless remain within the coverage of existing requirements addressing workplace chemical risk management. Some comments are
in order concerning the relationship between the new REACH regulation and
existing EU provisions for regulating workplace exposure to hazardous chemicals.

REACH AND EXISTING WORKPLACE CHEMICAL
RISK REGULATION

REACH belongs in the category of EU provisions that deal with the functioning
of the internal market; that is, those made under Articles 94 and 95 of the EC
Treaties. It will repeal, incorporate, or amend existing directives and regulations
on the marketing and use of chemicals. It therefore replaces Regulation 793/93
on the evaluation and control of existing substances and Directive 76/769
and associated directives concerning restrictions on the marketing and use of
dangerous substances and preparations. The restrictions themselves will remain in
force but are to be found in an annex to REACH. Directives 67/548 and 1999/45
on the classification and labeling of dangerous substances and preparations will be
amended to bring them in line with REACH, which will also take over current
requirements for Safety Data Sheets that were part of Directive 91/155. Moreover,
it is an EU regulation, rather than a directive. As such it has direct effect on the
legislative frameworks of member states (that is, it does not require national
legislative provisions for its implementation).

However, there is little duplication between REACH and existing occupational
health and safety provisions on chemical risks. Unlike the directives made under
Articles 94 and 95 of the EC Treaty, those made under Article 137 of the EC
treaties—the Chemical Agents Directive and the Carcinogens Directive—will
remain in force after the introduction of REACH, and the requirements of both
sets of provisions will need to be met. Ideally therefore REACH will build on
existing workplace provisions; it has been suggested that it might even help
to plug gaps that exist in them by providing a further opportunity to remind
employers of their obligations (Pickvance et al., 2005).

However there are a number of concerns that regulatory agencies responsible for OHS surveillance have expressed regarding the interface between REACH, the Chemical Agents Directive, and the Carcinogens Directive. For example in a paper presented at the SLIC (Senior Labour Inspectors Committee) plenary meeting in Vienna in March 2006, the Deputy Director of the HSE envisaged a number of potentially difficult situations (McCracken, 2006). They included circumstances where a manufacturer or importer provided instructions for supported uses of a chemical product that are different from those resulting from the user's existing controls developed under CAD and CMD. If this were to happen, national regulators would be faced with some difficult decisions on which regulatory provisions they should require compliance. It is unclear at present whether a member state could require higher standards than those set by REACH, such as might be the case where exposure limits differ in different member states. There is also some concern that the measures required by REACH may not be specific enough to cover some of the circumstances of individual workplaces. The REACH provisions are also not related to other workplace requirements on risk assessment and management, such as those in national provisions implementing the EU Framework Directive. Furthermore there are a number of specific situations in which REACH will not apply and the CAD and CMD requirements will remain the only EU provisions in place. These include:

- on-site intermediates and products generated *in situ,*
- byproducts,
- polymers,
- regime-controlled products (such as medicines, cosmetics, etc.), and
- substances produced in quantities of less than 1 tonne annually.

*   *   *

In recent years the EU system for regulating the production and use of chemical substances has undergone a major overhaul. While the content of the regulation that comes into force in 2007 is a much reduced version of the original proposals, the new system introduced under REACH is intended to have widespread impact across the spectrum of the life cycles of chemical substances, offering increased protection for human health and the environment and reversing the burden of proof concerning the safety of such products from the regulatory authorities to the industry. At the same time it is argued that it will increase innovation in the chemicals industry, maintaining and enhancing its competitiveness and preventing fragmentation of the internal market while increasing the transparency of risk assessment and communication. As far as chemical risk management in small firms is concerned, there are several innovations in REACH, especially its focus on risk communication in supply chains, which could have some impact on current practices. However, its effect will be influenced by the ways in which these matters are addressed and supported in the implementation of existing national regulatory frameworks.

CHAPTER 3

National Regulatory Strategies on Chemical Risk Management

In all European countries there are national regulatory strategies on the management of chemical risks at work. Indeed this might be anticipated given the scale of use of chemical substances and the extent of the associated health and safety problems discussed in Chapter 1. It might be further anticipated that as a consequence of membership in the European Union there would be a degree of convergence between these strategies among different member states as the effects of harmonization are felt. This is also the case. However, such convergence does not mean that there are no longer significant differences between national approaches to workplace chemical risk regulation. As this chapter demonstrates, such differences form an important feature of the institutional implementation of chemical risk management regulation.

Although legal regulation of chemical risk management features prominently in regulatory systems in all countries, it is questionable whether such regulation has dealt adequately with all the situations in which exposure to hazardous substances is experienced at work, especially in small enterprises.

A main concern of this chapter is the extent to which regulatory strategies address, or are relevant to, the use of hazardous substances in these enterprises and in related forms of work. It begins by outlining these strategies in each of the countries studied. It then reviews research that has drawn attention to the limitations of their coverage and operation. Current political and economic trends that undermine the primacy of regulation as a means of controlling chemical risks are also noted. The chapter concludes with a discussion of the appropriateness of current regulatory approaches in the light of their effectiveness and questionable continued political support.

Features in common in the six countries studied can be especially linked to the harmonizing effects of transposition of the Framework Directive and its related directives on chemical and carcinogenic agents. Provisions on workplace chemical risk management in the countries studied are, to varying degrees, applications of generic regulatory strategies that have followed transposition of the Framework Directive. The same relationship between these generic and specific strategies is evident at national levels as that found between their sources at the EU level. Thus, all countries have framework legislation in which generic provisions are laid down on systematic health and safety management and requirements on employers to undertake risk evaluation and control with the aid of competent advice and the involvement of workers and their representatives are spelled out. Within such a framework, they also have provisions aimed more specifically at employers' responsibilities to manage chemical risks that are supported by duties on manufacturers and suppliers to provide sufficient information to allow both an awareness of the nature of the hazards of their products and the means with which they can be used safely.

Together these provisions require that manufacturers and suppliers provide users with information on labels and in SDSs and that employers use this information in broadly similar ways in their approaches to systematic chemical risk management. They are required to keep inventories of chemical products used, to provide their workers with information and training to ensure they are aware of the hazards of chemical products, and to enable safe use. There is some variation on requirements specifying the form in which such information is made available to workers. Employers are further obliged to assess the risks of using chemical substances. Again, there is some variation concerning the detailed means of doing so—for example, on the extent to which measurements in relation to OELs are required—but the overall approach is essentially the same. Similarly, the approach toward monitoring and controlling exposure to hazardous substances follows the same hierarchy of preference in all countries. It begins with due consideration of the elimination or substitution of the hazardous substance or process and is followed in descending order of preference by controls such as enclosure, local exhaust ventilation (LEV), general ventilation, systems of work and the use of personal protective equipment where other measures cannot be applied.

In practice, the application of these requirements has been shown to vary enormously across industrial sector, establishment size and in relation to the hazards and processes encountered in all countries. This appears to be true for the generic regulatory approaches to systematic risk management, as well as in relation to the more specific measures on chemical risk management. For small enterprises there is a growing body of evidence pointing to the limited operation of measures on systematic risk management in all countries. This is especially true of the arrangements to deliver the basic requirements of the Framework Directive, such as those on risk assessment and control, competent advice and worker participation (Walters, 2001). Reasons for the poor application of these measures have been ascribed to two broad sets of conditions. First, the multifaceted lack of resources within small enterprises themselves, which means that owner/managers and their workers have neither the will nor capacity to implement and operate measures based on models that mainly reflect the experience of large enterprises. Second, the limited development of supportive infrastructures for preventive health and safety in relation to small firms, including in most countries the weak presence of trade unions; poor uptake of prevention services; and insufficient resources for adequate regulatory inspection and control.

Against this backdrop, there is evidence of several specific weaknesses common to the application of regulatory strategies in chemical risk management in small firms in the countries studied. They include the poor delivery of mandated suppliers' information on hazards and safe use of their products. There is further evidence from several countries indicating that owner/managers neither understand the information with which they are supplied nor do they pass it on in a form that will help their employees either to use the products safely or to appreciate the risks to which they may be exposed if they don't.

These basic failings in turn lead to others. There is evidence that assessment of chemical risks required by regulation is at least as poor and incomplete in relation to these products as it is for health and safety risks more generally; and that management systems to ensure that such procedures are undertaken are far less developed in small enterprises than they are in their larger counterparts. There is also a suggestion in some countries that chemical risk management may in fact be worse than risk management more generally because of the more technical nature of the understandings and support involved. In relation to some of the specific regulatory means for ensuring control of exposure to hazardous chemicals, such as the role of OELs, although they are a feature of regulatory requirements in all countries and, central to the development of the strategic thinking behind the regulatory instruments at the EU and national level, the evidence of their application, such as it is, demonstrates that measurements around OELs are seldom a feature of approaches to dealing with chemical risk management in small enterprises. This is for the simple reason that employers in these enterprises frequently do not possess the skills or understanding to appreciate the need for them, the capacity to undertake them, or access to expertise that could do so on their behalf. Nor are national health and safety infrastructures adequate to support such measurement or to monitor to ensure that it is undertaken correctly.

The challenges presented by these observations are considerable, but there is nothing especially new about them. It is clear from the review of approaches at EU and national levels that they have been recognized for some time. Responses to them in the countries studied have, in the main, not been concerned with fundamental regulatory changes. Rather, they have taken more instrumental forms, with an array of programs and tools designed to make chemical risk management more accessible to small firms. Where there has been change at a regulatory level such as in the UK and in Germany, it has tended to reflect the pragmatic views of the health and safety authorities concerning the capacity of small firms to address the complexity of traditional approaches to the monitoring, evaluation, and control of hazardous substances. As a result, regulatory frameworks have been slightly modified to accommodate generic approaches to exposure assessment and control that are deemed to be more practicable to achieve in a small-firm setting.

CHEMICAL RISK MANAGEMENT REGULATORY STRATEGIES AT NATIONAL LEVELS

What follows is not intended as an exhaustive description of regulatory provisions on chemical risk management in the six EU countries studied. The aim is rather to explore their relevance to improving the management of chemical risks in small enterprises. In each country a brief description of the regulatory framework is used to introduce an analysis of the extent to which provisions and the strategies for their implementation and operation are cognizant of the needs of small enterprises. In addition, as there is now a highly developed strategic approach to regulating chemical risk management in place at the EU level, a further aim of the following section is to consider its influence on regulatory developments in the countries studied and the impact on regulating chemical risk management in small enterprises.

Austria

Although Austria is a recent member of the EU, the influence of EU regulatory strategies for health and safety generally and for chemical risk management in particular are clearly evident. As with most other countries, relevant provisions concerning the regulation of workplace chemical risks can be found in the occupational health and safety elements of labor law and in other laws that deal with regulating chemicals with regard to their effects on man and the environment, in which some OHS aspects are also addressed indirectly.

The Health and Safety at Work Act 1994 (*ArbeitnehmerInnenschutzgesetz— ASchG* 1994) and its attendant ordinances provide the main framework for regulating health and safety at work in Austria. The management of chemical substances is covered by Section 4 of the Act, concerning "dangerous substances." The Chemicals Substances Act (*Chemikaliengesetz—ChemG* 1996) and the Chemicals Substances Ordinance (*Chemikalienverordnung—ChemV* 1999) contain obligations regarding the use of dangerous substances, products, and goods more generally, some of which apply to handling chemical substances at the workplace.[1]

The requirements of OSH (Occupational Safety and Health) law in relation to chemical substances are directed toward employers and their employees, while

---

[1] The Federal Ministry of Economics and Labour is in charge of labor law: www.bmwa.gv.at/EN/Topics/Labourlaw/, the Federal Ministry of Agriculture, Forestry, Environment and Water Management is in charge of chemicals law: www.lebensministerium.at/

those of the Chemicals Substances Act (CS) and Ordinance are mainly addressed to manufacturers, importers and enterprises using them (i.e., employers). Under OSH law, workers' representatives (or all workers if there are no representatives) are entitled to participate in all OSH matters (OSH Act, 1994:13), including the selection of chemicals, information on OSH effects (*ArbVG:92a/1*), and they are entitled to receive advice from preventive experts, who have to be involved in all OSH matters (OSH Act, 1994:76/3,4; 81/3,4).

Occupational chemical risk management regulation in Austria is structured around substitution, labeling, suppliers' information (i.e., SDSs), information for workers, chemical inventories, risk assessment, control measures, and exposure limits. Additionally, there are specific regulations regarding work with certain hazardous chemicals or groups of such chemicals, which as a rule, contain the same or similar kinds of demands, sometimes complemented by specific obligations regarding training, measurements of exposures and medical monitoring. There are also further obligations relating to specific notifications or permissions; e.g., for the import of chemicals or for the handling and transport of chemical waste.

The general requirements under these categories are shown in Table 3.1. In addition, basic procedures for chemical risk management are given in publications of the Central Labour Inspectorate and of the *Allgemeine Unfall-versicherungsanstalt (*AUVA). For risk assessment, a procedure is described in AUVA (2005b), including a simplified model of risk estimation (a risk matrix with 5 risk classes and 4 severity-of-harm classes). Risk assessment for chemicals is specified in AUVA (2006), including a simplified risk estimation and substitution model, in guidelines for risk management and assessment of chemicals (BMWA, 2004a; also in AUVA, 2002), as well as in a leaflet with procedures regarding limit values and carcinogenic substances (BMWA, 2004b). Risk assessment regarding dusts is specified in AUVA (2003b), including a simplified risk estimation with four risk classes (severity of harm depending on the ratio of the particle concentration and the respective limit value, on the risk category, and compliance with given peak concentrations).

Adequate operation of all these measures in small enterprises cannot be inferred simply from their existence on the statute book. In Austria, as in other countries, the move toward greater emphasis on regulating more systematic OHS management has not occurred without some concerns about the nature of this change and its implications for the status and stringency of both national and EU regulation as well as about issues of flexibility, voluntarism and the role of compulsion in its achievement. Representation of the interests of small enterprises in the debates on modern OHS regulation has tended to focus around issues of the cost-effectiveness and appropriateness of what are perceived as more "bureaucratic" approaches to compliance with health and safety standards. Beneath such concerns however are important questions about the capacity of small enterprise owner/managers to implement regulatory requirements for OHS

Table 3.1 The Regulatory Framework for Chemical Risk Management
at the Workplace in Austria

Risk management strategy	Regulatory provision
Substitution	The OSH Act stipulates a chain of measures in order of priority regarding the use of dangerous substances. Such measures include, as a rule, substitution whenever possible, reporting, and banning use. Substances that are mutagenic or toxic for reproduction must not be used if an equivalent work result is technically feasible and achievable with safer chemical substances or, if not possible, with less dangerous chemical substances or work processes. This applies to all carcinogenic and other dangerous chemical substances if the efforts inolved are economically justifiable (OSH Act, 1994:42, in combination with OEL Ordinance, 2003:11).
Labeling	The manufacturer or importer (the supplier) must label dangerous chemical substances and products in order to give easily understandable (in German), clearly visible, and lasting information on the risks involved (ChemG, 1996:24; ChemV, 1999:13-24; or equivalent regulations as the Biocide Act, 2000:24 or the AWG 2002). Each employer is responsible for ensuring that employees handling dangerous chemicals are acting according to the labeling. Generally, the employer should be able to rely on labels being correct and complete (OSH Act, 1994:41/4).
Material Safety Data Sheets (SDS)	The manufacturer or importer (the supplier) has to provide more detailed information about dangerous chemical substances and products in SDS to enable the employers to take necessary preventive measures:[a] SDSs are prescribed for most chemicals of the ChemG 1996 and for biocides, but not for medicaments, cosmetics, or explosives. Information should be in German, provided not later than at first delivery, updated if necessary, free of charge, and as hard copy or electronically (ChemG, 1996: 25; ChemV, 1999:25). The content of SDSs has to be correct and complete according to ChemV 1999: annex F (consistent with EC regulations). Employers or their preventive experts are obliged to implement the preventive measures written in the respective SDS.

[a]SDSs are prescribed for most chemicals of the ChemG 1996 and for biocides, but not for medicaments, cosmetics, or explosives.

Table 3.1 (Cont'd.)

Risk management strategy	Regulatory provision
Worker' information	Workers must be informed by the employer about the risks to their health and safety, as well as about risk-prevention measures (OSH Act, 1994:12). Each employer has to make SDSs available to employees involved at any time (OSH Act, 1994:12/5; ChemG, 1996:25/6). Employees must work according to these instructions and information (OSH Act, 1994:15). In addition, workers must be given workplace-relevant instructions in accordance with the state of their experience (OSH Act, 1994:14): If necessary, such instruction (*'Unterweisung'*) must be given regularly and if changes have taken place, e.g., new chemicals or processes are used, as well as after (near) accidents. Briefing must include action- and behavior-orientated instructions and must be seen as specific training meeting the needs of a certain workplace, task, and risk. The instruction has to be in the native language of the workers. The employer must be able to furnish evidence of having given such instruction. For some areas, special instruction duties apply.
Risk assessment	Employers must determine whether each of the chemicals they use or store is of a dangerous type, determine their properties, assign such substances by groups, and assess the hazard. They must also evaluate the work processes, the way the chemicals are handled, the duration and level of exposures, as well as protective measures that have to be considered. To do so they may refer to suppliers' information (labels, SDSs, technical instructions, etc.), to practical experiences, monitoring results, and scientific findings. Employers are required to conduct risk assessments (*Evaluierung*) regularly, but especially after the occurrence of accidents, near-accidents, work-related diseases, when new equipment or new chemicals or new processes are implemented, when new findings become known (OSH Act, 1994:4.41). The employer has to ensure the participation of safety representatives (OSH Act, 1994:11/6), the works council (ArbVG:92a/2), or of all workers (if there are no such representative institution, OSH Act, 1994:11/2), and of preventive experts (OSH Act, 1994:76/3, 81/3).

Table 3.1 (Cont'd.)

Risk management strategy	Regulatory provision
Risk assessment (cont'd.)	All enterprises (including small enterprises) were required to implement a first risk assessment by July 2000. The social partners agreed not to regulate the risk assessment by ordinance. Therefore, there is no specific procedure for its conduct that is prescribed by the authorities (AUVA, 2005c). But by the OSH Documents Ordinance 1996, the type of safety and health protection documents are specified (see also OSH Act, 1994:5), an inventory of dangerous chemicals, an inventory of work equipment to be controlled, specific risk assessment regarding pregnant/breastfeeding women, and listing of workers' OHS instructions are all obligatory. There are simplified obligations for companies with fewer than 10 employees. For worksites with similar conditions, the documentation of the risk assessment and the hazard and stress profiles can be combined.
Inventory of (dangerous) chemicals	Employers are required to have an overview of dangerous chemicals used or stored within companies and to compile an inventory of all the dangerous chemicals as an annex to the safety and health protection documents of the enterprise (OSH Documents Ordinance, 1996:2/3). It is recommended good practice to list all chemicals and to take the opportunity to sort out unnecessary chemicals and thus to save time and money. It is also seen as good practice to develop purchasing routines for chemicals in which OSH-relevant criteria should be considered alongside other factors such as technical aspects and price.
Control measures (e.g., arising from risk assessment)	Following risk assessment, employers are responsible for implementing control measures according to the standard hierarchy (OSH Act, 1994:43, 44): substitution of chemicals and work processes; encapsulating dangerous chemicals; minimizing the amounts of dangerous chemicals, the number of workers involved, and the exposures involved; control and elimination of chemical risks at the source; separating workers from risk sources; ventilation and, only as a last resort if the above measures are not effective, the use of personal protective equipment by the workers.

Table 3.1 (Cont'd.)

Risk management strategy	Regulatory provision
Control measures (e.g., arising from risk assessment) (cont'd.)	General OSH principles also apply (OSH Act, 1994:7), including risk prevention, risk control at the source, consideration of the human factor and of the state of the art, integrated planning of risk prevention, priority of collective protection measures over individualized ones; and proper working instructions.
Specific measures regarding very dangerous chemicals	There are special provisions for substances that are carcinogenic, mutagenic, or toxic for reproduction, in which they may be used only within closed systems, wherever applicable, according to the state of the art and the type of work (OSH Act, 1994:42, 43). Documentation of all workers exposed must be kept and communicated to the appropriate Social Insurance bodies (OSH Act, 1994:47).
Exposure control (OELs)	OSH Act 1994:45 and OEL Ordinance define the Occupational Exposure Limit Values (OEL = MAK-Wert, *Maximale Arbeitsplatz-Konzentration*) and Technical Guidance Concentrations (= TRK-Wert, *Technische Richtkonzentration*). In current practice, TRK levels are set only for carcinogenic agents. The values are regularly updated and listed in the OEL Ordinance. In principle, concentrations of dangerous chemicals in the workplace air should kept as low as possible according to the state of the art (OSH Act, 1994:45/3, 4 , 7). Therefore, it is not sufficient to merely not exceed OELs. OSH Act (1994:46) and the still-to-be-enacted Measurements Ordinance, which will regulate technical measurements. Results and documentation of exposure measurement have to made available to safety representatives (OSH Act, 1994:11/7), preventive experts (OSH Act, 1994:76/2; 81/2) and works council (ArbVG:92a/2).
Health surveillance	Pre-employment medical screening is required under OSH Act (1994:49). Follow-up tests are further required in many cases involving exposure to chemical substances (e.g., lead, benzene, toluene, etc.).

management that were developed around assumptions mostly reflecting the experience of larger enterprises. It is indeed questionable whether they have the capacity in terms of time, staff, expertise and interest to deliver systematic OHS management without further support. Chemical risk management is no exception to this and provides an illustration of the operational problems encountered in small enterprises when risk management requires technical knowledge and understanding that are beyond the capacity of many owner/managers.

Review of what is known of the experience of the operation of the elements of the regulatory approach to chemical risk management in small enterprises confirms this. In terms of suppliers' information, for example, labeling chemical products with clear hazard and risk information is fundamental to appropriate risk management, yet the ECLIPS study in Austria revealed considerable deficiencies in this area with more complaints about risk and safety phrases than on average in the EU (UBA, undated). Further observations show that in Austria, users frequently find they must request up-to-date and correct SDSs from suppliers, rather than being supplied with them. Equally significant for small enterprises is the evidence that parts of the SDSs are not understood. A study evaluating the usefulness of SDSs concluded that they provided little information on protection measures, their texts were too long-winded and too technical, and that the information provided often contradicted the user's experience. As a result the information supplied was often perceived by users (employers) to be exaggerated. A large number of employers from SMEs in Austria were not even aware of the existence of the SDSs, and even when they were, they rarely consulted them, and users also rarely asked for additional information from suppliers. Interviews with suppliers showed that when drafting SDSs, they took little account of the ability of SMEs to understand them (EU OSHA, 2002a, p. 12; Geyer et al., 1999; Geyer & Kittel, 1999).

While written work instructions (*Betriebsanweisungen*) for dangerous chemicals are not prescribed explicitly by law, many larger enterprises use them. If responsible persons in smaller enterprises lack the knowledge and understanding of SDSs and other information sources as evidence indicates, they cannot produce appropriate instructions. A similar situation is likely regarding oral instructions concerning more complicated substances or mixtures. It is unclear to what extent practices of using purchasing routines in which OHS is a consideration are implemented in small enterprises, but it seems unlikely that the preconditions would exist to inform and encourage such practices in small enterprises.

In 1998 the Labour Inspectorate judged the quality of risk assessment as "good" within 63% of the companies it investigated, but the results were not analyzed according to sector or to the size of the enterprises (BMAGS, 1999, p. 104). It is widely held that small enterprises have problems accomplishing the risk assessment process and its documentation, a situation supported by the many representations small enterprises and their organizations have made concerning the "bureaucracy" of risk management requirements. According to sources within the Labour Inspectorate, a common experience with small enterprises is their practice of filling in templates for risk assessment and archiving this sometimes large document so it can be produced during inspections. This practice doesn't provide a good basis for risk communication within companies.

Reasons for the poor compliance with the regulatory requirements identified in Table 3.1 have been linked to the general lack of OHS infrastructure in both company operation and personnel in small companies compared with larger organizations. As a consequence, at best, SMEs rely on external preventive experts, and management of OSH is left to them. Many employers therefore do not recognize OSH as an activity that is required to come from within the company and its staff as part of a continuous process. This is thought to be a main barrier to the implementation of OSH regulations, as there is not only a lack of expert competence but also a lack of competence in communication and implementation. In addition to the absence of responsible personnel with relevant prevention expertise, very often SMEs also have limited financial scope, which affects human resources and the possibility of investment. This is especially so for those in weak economic situations and in sectors with structural limitations such as are found in textiles and in construction (ÖNBG, undated, p. 19ff; Kranvogel et al., 2000, p. 36).

Experts in the AUVA see the information deficit and the opinion that OSH is expensive and labor-intensive as barriers to the practical implementation of preventive elements in SMEs, and they conclude that there are still many gaps in SMEs regarding OSH (Bochmann et al., 2004, p. 22). They further estimate that these gaps lead to specific problems in managing chemical risks, especially in those enterprises where chemicals play a peripheral and infrequent role in production (Bochmann et al., 2004, p. 40).

Inspection by authorities is seen as a necessary contribution to improving chemical risk management in small enterprises, but alone it is not sufficient to address the problem. The lack of funds and personnel in the labor inspectorates prevents comprehensive coverage and control. For instance, apart from external workplaces and construction sites, the Labour Inspectorate of the BMWA inspects 22% of all worksites registered with them or 20% of the worksites with up to 50 employees (BMWA, 2004c, p. 92). In the year 2004 only 1.2% of the 76,160 "specific checks" of the Labour Inspectorate applied to chemical substances (BMWA, 2005).[2]

---

[2] However, handling and management of chemicals would also have been included in the extensive 41,487 "inspections" of entire companies and by other specific checks such as the 3,222 checks of work processes and workplaces. Unfortunately it is not possible to estimate to what extent, because no details of the chemical-related aspects of such inspections are available.

Regulatory strategists in Austria are not unaware of this overall situation or that it requires a response. To ensure a systematic OSH approach in smaller enterprises, there is a need for more public OSH information and awareness activities for better assistance and qualification structures, for closer cooperation by the institutions involved, for the identification of good practice examples, for employers' round tables, and for monetary incentives, which reward safe and healthy companies, for example, by lower accident insurance contributions (Kranvogel et al., 2000, p. 40ff).

It was to address some of these challenges posed by risk management in small enterprises that in 1999 the AUVAsafe system was established. It provides a free OHS service for enterprises with up to 50 employees. This represented a fundamental strategic change regarding smaller enterprises and Chapter 5 considers it in more detail.

Germany

The regulatory context of chemical risk management in Germany is complicated by the so-called dual system of health and safety regulation, the federal nature of the German state, and the sheer size and complexity of German industry. This requires some digression to describe its basic elements if their relevance to chemical risk management is to be appreciated. In recent years the overall health and safety system in Germany has been subject to considerable policy development as efforts have been made to modernize. This has resulted in current approaches that are a mixture of the traditional German model and newer, more "European"-style strategies, which nevertheless have particular German features.

The dual system gives sectoral insurance associations (*Unfallversicherungsträger: Berufsgenossenschaften and Unfallkassen*) a powerful rule-making and inspection function, which operates alongside that of the state. Additionally, since the German system is a federal one, regulation occurs at both national and state levels. In both the private and the public sector the insurance associations are empowered to derive autonomous legislation within their legal remit. Such legislation produced by these insurance associations is limited to the prevention of accidents at work and on the journey between home and work, on occupational diseases and on work-related risks. Legislation passed by the assembly of an insurance association has to be (formally) acknowledged by the appropriate federal ministry.[3] Although this sort of legislation is binding only for those enterprises that are members of the respective insurance association,

---

[3] In the recent past this has been the Ministry of Economy and Labour and previously it was the Federal Ministry of Labour and Social Affairs. Since 2006 further changes instituted by a new government mean that the economy and labor are no longer part of the same ministry and a Ministry of Labour and Social Affairs has been reestablished and placed in charge of occupational health and safety.

harmonizing its main features avoids major discrepancies between obligations in the various insurance associations.[4]

Approaches to chemical risk management in Germany are present at both federal and state levels and prominent at sectoral level, especially as a result of the activities of the sectoral insurance associations. Their engagement has contributed to a tradition of measuring exposure that is probably more embedded and substantial in terms of the exposure data it has generated than anywhere else in the EU. These infrastructural features, combined with Germany's size and complexity and its position as the major industrial economy in the EU with the largest chemical industry, make for a rich and varied array of approaches to supporting chemical risk management.

Partly because of the complexity of its structure and the traditions of prescriptive regulation it generated, modern process-based health and safety regulation took hold relatively late in Germany, with measures effectively implementing the requirements of Framework Directive 89/391 not introduced until the Occupational Health Act 1996 (Walters, 2002) and national guidelines for systematic health and safety management published in 2003 (BMWA, 2003). In parallel, systematic health and safety management targeted at small firms has been developed at the federal state level as well as by insurance associations (for example, LASI (*Länderausschuss für Arbeitsschutz und Sicherheitstechnik*), 2001; BAYERN (*Bayerisches Staatsministerium für Arbeit und Sozialordnung*), 2001; SACHSEN (*Sächsisches Staatsministerium für Wirtschaft und Arbeit*), 2002; SMS (*Sicher mit System*), 2005). At the same time, the Work Safety Act (*Arbeitssicherheitsgesetz*) 1973, addresses the implementation of occupational health and safety services in enterprises. Employers are obliged to delegate specified tasks either to occupational physicians or to occupational hygienists. Both experts must support employers in their duties regarding health and safety and they must cooperate with the works council. It is left to the discretion of the enterprise—to a consensual decision by employer and works council—how the employers' obligations are to be realized: the medical and safety experts can be employed by the company, they can be hired as individual experts, or the task can be commissioned to an external service. Whereas the tasks of both types of experts are defined in the act, the time to be spent by them on the specified tasks is prescribed in provisions issued by the respective insurance association.

In 1992 the Federal Ministry of Labour and Social Affairs (BMA) decreed that by the end of that year the mandatory employers' liability insurance associations

---

[4] See Walters (2002) for a fuller description of the German health and safety system, but also note that currently the system is undergoing significant change as efforts are made to produce a more unified national strategy for the working environment, among other things this will reduce the number of insurance associations through various planned amalgamations.

should develop approaches for the obligatory coverage by medical experts of all enterprises with at least one employee (BMA, 1992). When in 1996, with the enactment of the Occupational Health Act, the previous exemptions for small enterprises from the obligatory coverage by medical and safety experts were repealed, several insurance associations established technical services to complement already-existing medical services in order to provide the necessary expertise, particularly for small enterprises. However, any enterprise is free to subscribe to the service of its choice and is not obliged to use the service connected to its insurance association. As the minimum number of hours per year for which occupational health and safety services have to be subscribed to is dependent on the number of employees in the enterprise, particularly in small and micro-enterprises, the contractual service hours are minimal and for many enterprises not at all sufficient for the tasks to be covered by the services. As a consequence, branch organizations of SMEs have complained about additional costs for services, which did not result in any tangible benefits but were conceived by many enterprises only as an additional bureaucratic burden.

Because this problem of too few service hours for SMEs became apparent while consideration of the transposition of the EU framework directive began, research on the development of more intelligent models of service coverage for SMEs was commissioned in the early 1990s. Since the mid-1990s various approaches have been evaluated (for example: Barth, 2000; Boldt, 1997; Heeg, 2002; Kliemt, 2003; Schulte et al., 2004). One such approach, the so-called employer's model (*Unternehmermodell*), was particularly favored by the employers' liability insurance associations. Originally developed by a single insurance association in 1983 as an alternative to obligatory coverage by external safety experts (Bieneck, & Rückert, 1992; Diekershoff, 1989; Grünewald, 1989), it was adopted and promoted by an increasing number of insurance associations. In 2005 a revised model regulation for coverage by medical and safety experts was agreed upon and has since been implemented by most insurance associations with some minor modifications.

Two types of coverage of occupational health are intended: standard coverage (*Regelbetreuung*), and alternatively, demand-oriented coverage. For enterprises up to 10 employees, standard coverage consists of two elements: basic coverage and additional cause-related coverage. The latter is only required for certain, explicitly defined situations. The number of contractual service hours are not specified for basic coverage or for cause-related coverage. For enterprises above 10 employees, the old system of prescribed contractual service hours per employee has been retained. As a concession to employers, prescribed service hours are limited until 2008 when they will be revised.

The second type of coverage, the alternative "employer's model," is limited to enterprises with up to 50 employees and in some sectors only up to 25 or 30 employees. It entails a number of training courses for the employer to provide basic occupational health and safety skills and to motivate the performance of necessary risk-reduction measures. Based on this training, employers are supposed to be qualified to decide for themselves about the necessity and extent of external coverage. In addition, they are obliged to hire cause-related coverage, which is required for the same situations defined as part of standard coverage for enterprises of up to 10 employees.

With regard to hazardous substances, the legislative provisions have been subject to recent major revisions in the form of the Hazardous Substances Ordinance, 2005, made under the Occupational Health Act 1996 and the Chemicals Act 1980. It introduced new, specific obligations for risk assessment, deals with obligations regarding both the marketing of chemicals and their use in the workplace, and transposes relevant parts of a range of EU directives, as can be seen in Table 3.2.

Predecessors of the present ordinance can be traced back to the 1930s. But in 1986 the first ordinance with the title of Hazardous Substances was used to transpose parts of EU directives on the classification and labeling of chemicals into national legislation. Subsequently, the ordinance has been changed to transpose either amendments to existing EU directives or evolving EU legislation like the Carcinogens Directive.

In 1997, when the outline of the incoming Chemical Agents Directive (CAD) was discernible, the Federal Ministry of Work and Social Affairs decided to utilize the transposition of this directive for a major overhaul of the existing Hazardous Substances Ordinance. One reason for the overhaul was the view that existing provisions were oriented toward conditions and structures found in large industrial enterprises, particularly in the chemical sector, while structural deficits in occupational hygiene, often due to lack of expertise, were mainly observed in SMEs.

It took almost seven years to complete this task. Some aspects of the CAD were already found in the previous version of the ordinance and in a more elaborate form: in the set of more than 60 Technical Guidance Documents (*Technische*

Table 3.2 Transposition of EU Directives in the Hazardous Substances Ordinance

Issue	EU directive origin
Classification and labeling of substances	67/548/EEC
Classification and labeling of preparations	1999/45/EC
Safety Data Sheet	91/155/EEC
Restrictions of chemicals (partially)	76/769/EEC
Protection of workers from chemical agents at work	98/24/EC
Protection of workers from carcinogens or mutagens at work	2004/37/EC
Protection of workers from asbestos at work	2003/18/EC

Regeln für Gefahrstoffe—TRGS), which underpin the ordinance. Because of the continuous adaptation process of the ordinance and these guidance documents, most new features introduced by the 2005 revision do not constitute a major challenge for enterprises with good occupational health standards. Some changes are adaptations to the risk assessment formalism familiar from the Occupational Health Act itself; others were introduced in previous guidance documents; while others are intended to make it easier to fulfill the obligations of the ordinance, particularly for SMEs. It is not concrete tasks that are changed by the 2005 ordinance but more the structure of the process in which they are embedded and, in part, some terminology. Its main features include the following:

Marketing of Chemicals

Manufacturers and importers of chemicals are obliged to classify and label them. The same obligation applies to formulators. If they put a chemical classified as hazardous on the market, they have to provide their customers with a Safety Data Sheet (SDS).

Recent studies have demonstrated deficits regarding these obligations. Whereas general compliance is good, which means that labels are applied and SDSs are provided, the quality of the information given was found to be less consistent.

As part of the ECLIPS study (CLEEN, 2004), the Occupational Health Authorities of eleven federal states and the Federal Institute of Occupational Health (FIOH) assessed 929 safety data sheets provided by 395 manufacturers. The assessment was mainly limited to assessing the completeness of information. Less than 30% of SDSs contained relevant details on concrete risk management measures, such as type and material of protective gloves, type and specification of RPE (respiratory protection equipment), or on those uses for which specific precautionary measures are necessary. Information on probable exposure levels under recommended use conditions were given in less than 10% of the SDSs assessed (LASI, 2003).

As a consequence, the competent authorities on occupational health and safety of the 16 federal states have established a coordination group to improve the quality of labeling and of SDSs, and to follow up justified complaints about insufficient SDSs. No figures are available on the numbers of such official complaints, but it is likely that they are filed predominantly by SMEs, since major companies are more able use their purchasing power as a lever to receive direct responses to their complaints from their suppliers. However, with the federal structure of Germany as it is, following up complaints filed with the authorities may be a time-consuming affair. For example, if a user with a complaint about the supply of a chemical is situated in one state, they must address the complaint to the factory inspectorate of that state. However, if the supplier is situated in another federal state it has to be approached by the competent authority of that state. As a result, response times may limit the usefulness of answers required for purposes of risk assessment.

Additionally, the question of the limited usefulness of SDSs for SMEs that often lack both expertise and time to extract the information relevant to their specific use pattern of the specific chemical is also thought to be as problematic in Germany as in other countries.

Use of Chemicals at Work

Legally, a risk assessment has to be performed before any work involving hazardous chemicals can be undertaken. The responsibility for this risk assessment lies with the employer, but the recent version of the ordinance states that the person who performs the risk assessment has to have the necessary expertise. This implies that for most enterprises the employer will have to commission this task. The Works Council has the right to participate in the risk assessment process. Any control measures derived without its knowledge or consensus can, in principle, be legally contested. However, of course, active Works Councils are associated with large rather than small enterprises.

An assessment must be made to determine whether hazardous chemicals are involved in, created, or released during the performance of any task. If none of these criteria are met, no risk assessment is necessary under the ordinance. Otherwise the formal risk assessment procedure has to be followed, starting with the evaluation of the risk; that is, the product of the hazards as intrinsic properties of the substances and of the exposure situation resulting from the use pattern of the chemicals during the task. Each hazardous chemical that poses more than a minimal risk has to be listed in an inventory (*Gefahrstoffverzeichnis*).

If the chemicals in question are purchased, the necessary information on the intrinsic properties should be available from both the label and the SDS. Whereas according to the old version of the ordinance, the user could rely on the information communicated in the SDS, this clause has been omitted from the current version: it is part of the user's responsibility to identify inconsistencies in the SDS. In such a case, the user is expected to contact the supplier for clarification. If, however, the respective chemicals are produced in the enterprise or are generated during the process, then the necessary information has to be compiled by the company itself.

With the transition to the current version of the ordinance, a major shift of focus has occurred with regard to two issues. The first one is a shift from a hazard-based approach to a risk-based one. Previously, attention was directed primarily at the hazards (the intrinsic properties) of the chemicals used. Now, with the focus on the task, the conditions under which chemicals used are accorded a more prominent role, which should result in a more differentiated control regime. For tasks that involve open use of substances, as predominantly will be the case for many SMEs, this is unlikely to result in simplified control measures. The second issue for which a shift of focus has occurred is an equal treatment of substances both with and without an occupational exposure limit (OEL) under the obligations of the ordinance. In contrast, under the previous version, only exposure levels for substances with an OEL had to be determined and the application of personal protective equipment was demanded only when it was exceeded.

Appropriate control measures have to be derived and implemented. When selecting these measures, in general the standard order of priority—substitution, technical measures, collective and organizational measures, personal protective measures—has to be followed. However, in order to offer incentives for the use of less harmful chemicals or for designing tasks that lead to lower risks, an approach based on so-called protection classes (*Schutzstufen*) permitting reduced control measures for lower risks has been incorporated into the ordinance. This approach will also be supported by a new tool, the Easy-to-use Workplace Control Scheme (*Einfaches Maßnahmenkonzept*) developed by the Federal Institute of Occupational Health (*Bundesanstalt für Arbeitsschutz und Arbeitsmedizin—BAuA*) (BAuA, 2005). The scheme, modeled on the British COSHH Essentials, is aimed at enabling SMEs to derive risk-reduction measures for risks posed by chemicals for which no OEL has been set. The scheme is intended to be underpinned by a catalog of control guidance sheets (*Schutzleitfäden*) or model solutions (*Modelllösungen*), the first of which were published in 2005 and also based on selected Control Guidance Sheets from the British scheme, which have been translated, adapted to the German situation and tested in a number of workplaces.

With the protection class approach, which foresees four risk bands for toxic hazards, a tiered system of control measures is introduced. For low risks, defined as the use of small amounts of hazardous substances that are not labeled with skull and crossbones and the use of which results in only a low and short-term exposure, good occupational hygiene practice is deemed sufficient and substitution is not demanded.

In the next risk band, which also applies for chemicals labeled without skull and crossbones, but for which no limitations with regard to amount of substance or to exposure apply, substitution is recommended but is not obligatory. If, however, a possible substitution is not performed, the reasons have to be documented. In addition to good occupational hygiene practice, control measures have to be implemented, following the standard order of priority but with one exception: in the choice of technical control measures, a closed system does not take precedence over a local extraction system if the same level of protection can be achieved with either. However, it has to be established that the control measures implemented are effective, otherwise the measures for the higher risk band will apply. For substances with an OEL, the efficacy of control measures is considered as sufficient when the exposure level is kept below the OEL. Criteria for substances without an OEL are addressed in the Easy-to-use Workplace Control Scheme.

More stringent measures apply for high risks, mainly for the use of chemicals labeled with skull and crossbones. Here, substitution is obligatory, and if this is technically not feasible, the standard order of priority for control measures has to be followed, starting with a closed system.

Finally, for carcinogens, mutagens, and substances toxic to reproduction, which are in the fourth and highest risk band, some additional obligations apply, as demanded by the Carcinogens Directive. For these substances, however, no simple answer regarding the efficacy of the control measures can be given because of the current lack of criteria on what constitutes an adequately controlled risk. Under the previous version of the ordinance, technical-based OELs, so-called TRK (*Technische Richt Konzentrationen*) values, existed. Keeping the exposure levels below them had the legal consequence that personal protective equipment did not have to be applied. Since the risks associated with these TRK values were so diverse, founding identical legal consequences on them irrespective of their underlying differences was considered counterintuitive and, thus, this type of OEL was abandoned in the new version of the ordinance. Up to now, no new tools for the evaluation of an adequately controlled risk with regard to carcinogens and mutagens have been derived, and consequently, enterprises must decide on their own whether the previously achieved level of exposure is sufficiently low and can be considered as adequately controlled or whether additional control measures are needed, such as personal protective equipment.

The results of the risk evaluation, including the measures derived, have to be documented in writing. According to the ordinance, unless the risk evaluation is finished, the derived measures have been implemented, and the documentation performed, no task involving hazardous substances may be started. Additionally, the risk assessment process includes regular checks on the correct performance of technical control measures and on the necessity of updating the risk evaluation if new conditions are given or if the results of medical surveillance or the incidence of diseases indicate the inadequacy of the previous evaluation. In the previous version of the ordinance, instead of the latter provision, there was an obligation to adapt the control measures of a work process in accord with technological progress and within a reasonable period of time.

Organizational measures of particular interest include informing workers, for which several approaches are obligatory; national obligations that go beyond the minimum requirements of the CAD include:

- written work instructions (*Betriebsanweisungen*) in the workers' language to be posted in workplaces where tasks including hazardous chemicals are performed;
- workers to be instructed verbally at least once a year on the chemicals-related hazards they encounter and on the control measures they have to apply;
- workers to be instructed on the correct and adequate performance of those tasks that include hazardous chemicals and additional requirements when certain particularly hazardous substances are used or certain high-risk tasks are performed;

• workers to have access to the inventory of hazardous chemicals and to the SDSs of all hazardous chemicals they work with and to receive advice on medical and toxicological issues.

Medical surveillance is obligatory for certain tasks and for exposures above specific limits for some defined chemicals. For other tasks or in case of exposure to particularly hazardous chemicals, workers are entitled to medical surveillance, which has to be facilitated by their employer.

Application in Practice

When comparing the obligations described above with a variety of real-life observations, a different picture emerges. Reports from factory inspectorates, surveys of works councillors and results of research projects collectively demonstrate wide gaps between reality and legal duty for some of the issues covered by the ordinance, while for others the level of compliance seems to be reasonable. Since none of these observations are based on a systematic survey, or can be considered as representative, only a qualitative impression can be given.

For example, recent reports and surveys show that in only about 30% of all enterprises is the obligation to perform a risk assessment, including one for risks posed by chemical agents (introduced by the Occupational Health Act of 1996), taken seriously. For instance in the federal state of Hesse, in only about one-third of all enterprises with more than 10 employees had a risk assessment been completed by early 2001.

A survey of more than 3,500 works councillors in both the private and the public sector, performed in 2004, showed that in only 50% of the surveyed enterprises had a risk assessment been performed, with a clear trend toward higher performance rates in larger enterprises, as shown in Table 3.3 (WSI, 2004).

It is likely that the situation in enterprises without a works council will result in fewer risk assessments. Furthermore, it is to be expected that outside the chemical sector, the extent of general expertise with regard to hazardous chemicals will diminish with reducing the enterprise size. In small enterprises

Table 3.3 Risk Assessments and Enterprise Size
(WSI, 2004)

Number of employees	< 51	51–100	101–200	201–500	501–1,000	> 1,000
Performance of risk assessment (%)	29	38	47	53	55	61

this situation cannot be remedied by the general obligation under the Work Safety Act to have access to occupational hygienists, since the time budget allocated to them is insufficient, because it is proportional to the number of employees.

At a symposium on OELs and chemical exposure in the workplace in 1998, a leading expert for the insurance association of the chemical sector (*Berufsgenossenschaft der chemischen Industrie—BG Chemie*) suggested that despite the tradition of exposure measurements in Germany, they were likely to have been performed in less than 1% of all enterprises since the enactment of the Hazardous Substance Ordinance in 1986. Consequently in his opinion, knowledge on exposure to chemicals in German enterprises was far from comprehensive (Bartels, 1998).

These and other weaknesses in the application of regulatory strategies on chemical risk management in relation to SMEs were elucidated in a seminal study based on 100 interviews in 1994 (Voullaire & Kliemt, 1995). Half of these interviews were conducted with experts from various institutions, addressing occupational health in general and chemical risks in particular, the other half were conducted with owners of SMEs in selected branches and industries in which chemicals were regularly used. The study, commissioned by the Federal Institute of Occupational Health, not only presented the problems with regard to the central obligations of the ordinance but also addressed the necessity of external support for the management of chemicals in SMEs and noted a wide range of issues that should be further pursued by the various actors in the field. Its findings were generally acknowledged by the occupational health community helping to bring together various ideas for developing support for SMEs on tackling chemical risks and providing an impetus for the initiation of concrete projects and the development of support tools.

Ten years later no clear picture exists of the effects of these efforts. Impressionistically, it seems that the systematic approach to risk assessment has still to take root in SMEs, a view that is supported by the observations of various factory inspectorates and researchers. At the same time it has been vigorously argued that the dissemination of certain tools, in particular written work instructions and regular oral instructions based on these, has made some progress. This latter view was expressed during the discussion of the drafting of the current version of the ordinance, when experts representing the different stakeholders and the occupational health institutions defended the further existence of such written instructions.

The Netherlands

The regulatory provisions outlined in Table 3.4 indicate that in the Netherlands, as in all the other countries in the study, much of the law regulating the management of workplace chemical risks is located within the wider regulation of

Table 3.4 Summary of Dutch Legislative Provisions on
Chemical Risks

Legislation	Responsible ministry	Responsible for enforcement	Obligations for companies (employers)	Obligations for suppliers
Labeling	Housing, Spatial Planning and the Environment; Health, Welfare and Sport	Food Authority, Environmental Inspectorate	(derived in OSH decree) to label internal products as well.	To classify chemical substances and products and label correctly
SDSs	Social Affairs and Employment	Environmental Inspectorate, Labour Inspectorate	(derived in OSH decree) to adapt the SDS information in instructions understandable for employees.	To provide SDSs with information for employers
Chemical agents	Social Affairs and Employment	Labour Inspectorate	Risk assessment on exposure of substances, taking measures according to the national occupational hygiene strategy.	
Flammable/ explosive substances	Social Affairs and Employment	Labour Inspectorate	Make a risk assessment (in an Explosion Prevention Document), taking preventive measures, classify hazardous zones.	

health and safety management required under the *Arbobesluit*.[5] In addition, there is a broad range of further provisions relating specifically to chemical substances, some of which are especially significant for chemical risk management in small enterprises. They include special decrees implementing EU directives on labeling and on safety data sheets (such as the *Wet Milieugevaarlijke Stoffen*—the Environmentally Dangerous Substances Act) that are enforced by agencies such as the

[5] In the Netherlands the Framework Directive is implemented in the *Arbowet*, Occupational Safety and Health Act. The individual directives are implemented in the corresponding *Arbobesluit*, OSH decree.

Food Authority and the Environmental Inspectorate. These led to requirements, enforced by the Labour Inspectorate, on employers under work-environment legislation concerning labeling internal products and on adapting information into instructions understandable to employees. Another significant feature of national approaches to addressing the risks posed by hazardous substances in the Netherlands is the attention that has been paid in national discourse to the concept of substitution. Derived originally from concerns in relation to the environmental effects of chemical hazards, debate over substitution strategies has been prominent in several areas of occupational exposure, especially, for example, in relation to volatile organic solvents in paints, inks and glues as well as in relation to carcinogens.

In summary, as Table 3.4 indicates, companies are required to undertake risk assessment of chemical hazards and to make registers of the substances they use. Employers are further required by work-environment legislation to instruct employees on the risks of chemicals in use at their workplace and on the control measures in place, but there are no special provisions to implement this requirement. There is considerable variation in practice, ranging from situations in which SDSs are simply filed and in theory therefore available for consultation by employees, to situations in which employers provide written practical instructions to carry out specific tasks that use chemicals (similar to that required by law in Germany). In recent years an increasingly common practice has been to make workplace instruction charts or cards derived from the information on the SDSs; there are software programs available that produce these instruction charts automatically. Ideally such charts or cards should consist of information both about the chemical product and the situation concerning its specific use at the workplace itself. However, many describe only the chemical hazard, personal protection and first-aid measures. Despite such limitations, there seems to be a gradually improving trend in the quality of such instruction cards.

A feature of the Dutch regulatory approach is the potentially significant role to be played in chemical risk assessment by external occupational health services, since under the Work Environment Act, until July 2005, all employers were required to contract with such services to provide them with support for managing the work environment and approving the workplace risk assessment that companies are also obliged to undertake. In addition, the external occupational health services (and also internal ones where they existed) were required to be certified as to their competence to offer a range of at least four OHS disciplines, one of which was occupational hygiene. In theory, the involvement of the occupational health services should result in highly developed and competent risk assessment and control of chemical hazards in all enterprises. However, this does not seem to have been the case in practice. Despite the mandatory contracts of SMEs with OSH services, a survey of the views of representatives from sectors in which the use of chemicals was greatest suggested they were of little help in chemical risk management in the small enterprises (Nossent et al.,

2003b). This finding was confirmed by a further study on a more general use of risk assessment, which also reported poor implementation and a limited role for OHS services in relation to small enterprises (Van Heemskerk et al., 2003).

Recent changes to the law on occupational health services have been introduced to achieve better conformity with EU provisions. They came into effect in July 2005, and it is too soon to be certain of their effects. They are thought likely to result in some liberalization of the market for occupational health services for enterprises with more than 15 employees and fewer obligations on risk assessments and contracts with occupational health services for those with 15 or fewer employees. Neither of these developments is likely to improve the present situation in relation to chemical risk management.

It is believed that the highest exposure to hazardous substances occurs in small enterprises. As mentioned previously, there is some evidence for this found in secondary analyses of the annual national survey of workers' self-reported experiences of their work environment that indicates an inverse relationship between workers' skin and respiratory exposure to chemical hazards and their workplace size (Kremer, 2005). In addition, as the above outline of compliance with existing provisions indicates, it is known that small enterprises present considerable challenges for regulating chemical risk management.

The Dutch authorities have developed a number of strategic approaches to address these challenges. Demarcation between these strategies and the tools designed to implement them is somewhat arbitrary. In this chapter the strategies are outlined, while a more detailed discussion of the tools to implement them is presented in Chapter 5.

There are several programs concerning chemical risk management relevant to small enterprises. They include the *Strategienota Omgaan met Stoffen* (SOMS) program, initiated by the Ministry for Housing, Planning and the Environment in 1998, and its successor, the Ministry of Social Affairs and Employment's *Versterking Arbeidsomstandighedenbeleid Stoffen* (VASt) program, which is specifically aimed at small enterprises and requires employers in sectors with previously identified relatively high risks from hazardous chemicals to prepare action plans for their reduction at the sectoral level. Each action plan should contain sectoral improvement activities regarding

- substances, exposure, and measurements;
- communication in the supply chain; and
- the knowledge infrastructure.

By March 2006, 25 action plans had been written and 24 had started. Evaluation will be completed by the end of 2007.

Another major Dutch strategy initiated by the Ministry of Social Affairs and Employment aimed at improving systematic approaches to OHS in general, but with some overlapping relevance to chemical risk management, is the introduction of work covenants (*Arboconvenanten*). These are agreements between employers and trade unions at the sectoral level, supported by the Ministry, setting voluntary targets for improvement of a range of health and safety issues relevant to the sector, which are considered achievable by their signatories. There were 62 such covenants at the beginning of 2005. Handling hazardous chemicals is one of the issues identified in the action plans of 14 of them (Jongen et al., 2003).

The effects of the covenants are monitored through measurements at the start and the end of the programs, and a recent report from the Ministry of Social Affairs and Employment summarizes their results (Ministry of Social Affairs and Employment, 2005). Examples of chemical risks addressed in the covenants include solvents in the paint sector, cytostatics and anaesthetics in hospitals and solvents in the building and metal-processing industry. However, the scope of the Ministry evaluation report does not allow an extensive discussion of the effects of the covenants with respect to the management of these chemical risks.

The Dutch chemical industry pursues the international industry's Responsible Care program, within which the notion of product stewardship supports the sound management of safety, health, and environmental effects of products through their entire life cycle. It is therefore a supply-chain strategy that is *inter alia* aimed at supporting chemical risk management in all situations in which the industry's products are used. Although not designed specifically for this purpose, it should nevertheless contribute significantly to the parallel strategies of the state and other actors described here in relation to chemical risk management in small enterprises. In particular it is aimed at increasing confidence between users and their suppliers and is intended to support innovation through cooperative approaches. Recently the Dutch chemical industry has evaluated its responsible care program (VNCI, 2005). However, there is no specific evaluation of the program in relation to its impact on improved chemical risk management in small enterprises.

Spain

In Spain statutory regulation of chemical substances is extensive and complex. There are, for example, rules that:

- prohibit or limit the use of specific chemicals;
- require an authorization (or a report to the controlling authorities) to start and continue an activity, which involves use of specific chemicals or specific waste emissions;
- set objectives in terms of waste and polluting emissions;
- protect the health and safety of workers exposed to chemicals;
- provide information about risks and regulate the registration, assessment, classification, labeling and packaging; and
- develop a framework for environmental information and environmental action.

The constitutional basis for worker protection is found in Article 40. 2 of the Spanish Constitution. Compliance with European legislation resulted in the Act on Prevention of Occupational Risks 1995,[6] which established the general principles of modern OHS regulation. The law sets the obligation of employers to grant the protection of the health and safety of all their employees against any risks derived from their work. It also imposes an obligation on employers to comply with such principles by implementing preventive actions following a hierarchical structure that aims at the elimination of risk when feasible as first choice; then only when elimination is not possible, it orders the reduction of risk, dealing with it at the source, taking into consideration technological advances and replacing the dangerous processes with less harmful or harmless practices.

These general principles have also been developed in the domain of specific chemical risks. The general plan sets environmental and biological limit values, which are understood as threshold values beyond which there are possibilities of risk for human health. The following specific measures are found.

Information and Training (RD 374/2001[7]: Article 9)—The employer has to ensure that workers and their representatives receive adequate training and information regarding the risks posed by the hazardous substances existing in their workplaces, as well as regarding the prevention and protection measures that must be applied. This requirement covers in particular:

- results of risk assessments;
- information on the hazardous chemicals existing in their workplaces, including name, health and safety risks, and OELs;
- training and information on precautions and measures to protect themselves and other workers; and
- Safety Data Sheets provided by suppliers.

Participation (RD 374/2001: Article 9)—The employer has the duty to consult workers and facilitate their participation in any issue regarding the protection of their health and safety.

Risk Assessment (RD 374/2001: Article 3)—The employer has a duty to determine, in the first place, if there is any hazardous chemical substance in the workplace. If this is the case, the employer must carry out an assessment of the risks to the workers health and security posed by these substances.

---

[6] *LPRL Ley 31/1995 de Prevención de Riesgos Laborales*

[7] *RD 374/2001: Real Decreto 374/2001, de 6 de abril (BOE n° 104 de 1 de mayo de 2001) sobre la protección de la salud y seguridad de los trabajadores contra los riesgos relacionados con los agentes químicos durante el trabajo.* Transposition of Directive 98/24/CE.

Measurements of exposures (RD 374/2001: Article 3.5)—As a part of the risk assessment, the employer is responsible for carrying out measurements of exposures whenever needed. Exposures should be compared to OELs and specific prevention, and protection measures should be implemented if OELs are exceeded.

Prevention principles to follow (RD 374/2001: Article 4)—The employer has the duty to eliminate or reduce to a minimum the risks posed by hazardous chemical substances.

Substitution (RD 374/2001: Article 5.2)—When the risk assessment shows the need to adopt specific prevention or protection measures, the employer has the duty to avoid the use of the hazardous substance, substituting it with another one or one with a chemical process that is not hazardous or is less hazardous according to the conditions of usage.

Identify carcinogenic and mutagenic substances (RD 665/1997[8]: Article 3)— The employer has the duty to identify carcinogenic and mutagenic substances, avoid them, and assess the risk of those that have not been avoided.

Eliminate carcinogenic and mutagenic substances (RD 665/1997: Article 4)— The employer has the duty to substitute carcinogenic and mutagenic substances with other chemicals that are not dangerous or are less dangerous.

Implementation of prevention and protection measures (RD 374/2001: Article 5.2)—If the nature of the activity does not allow the elimination of the hazardous substance, the employer has the duty to reduce the risk to a minimum, implementing the following measures by order of priority:

- isolate the hazardous substance;
- ventilation and other collective protection measures;
- individual protection measures.

Measures to avoid fires, explosions, or dangerous chemical reactions (RD 374/2001: Article 5.3 & Article 5.4)—The employer has the duty to adopt technical and organizational measures in order to protect the workers from these risks.

---

[8] *RD 665/1997: Real Decreto 665/1997, de 12 de mayo, sobre la protección de los trabajadores contra los riesgos relacionados con la exposición a agentes cancerígenos durante el trabajo. BOE núm. 124 de 24 de mayo.* Transposition of Directive 90/394/CEE.

Health Surveillance (RD 374/2001: Article 6)—When the risk assessment shows the existence of a risk for the workers' health, the employer has the duty to carry out the surveillance of the heath of those workers.

Emergency measures (RD 374/2001: Article 6)—When the risk assessment shows the existence of a risk of accidents, incidents, or emergencies due to the presence of a chemical substance, the employer has the duty to plan the activities that will be developed in these cases and to provide the measures that will be needed.

Prohibitions (RD 374/2001: Article 6)—Some chemicals are prohibited from use while some are prohibited from use in certain applications. The list is included in Annex III of this regulation.

Reporting accidents, ill-health, or incidents (Orden 16.12.1987[9])—Whenever an accident, ill health, or incident has occurred, employers have the duty to report it to the Labour Inspection Authorities. The employer is responsible for the follow-up and action to prevent something similar from happening again.

Elaborate and keep documents (LPRL: Article 23)—The employer has the duty to elaborate and keep the following documents: risk assessment and its resulting prevention plan, results of measurements of exposures, results of health surveillances, and a register of accidents and worker illness.

In addition to these laws, as in other countries, there are regulations aimed at the marketing of chemical substances. The general approach requires those who market new chemical products to:

- study their intrinsic characteristics and risks;
- communicate the result of research to the authorities, who must evaluate the risks; and
- provide the consumers with full information about the products' characteristics, their intrinsic hazards, the possible risks, and the ways to prevent them through labeling and chemical safety data sheets.

Failure to comply with these regulations is reported to the Health Council in the Regional Government where the manufacturers or importers are registered. It files the case and has the authority to sanction the company or to request the correction of the detected mistakes. It is also possible to file the report with the Ministry of Health or other regional authorities since both have channels to forward the report to the competent health authority. The main provisions are listed in Table 3.5.

---

[9] *Orden 16.12.1987 Nuevos modelos para la notificación de Accidentes de Trabajo.*

Table 3.5 Spanish Provisions Controlling the Marketing of
Chemical Substances

R.D. 363/1995, on the registration, classification, packaging and labeling of dangerous substances.	Separates existing substances (substances available in the European market before the September 18, 1981) and new substances (substances introduced in the market after that date). For the first ones, the only obligations are to check if they are included in Annex I and if so, comply with labeling and packaging requirements expressed in it. It is mandatory to note the use of new substances and to conduct research to determine their characteristics and to label and package them accordingly.
R.D. 255/2003, on Classification, packaging and labeling of dangerous preparations	Regulates preparations in the same way as R.D. 363 does for substances, with the important exception of notification.
R.D. 1054/2002. Chemical products.	Regulates the assessment process for the registration, authorization and marketing of biocides.

Note: Some products, such as bleach, pesticides, detergents, solvents and adhesives, paints and varnishes have their own specific regulations for classification, labeling and packaging and in some cases even for manufacturing and marketing.

Despite the fact that Spain is Europe's fifth-largest producer of chemical substances and an economy with one of the highest proportions of small enterprises in Europe, with almost 90% of the enterprises in the chemicals industry having fewer than 50 workers, there are no special strategies for addressing the known problems of chemical risk management in small enterprises.

In the opinions of health and safety specialists and trade unionists, awareness of chemical risks among workers and employers is poor. There is some support for this view in the findings of the 5th National Survey on Working Conditions. Responses to questions in this survey about what are considered disturbing working conditions, polluting agents were ranked 13 in a 14-item list (INSHT 2004). Worker health and safety representatives appear to be more concerned than others. In a survey carried out by the trade union research institute, ISTAS (CC.OO.), worker health and safety representatives were interviewed about the major risks in their enterprises. Exposure to toxic products was listed among the top seven risks in the industrial sector, with an increased level of concern if the work environment was affected by dust.

Opinions of specialists suggest that as in other countries, suppliers' information on chemical risks provided on labels and SDSs to users in Spain is insufficient for purposes of risk assessment and management. The additional limited knowledge of chemical risks and approaches to addressing risk management among users in combination with the poor supply of information from suppliers consequently is thought to lead to poor risk management of chemical substances. These weaknesses of information and competence are thought to be greatest in small enterprises for all the reasons identified in the other countries in the study, although there is no detailed study to verify these suppositions in Spain.

Regulatory approaches to addressing these issues are poorly developed. Considerable emphasis placed on raising awareness of health and safety generally through the provision of training and a national strategy exists to disseminate such training to employers and workers throughout the economy. In the Plan for Preventive Activities (2003-2005) of the Social Security system, there was provision for training to be managed by the Mutual Insurance Associations (the *Mutuas*), aimed specifically at small enterprises and including employers, workers, appointed safety delegates, self-employed workers and health and safety representatives among its targets. Training on specific risks including those of chemical substances was part of this provision; however, its uptake or effect does not appear to have been analyzed.

Sweden

Swedish regulatory approaches typify the combination of procedures for systematic work environment management (SWEM) with specific and detailed rules for particular exposures. The main strategy evident in regulatory approaches to chemicals used at work is to effect a shift from detailed rules for specific substances and some general demands for good housekeeping and hygiene, to a more comprehensive set of rules reflecting the demands for chemical proactive risk management that are combined with specified rules for specific substances. If the provisions on SWEM and proactive chemical risk management are compared, the requirements for chemical risk management are often more detailed and demand more work from employers than SWEM. This is the case with the methods for risk evaluations.[10]

Sweden has had laws and provisions concerning chemical risk management for many years (Lofstedt, 2003). The present provisions, Chemical Hazards in the Working Environment, AFS 2000:4, are based on previous provisions found in Dangerous Substances, AFS 1985:17, revised in AFS 1994:2 and also reflect the process of adapting Swedish legislation to EU directives, which began well

---

[10]In relation to SWEM, under AFS 2001:1, risks should be judged to be severe or less severe. By comparison, in AFS 2000:4 Chemical Hazards in the Working Environment, risk evaluation is described in detail as a very complex process in which many different aspects have to be considered.

before Sweden joined the EU in 1995. Originally, legislation[11] focused on substances, establishing occupational exposure limits (OELs) and measuring exposure. Demands for good practice were also included, such as cleanliness and tidiness; hygiene; technical preventive measures; information to workers about risks and protective measures; and requirements on work premises, storage and fire hazards.

In keeping with the general trend in Swedish legislation on SWEM, more recent provisions have highlighted proactive risk management with requirements on documenting the chemical substances used at the workplace as well as on risk assessment and with a requirement that such actions should be kept up-to-date, which in turn implies that some kind of proactive systematic chemical risk management is undertaken. In parallel with these general demands, there are also provisions relating to substances or groups of substances that usually include more detailed requirements for handling and use. Such regulations have been issued for:

PCBs	AFS 1985:1 and SFS 1985:83
Oils and waste oil	AFS 1986:3 and SFS 1993:1268
Synthetic inorganic fibers	AFS 2004:1
Quartz	AFS 1992:16
Lead	AFS 1992:17 (changed in AFS 2000:14)
Motor fuel	AFS 1992:18
Thermosetting plastics	AFS 1996:4 Härdplaster (changed in AFS 2000:28)
Asbestos	AFS 1996:13 (changed in AFS 2000:26)

Apart from specific technical or organizational measures, general requirements commonly apply to medical examinations, exposure measurements in relation to OELs, and education and training on safe handling. However, as the trend is toward more general provisions, older measures on specific substances are merged or repealed if their requirements are covered by those of more recent general ones.

The basic elements of chemical risk management are provisions directed toward manufacturers, suppliers, employers and employees who use chemical products in the course of their work. They are found in *Chemical Hazards in the Working Environment*, AFS 2000:4[12] and are summarized in Box 3.1

In the main, there is no regulatory distinction between small and large companies. The same requirements apply to both since they are tailored to risks rather than to the size of the organization that is required to manage them. Increasing risk therefore increases the stringency of the regulatory provisions, regardless of the size of the company. Only in one provision, AFS 2001:1, are the requirements concerning documentation of SWEM reduced for the smallest

[11]See Council Directive 80/1107/EEC and Swedish provisions AFS 1985:7 Dangerous Substances.
[12]http://www.av.se/english/legislation/afs/eng0004.pdf

Box 3.1—Swedish regulatory requirements on managing chemical hazards at work

Labelling (AFS 2000:4, section 24): Manufacturers must label chemical products with short and easily understandable information about the risks (including risk phrases). Also found in the Environmental Code, ordinances based on it and provisions issued by the Chemicals Inspectorate.

Understanding labelling (AFS 2000:4, section 23): The employer has a duty to ensure employees that handle chemicals have sufficient knowledge of labelling in order to understand what potential risks there are in the handling of the chemicals. The means of acquiring this knowledge are not prescribed.

Provision of material safety data sheets, SDS: The manufacturer must provide detailed information about the chemicals in SDS (also required under the Environmental Code as well as in ordinances and provisions issued under it).

Understanding and use of SDS (AFS 2000:4, section 23): Employees must have access to and the skills to read and understand the SDS. The manager is responsible for SDS being used to find out if there are any special requirements on the handling of the chemical product, e.g. specific regulations that may apply or restrictions in the use and handling of the chemical. The employer is responsible for ensuring that employees that handle chemicals have the required knowledge about SDS and use the information available. The means of acquiring this knowledge are not prescribed.

Compilation of a list of chemical products used and stored (AFS 2000:4, section 38): Employers must know what chemical products are used within the company and compile a list of the dangerous chemicals (labeled chemicals).

Risk assessment (AFS 2000:4, section 4): The employer has a responsibility to ensure that risk assessments are undertaken in relation to chemical products handled. The risk assessment must cover the inherent risk of the chemicals, the way they are handled, the duration of the exposure and protective measures to be considered. The risk assessment must be communicated to the employees using the chemicals. Involving employees in risk assessment of the chemicals they use is considered good practice.

Measurements of exposures (AFS 2000:4, section 4): As a part of the risk assessment, the employer is responsible for carrying out measurements of exposures whenever needed. Exposures should be compared to OELs and control measures of some kind should be implemented if OELs are exceeded. It is good practice to implement control measures if OELs are considered even likely to be exceeded.

Control measures (AFS 2000:4, section 5 and 10): The employer is responsible for implementing control measures when the risk assessment indicates they are required. There is a hierarchy of control:
- Substitution of the dangerous chemicals for less dangerous ones, or methods that require use of no or less hazardous substances, where possible.
- Control through measures close to the source, e.g., integrated exhausts.
- Enclose and ventilate in order to reduce emissions from the source.
- Separate the source from other activities.
- Conduct of work during hours when others will not be affected by the work.
- Use of personal protective devices.

Box 3.1 (Cont'd.)

Safety instructions (AFS 2000:4, section 11): The employer is responsible for the provision of work instructions. If working procedures, such as the use of personal protective equipment etc. are essential for safe work with chemicals, instructions have to be in writing. Employees are required to work according to these instructions.

Reporting accidents, ill-health or incidents (AFS 2000:4, section 7): Whenever an accident, ill health or incident has occurred, employees have to report it to management. The employer is responsible for the follow-up and action to prevent something similar from happening again.

The following recommendations are made in order to help compliance with the above requirements:

Sorting out of unnecessary chemicals: It is recommended that chemicals that are not in use are identified and only those really necessary are retained to reduce the work of compiling the list of all chemical products used in the company and evaluating their risks.

Purchasing routines for chemicals: In order to have control of the chemicals used in the company, purchasing routines for chemicals are recommended. This helps ensure:
- Purchase of hazardous chemicals is controlled.
- Whenever new chemicals are purchased the routines followed include:
  o Access to and use of SDS.
  o Adding the chemical product to the list.
  o Risk evaluation of the handling of new chemical products.

Other requirements:
There are additional regulations regarding work with specified hazardous chemicals or groups of chemicals. There are also restrictions for the use of many chemicals. Some chemicals are prohibited from use while some are prohibited from use in certain applications. A data-base of these chemicals can be found on the web-site of the Chemicals Inspectorate, www.kemi.se. Another list of chemicals known as the OBS-list contains substances that ought to be considered for substitution or reduced use, but for which there are no regulations demanding their ceased use.

---

companies (with fewer than 10 employees), reflecting a desire to reduce administrative burdens without reducing the level of protection provided.

Difficulties in developing chemical risk management in small companies are well known (Norrby, 1997). Consequently, small companies are often in focus when developing information, work materials, and guidelines for these purposes. Reasons for this can be found in the scattered research on how the basic elements of risk management regulation, summarized in Box 3.1, operate in small companies. There is no single study that grasps the entire range of problems encountered, but collectively they give a picture of the extent of the challenge.

As in other countries, regulatory strategy emphasizes substitution as a first principle. While the legislative demands do not distinguish between company size, studies suggest that there is much more limited knowledge in smaller companies concerning substitution and control measures than present in their larger counterparts. For example, in a qualitative study of 11 companies, six of which were small, interviews revealed major differences. The small companies in general substituted dangerous chemicals based on recommendations from their suppliers. They did not themselves identify which chemicals ought to be substituted or actively seek less hazardous chemicals. Large companies were in general more ambitious, especially if they used a lot of dangerous chemicals (Alvarez de Davila & Cerne, 1999).

The ECLIPS study on SDSs showed there are many deficiencies in those provided by chemical manufacturers and suppliers in Sweden, with only 20% of SDSs without any deficiencies (CLEEN, 2004). A recent Swedish study on SDSs for degreasing agents, which included use in small enterprises, further concluded (Swedish Chemicals Inspectorate, 2004):

> Even SDS that were judged to comply with the regulations and thus considered to be sufficiently good by the authorities, did not necessarily leave advice that was concrete enough to assist the user to plan for appropriate handling of the chemicals.

Given such findings, the information base for chemical risk management in small companies is clearly problematic, a finding that is further confirmed by research on labeling.

Early studies in both Sweden and Denmark showed considerable variation in employees' understanding of basic signs on labels (Nordiska ministerrådets miljörapport, 1986, p. 7). While provisions on labeling chemical products have been further developed since these studies were conducted, there are many indications that understanding of labels remains poor.

A series of interviews in 2002 showed important differences between risk management of chemicals in small and large companies, in particular the absence of specialist staff and routines in smaller organizations and a concern with fulfilling broad regulatory requirements rather than more subtle aspects of chemical risk management (Alvarez de Davila et al., 2002).

In an inspection campaign in the autumn of 2003,[13] despite prior notice of inspection, and an instruction to be fairly open-minded in what they accepted as evidence of chemical risk management, inspectors nevertheless served notices to improve the chemical risk management in 59% to 81% of companies. They

---

[13]The results from the campaign have not yet been published. The information presented here is based on personal communication with Maria Cronholm-Dahlin at the Swedish Work Environment Authority.

investigated whether SDSs written in Swedish were available at the workplace and found that in the sectors examined (printing, construction, engineering, and carpentry), an average of every third company did not have access to Swedish SDSs for all its labeled chemical products.

There are no studies available on how employers and employees in small companies use and understand SDSs. However, it seems likely that many people who ought to read and use them do not; but the extent of this problem is unknown. One important application of SDSs is as background information for risk assessment. It is to support this, among other things, that employers are expected to keep inventories of substances used at their workplaces. The inspection campaign in 2003 investigated the existence of such inventories and the extent to which they were kept up-to-date. They found that more than 60% of inspected companies were not in compliance with requirements on the possession of an inventory or its being up-to-date.

The inspection campaign also investigated if workplaces undertook risk evaluations, documented them, and implemented control measures so identified. The results are shown in Table 3.6. During the campaign, 68% of inspected companies received at least one order from the inspectorate to improve their chemical risk management.

There are no statistics available on the extent of measurements of exposures in small companies, but in a statement in April 2005, the Swedish Work Environment Authority concluded that in many companies it is not possible to evaluate the risk due to lack of measurements (Trägårdh, 2005). It is also known that there has been an overall reduction in the measurement of chemical exposures in recent years. Indeed, the number of compulsory measurements reported to the Swedish Work Environment Authority has decreased by about 50% since the beginning of the 1980s (Trägårdh, 2005). This seems to be partly a consequence of reduced numbers of safety engineers with training in industrial hygiene measurement and partly a result of the decreased use of organic solvents following their substitution by water-based or high-solid formulas. It may also be because of more effective control of the most common exposures, for example through automation. There are however no studies verifying this. Another factor certainly affecting the extent of measurements is the decrease in the number of occupational health services during the recession in the beginning of the 1990s, when a considerable number of safety engineers left.

The Work Environment Authority has published brochures and books on practical control measures relating to the different provisions of the hierarchy of control set out in the legislation. There is only limited study of their impact in small enterprises. Other high-priority control measures such as extractive ventilation require expertise usually not available in small companies. There are scattered studies on the use of such control measures in different trades, often based on evaluations of inspection campaigns; they however do not present results in relation to size of company.

Table 3.6 Companies Without Correct Risk Evaluation During
an Inspection Campaign in Sweden, Autumn 2003

	Printing industries	Construction	Engineering industry	Carpentry	All
Inspected companies	124	1140	130	427	1821
Companies without risk evaluation	53	552	62	209	886
% no risk evaluation	43%	48%	48%	49%	49%
Companies having to undertake control measures	52	493	62	200	807
% in need of control measures	42%	43%	48%	47%	44%
Companies with insufficient documentation of risk evaluation	66	550	68	216	900
% insufficient documentation	53%	48%	52%	51%	49%
Companies with incomplete risk evaluation	171	1595	202	565	2593

There is no information on how small companies work with safety instructions, whether oral or written, but as we have already seen, weaknesses in SDSs (such as demonstrated in the study by the Chemicals Inspectorate and the ECLIPS study) suggest that it is probably not uncommon that written safety instructions are lacking or incomplete. Similarly, there is no information on how small companies identify what are necessary or unnecessary chemicals for their purposes or about purchasing routines for chemicals, yet they are important practical elements that would help facilitate chemical risk management work in small companies.

It is acknowledged that chemical risk management is a complex activity, requiring knowledge and skills to deal with for example, labeling, SDSs, risk evaluation and control measures. However, training on chemical risk management that is compulsory according to the legislative provisions is mainly related to work with a small number of specific substances for which there are special provisions, such as thermosetting plastics, asbestos, pesticides, some toxic drugs, and PCBs. In the more general provisions on dangerous chemicals, there are requirements concerning knowledge about risks and protective measures but not how it should be acquired. In practice this means that knowledge can be acquired through learning by doing, but there seems to be little cognizance of how this is done or with what results in small companies, other than the belief that such knowledge is limited.

Overall it can be argued that all this evidence related to the implementation of the regulatory strategies in small enterprises emphasizes their limited resources for health and safety generally and for chemical risk management in particular. This is further borne out by interviews conducted in 2002 with the authority, the social partners and a few small companies, in order to survey needs regarding the risk management of chemicals in small enterprises (Alvarez de Davila et al., 2002). They showed that important differences between risk management of chemicals in small companies compared with large companies were related to differences in the levels of resources they were able to devote to this matter. For example, large companies often had specialist staff occupied with risk management of chemicals and related questions with well-developed routines for risk management. When they approached the authorities, it was usually because they had subtle questions about such things as the interpretation of regulations. In contrast, small companies and micro-companies (with fewer than 50 and 10 employees, respectively) had considerably fewer resources and far less developed risk management. When they approached the authorities, they were seeking the answer to far more fundamental questions such as:

- Are we affected by the regulation?
- What exactly are we required to do?
- How should we go about fulfilling these requirements?

It is to address such questions that current chemical risk management tools are mainly directed.

The United Kingdom

In the UK regulatory approaches to achieving improved health and safety management generally are framed by the Health and Safety at Work Act 1974 (HSW Act) and the main provisions implementing the Framework Directive's requirements: the Management of Health and Safety at Work Regulations. Section 6 of the HSW Act and the Chemical (Hazard Information and Packaging for Supply) Regulations 1994 outline duties of manufacturers and suppliers to provide information on the safe use of their products. The provisions of the

Control of Substances Hazardous to Health Regulations deal with the chemical risk management duties of employers. These latter measures were first introduced in 1987 and implemented in EC Directive 80/1107/EEC on the protection of workers from the risks related to exposure to chemical, physical, and biological agents at work. While they applied specifically to hazardous substances, they exemplified the emerging British approach to regulating systematic health and safety management more generally. Central to the thinking behind them was a model of good practice in which systematic chemical risk management would operate through the adoption of an occupational hygiene approach to monitoring and controlling exposure to hazardous substances. Prevention or control of exposure was to be achieved through the application of the usual hierarchy of measures. The regulatory requirements to achieve this are summarized in Table 3.7.

The COSHH Regulations cover:

- substances designated as very toxic, toxic, corrosive, harmful, or irritant under the Chemicals (Hazard Information and Packaging for Supply) Regulations 1994 (CHIP);
- substances that have a Workplace Exposure Limit (WEL) (until April 2005), Maximum Exposure Limits and Occupational Exposure Standards (MELs and OESs);
- biological agents;
- any other dusts that exceed a specified concentration; and
- any other substance that creates a risk to health because of its chemical or toxicological properties and the way in which it is used at work.

Updated COSHH Regulations came into force on November 21, 2002, in order to implement the health requirements of the chemical agents Directive (98/24/EC). Other health requirements of the directive were implemented by the Control of Lead at Work Regulations 2002 (CLAW)[14] and the Control of Asbestos at Work Regulations 2002. The directive's provisions on safety risks, such as from fire and explosion, were implemented by the Dangerous Substances and Explosive Atmospheres Regulations 2002. Substantive changes included detailing the measures that the employer must take to prevent or adequately control the exposure of its employees to substances hazardous to health (Reg. 7) and extending the duties on employers with respect to health surveillance where an employee is found to have an identifiable disease or adverse health effect caused by exposure to a substance hazardous to health (Reg. 11).

[14]The Control of Lead at Work Regulations 2002, SI 2002 No.2676, Stationery Office.

Table 3.7 UK Regulatory Requirements on Chemical Risk Management

Regulatory source	Requirements
Health and Safety at Work Act Section 6	Manufacturers, suppliers, importers of substances for use at work shall ensure, so far as is reasonably practicable[a] that the substance is safe and without risk to health when properly used. They also have to arrange any necessary testing of the substance and make information available on the safety of the substance and conditions for its safe use.
The CHIP Regulations 1994	Implement EU system for classifying toxicology of substances, including R-phrases as listed in Directive 67/548/EEC as amended. Describes 16 categories of information suppliers are required to provide in SDSs.
The COSHH Regulations	Require: • prohibition of the manufacture, importation and supply of specified substances; • risk assessment to identify measures necessary to comply with the regulations; • implementation of the measures, and their subsequent maintenance and testing; • an approach to prevention or control of exposure, starting with elimination or substitution, then by controls such as enclosure, LEV, ventilation, systems of work and personal protective equipment; • monitoring of exposure in some circumstances; • health surveillance in some circumstances; • provision of information, instruction, and training to all persons exposed to hazardous substances; and; • arrangements to deal with incidents and emergencies.

[a]In Dugmore v Swansea NHS Trust and Morriston NHS Trust, the Court of Appeal confirmed on November 21, 2002, that employers have an absolute duty under reg. 7(1) of the COSHH Regulations to ensure that exposing employees to hazardous substances is prevented or—where prevention is not reasonably practicable—adequately controlled. The Court said that the qualification of reasonable practicability refers only to prevention and not to the secondary duty of adequate control. The judgement is not affected by new COSHH Regulations that came into force in November 2002 and 2005. In 2003 the Court of Appeal revisited and confirmed its Dugmore decision in Naylor v Volex Group plc.

The regulations were amended again in 2004.[15] Many of the amendments were designed to be helpful to SMEs. These included the new system of Workplace Exposure Limits, which took effect in April 2005, replacing a system of occupational exposure limits (OELs) that comprised MELs and OESs. Clarification was also made of what is meant by adequate control in Reg. 7. The regulations

[15]"The COSHH (Amendment) Regulations 2004," SI 2004 No.3386.

now state that where there is exposure to a substance hazardous to health, control of that exposure shall be treated only as adequate if:

- the principles of good practice for the control of exposure to substances hazardous to health set out in a schedule are applied;
- any workplace exposure limit approved for that substance is not exceeded; and
- exposure has been reduced to as low a level as is reasonably practicable if the substance carries the risk phrase R45, R46, or R49; is a substance or process specified in a schedule; carries the risk phrase R42 or R42/43; or is listed as an asthmagen or has been shown by a risk assessment to be a potential cause of occupational asthma (HSE, 2005b).

Additional measures on regulating chemical risks are found in the Control of Major Accident Hazard (COMAH) Regulations that implement the Seveso Directive. However, they do not concern us here.

There is a clearly documented development of strategic thinking in relation to chemical risk management that is particularly focused on the situation of small enterprises (Walters & Grodzki, 2006). From the 1990s onward, a growing body of research demonstrated that the majority of owners and managers in small enterprises where there was significant use of hazardous chemicals had little understanding of the detailed regulatory requirements that applied to them and limited knowledge of how to go about assessing and controlling the risks to which their workers were exposed (see for example, Research International, 1997; Russell et al., 1998). This caused the Chemicals Directorate of the HSE and the tripartite Advisory Committee on Toxic Substances (ACTS) to rethink the regulatory approach framed by the Control of Substances Hazardous to Health Regulations to take account of the realities of compliance among employers in small enterprises.

As a result, HSE policymakers gradually shifted the focus of regulating the management of the risks of working with hazardous chemicals in smaller enterprises away from occupational hygiene approaches in which measurement of exposure was implicated to more predictive and generic approaches to exposure specification and control. The HSE researchers and policymakers were not the only specialists interested in such issues during the 1990s. Similar approaches had been outlined for example in relation to aromatic amines and related compounds by Money (1992); for pharmaceutically active substances by Naumann et al., (1996); for volatile organic substances by Gardner and Oldershaw (1991) and for laboratory chemicals by the Royal Society of Chemistry (1996). They were also apparent in publications on occupational exposure bands for colorants (Chemical Industries Association (CIA), 1993) and subsequently in guidance from the Chemical Industries Association to its members on a wider range of hazardous substances (CIA, 1997; Guest, 1998). However, the significance of the contribution from HSE researchers and policymakers was in relations to the linked development of COSHH Essentials (described in Chapter 5). Their thinking was presented in 1998 in a series of papers published in the *Annals of Occupational Hygiene* at the same time as COSHH Essentials and was released in a trial paper version (see Brooke, 1998; Maidment, 1998; Russell et al., 1998).

An interactive electronic version of COSHH Essentials followed in 2002.[16] In 2003 the HSE completed phase 2 of COSHH Essentials, with the launch of a further 70 control guidance sheets, and in 2004 it issued Chemical Essentials, a demonstration CD-ROM combining workplace health and safety guidance from COSHH Essentials with additional guidance on environmental protection. At its launch, the HSC (Health and Safety Commission) chair, Bill Callaghan, said that employers, particularly small businesses, "need to recognize that the branded product they are using could actually harm their own health or that of their workforce." The tool, he added, was "in keeping with" the HSE's attempts "to develop channels of support and advice that can be accessed without fear of enforcement action" (HSC, 2004).

In 2001 the HSE commissioned a survey of the use of COSHH Essentials among companies with fewer than 250 employees (Wiseman & Gilbert, 2002). It found that just under 80% of the 500 firms in the survey that had purchased the paper version of COSHH Essentials had taken some action since purchase. Of these, the majority claimed to be confident of their risk assessments and ability to control chemical health risks. However, the survey population was biased toward manufacturing and the larger enterprises within its size range. More importantly, while it demonstrated the opinions of users, it did not provide objective information on the nature of the use to which the guidance had been put. Nor did the study allow comparisons to be made between the use of COSHH Essentials and other forms of guidance. The report of the survey noted that COSHH Essentials was thought to be one of the HSE's most useful pieces of SME guidance, but it was still not making inroads into smaller SMEs to the extent that the HSE had hoped and that such firms were underrepresented among its purchasers.

This finding helped to justify the launch of an interactive Internet version of COSHH Essentials. The HSE monitors the number of visits to the site and claims that there were as many visitors to the electronic form in three months as the paper version sold in three years. Unpublished figures obtained from the HSE indicated that by the end of July 2005, there had been 257,830 visitors, with 232,915 completed assessments. It is not known at present how many of these visitors are small firms. Despite the apparent significant access to the electronic COSHH Essentials however, it needs to be borne in mind that such figures say little about its actual use or of the supports and constraints to use. There is little information for example on the role played in this respect by incentives, access, or the role of enforcement in influencing employers to use COSHH Essentials.

[16]www.coshh-essentials.org.uk

Nor is much known concerning employers' occupational health and safety competence to use COSHH Essentials or how much they involve workers and their representatives in such use.

CONCLUSIONS: CONVERGING REGULATION BUT CONTINUING PROBLEMS

The gulf between regulation and compliance described in the each of the six countries studied leads to the need to consider the role of regulation in improving chemical risk management in small enterprises and to ask what exactly it is that regulatory strategy is attempting to achieve. Breaches of the regulatory requirements outlined in this chapter are either criminal or administrative offenses (or both) depending on the national regulatory system and the seriousness of the breach. Penalties are most commonly fines, the levels of which are usually defined in the relevant legislation. The extent of the use of such penalties in relation to chemical risk management and of enforcement in general in this respect in small firms is difficult to determine from existing records, but it does not seem to be a major feature of the enforcement scenario in any of the countries studied.

As Walters and Grodzki (2006) have argued, there are several reasons why enforcement of the regulation of chemical risk management may not be as prominent as might be expected given the indications of noncompliance evident in many countries. Some have to do with artifacts of the recording of inspection practice—it is likely for example that many actions involving chemicals are not recorded as such but rather as actions dealing with risk management more generally. However, there are other reasons that have to do with the degree of technical understanding and skill of labor inspectors and the resources available to support them that may militate against the use of enforcement actions in relation to chemical risk management. This leads to the conclusion that the low level of enforcement action on chemical risk management in relation to small firms is a real observation and not just an artifact of reporting (Walters & Grodzki, 2006).

Relatedly, regulatory strategies on chemical risk management have implications for the provision of support for employers that need technical assistance to undertake their obligations competently. In the case of small firms, this often means access to external expertise. Regulatory inspectorates (perhaps with the exception of those in Germany), rarely engage in proactive acts of monitoring themselves; instead it is undertaken by prevention services and a variety of other consultants. There are legislative provisions that oblige employers to use such services to support their management of OHS in most continental EU countries. Not surprisingly therefore, in most countries in this study such services are perceived as having a frontline role in supporting chemical risk management. However, their role in enabling employers in small enterprises to fulfill their regulatory duties is problematic, especially because of limited access. This seems to be the case regardless of the legislative provisions that control services and require employers to use them. It is generally acknowledged that as a consequence, employers in small enterprises are not serviced as well by external prevention services (Walters, 2001). It is therefore far from clear how useful such support is for the implementation of regulatory strategies on chemical risk management in these firms.

The above observations are especially relevant to the current approaches to regulation, because they help to inform the view widely held by regulatory policymakers: that improving health and safety in small enterprises is a challenge that cannot be met successfully solely through traditional regulatory means. As a consequence, an interest has developed in identifying and exploiting other ways to promote and sustain health and safety improvements that can supplement state-led inspection and control. This has prompted a host of initiatives in EU countries to identify actors and processes mainly in the market environment of small enterprises and in the networks of production in which they are located, in whose (largely economic) interests it is to promote and support health and safety improvements in such enterprises. Ways in which they and the processes with which they interact with small businesses can apply leverage to small enterprises to achieve such ends have been explored and widely promoted by state agencies. Approaches of this type are also evident in relation to chemical risk management and will be considered in greater detail in the following chapters. However, it is worth noting that the emphasis they place on the supply chain is itself not without problems when, as this chapter clearly shows, the quality of the information supplied through it continues to be found wanting.

It is also important to contextualize these policy orientations within a wider economic and political setting. They have occurred at a time when, at the EU level and in most member states, governance has struggled to develop appropriate regulatory responses to the economic pressures of globalization. As a result, there has been an increased interest in market-based reforms in which self-regulatory approaches have been encouraged, while state-led regulation, inspection and control have been contained, if not actually reduced (Walters, 2005). Therefore, while insights on the limited application of health and safety management systems and the finite nature of inspection and control strategies in relation to small enterprises need to be acknowledged, it is equally important to recognize the political motivators behind current governmental promotion of market-based, self-regulatory strategies addressing health and safety arrangements in small enterprises and related forms of work.

This is especially so in relation to chemical risk management where, at the EU level, the emphasis of REACH on supply-chain relationships between producers and users and on the two way communication of information concerning use is largely predicated upon notions concerning the market relationships of such actors and a belief in the potential of economic influences they might bring to bear on one another to improve practice in chemical risk management. The country-by-country experiences reported in this chapter demonstrate the extent to which such approaches are also in evidence at national levels. Although their rationale has an attractive plausibility, it is important to note that there is as yet very little evidence to support the efficacy of these approaches in practice. The extent to which this is the case in relation to the programs specifically set up in some countries to deal with achieving improved chemical risk management in smaller enterprises will be explored in Chapter 5. Before doing so however, it is important to consider something of the infrastructures in place to support modern approaches to improving chemical risk management in small enterprises. This is the subject of the next chapter.

CHAPTER 4

Managing Chemical Risks:
The Role of the Occupational Health
and Safety System

The need for support for small enterprise owner/management in implementing current regulatory approaches to chemical risk management is evident. Published accounts show that despite harmonizing strategies at European levels, there remain divergent patterns of national support for occupational health and safety in different member states (Walters, 2002). Therefore no one single model of institutional support is likely to have widespread international application in relation to supporting chemical risk management in small firms. The aim of this chapter is to review the range of institutional support in the countries studied and consider its adequacy in underpinning the application of the regulatory strategies outlined previously.

The chapter begins by examining the structures and actors in what might be termed the "health and safety system" in the countries studied; that is, the national, regional, or sectoral infrastructures charged by the state to monitor and support compliance with legal measures for the protection of workers' health and prevention of injury, along with the preventive services and social-insurance associations that are prominent in the health and safety systems of some countries. It includes an account of the somewhat anomalous situation in the UK in which neither statutory provision for prevention services nor social-insurance associations contribute to health and safety support, but where strategies on chemical risk management tailored to small firms are prominent nonetheless.

The chapter continues by reviewing the role of employers' and employees' organizations and other sector- and trade-based actors and processes in supporting small firms in their handling of chemical risks. Mindful of the supply-chain orientation of current European measures such as REACH, it examines the infrastructure of chemical supply, the structural aspects of health and safety management within supply chains for chemical products and their potential role in reaching risk management in small firms. It concludes with a discussion of common themes in the role of all these elements of national health and safety systems in supporting chemical risk management in small firms in the countries studied.

INSTITUTIONAL SUPPORT AT THE STATE LEVEL

Table 4.1 indicates the authorities at the national level who are responsible for the implementation of the legal framework on health and safety at work, including that for managing workplace chemical risks in the countries studied.

In several of the countries studied, the national regulatory authorities such as the HSC/E in the UK, the SWEA in Sweden, and the Dutch Ministry of Social Affairs and Employment, as well as other ministries, are a source of information and guidance on the implementation and operation of legal and quasi-legal requirements for which they are responsible for administering. In other countries there is a more formal separation of health and safety authorities at the state level and public institutions undertaking research and disseminating information on health and safety. In all cases a substantial part of the research and information dissemination concerns worker protection from the hazards of chemical substances. In those countries in which social insurance systems are legally mandated with preventive roles, these additional national and sectoral institutions undertake research and provide information on chemical risk management, some of which may be directed at small enterprises.

Although there is not a dedicated state institution for research and information dissemination on health and safety in the UK, substantial activity occurs, and a significant proportion of the annual budget of the regulatory agency (the HSE) is used for these purposes. It commissions research from independent organizations including commercial consultancy firms and universities. Much of this work was undertaken in-house but has since been outsourced following public-sector reorganization from the 1980s onward. The HSE produces and disseminates information on health and safety, such as COSHH Essentials, both in hard copy and, increasingly, via its Web site.

Similarly, in Sweden, while the Work Environment Authority (SWEA) deals with regulatory inspection of health and safety, it also produces information and guidance on chemical risk management. In addition, the Chemicals Inspectorate (*KemI*), is a supervisory authority under the Ministry of Sustainable Development, with a focus on chemical products and the companies producing them. At the same time there are several state-funded research organizations, such as the National Institute for Working Life (NIWL),[1] that provide support for ministerial-level political and regulatory activity as well as research and information for employers

---

[1] Research on which this book was based was largely undertaken before the 2006 elections in Sweden. One of the early announcements made by the new government concerned its intention to close the NIWL in 2007. It is unclear what, if anything, will replace its function of informing government on work environmental policy.

and employees. Additionally, there are research institutes jointly supported with industry such as the Swedish Environmental Research Institute (IVL).

In the Netherlands, the Labour Inspectorate, which is part of the Ministry of Social Affairs and Employment, enforces the regulation of health and safety. The Ministry also produces guidance materials and is supported in doing so by several research organizations, notably the Dutch Organisation for Applied Scientific Research Expertise (TNO), a large (5,500 employees), formerly state-funded national institute that undertakes research and information collation on a wide range of relevant subjects, including occupational exposure, OSH management systems and industrial safety. In addition, there are several other smaller research groups in universities and elsewhere with specialist knowledge on hazardous substances.

In other countries such national-level regulatory structures are supported by separate agencies undertaking research and information functions. In Germany, for example, the Federal Administration has acted on health and safety through two institutional structures: the department in charge of occupational health and safety within the Federal Ministry (until recently the *Bundesministerium fuer Wirtschaft und Arbeit—BMWA*), and a federal agency subordinated to it, the Federal Institute of Occupational Health (FIOH; *Bundesanstalt fuer Arbeitsschutz und Arbeitsmedizin—BAuA*). Political decisions and the shaping of framework conditions, including agreements with other institutional actors in the field, are part of the tasks at the ministerial level. The roles of FIOH are twofold: it provides the ministerial level with expert advice on policy contents; and it carries out research and development in the field, including model solutions for application in enterprises and practical advice on selected issues including chemical risk management. It has been involved in the development of guidelines for occu-pational health management systems (OHMS), targeted particularly at SMEs, and in providing a range of models of good practice, including simplified guide-lines and checklists on using hazardous substances (BAuA, 2004a, 2004b). It works jointly with other actors in relation to specific sectors or trades, such as the motor vehicle trade (BAuA, 1999; Kliemt & Voullaire, 1999).

Also important in terms of federal state support for chemical risk management is the Committee on Hazardous Substances (*Ausschuss für Gefahrstoffe—AGS*), an advisory body to the Federal Ministry of Economics and Labour. Its tasks and composition are defined in the Hazardous Substances Ordinance; they include drafting technical guidance documents on hazardous substances. It is legally an advisory body, but in practice its tripartite nature means that it is also used as a negotiating forum on technical details that affect the economic interests of businesses and the health interests of workers (Körber, 1998).

In Spain the National Institute for Occupational Safety and Hygiene (*Instituto Nacional de Seguridad e Higiene en el Trabajo—INSHT*) provides technical support for regulatory decision making at ministerial and inspectorate levels and at the same time promotes and implements training, information, certification,

Table 4.1 State Institutional Support for Managing the Risks of Hazardous Substances in the Workplace

Country	Ministry	Sub-department(s)/ Advisory bodies	Research institutes/ other bodies/institutions	Surveillance authorities
Austria[a]	Federal Ministry of Economics and Labour (BMWA)	Department III—Labour Law and Labour Inspectorates	Austrian Federal Environment Agency (Chemicals Dept.)	Central Labour Inspectorate
Germany[a]	Bundesministerium fuer Wirtschaft und Arbeit Federal Ministry of Economics and Labour (BMWA). From 2006, the Ministry of Labour and Social Affairs	Committee on Hazardous Substances (Ausschuss für Gefahrstoffe—AGS)	Bundesanstalt für Arbeitsschutz und Arbeitsmedizin (BAuA) Federal Institute for Occupational Safety and Health (FIOH).	Regional Offices for Industrial Safety Staatliche Amter Abeits-schutz
Spain	Ministerio de Trabajo y Asuntos Sociales (Ministry for Labour and Social Affairs	Commission Nacional de Seguridad y Salud en el Trabajo National Commission for Safety and Health at Work	Instituto Nacional de Seguridad e Higiene en el Trabajo National Institute for Safety and Hygiene at Work	Inspección de Trabajo Labour Inspectorate

Sweden	Ministry of Industry, Employment and Communication	Swedish Work Environment Authority (SWEA)	For example: Swedish National Institute for Working Life; IVL—Swedish Environmental Research Institute (a joint organization with industry)	Swedish Work Environment Authority—regional districts.
Netherlands	Ministerie van Sociale Zaken en Werkgelegenheid (Ministry of Social Affairs and Employment)	Directoraat-Generaal Arbeidsverhoudingen en Internationale Betrekkingen	For example: TNO, Dutch Organisation for Applied Scientific Research Expertise	Labour Inspectorate
United Kingdom	Department of Work and Pensions	Health and Safety Commission/ Health and Safety Executive	No national institute, Health and Safety Laboratory (formerly within HSE now contracted out), commercial research consultancy firms, universities, etc.	Health and Safety Executive/ Local Authority Environmental Health Departments

[a]The table is limited to state institutional support in relation to workplace chemical risk management. It presents an incomplete picture of the government departments and agencies involved in all aspects of chemical risk management. It is especially incomplete in the case of Germany and Austria, because it does not include the parallel structures of the insurance associations that are also present in both countries. Also in Austria there are other smaller labor inspectorates for special branches of industry, and the federal state level structure in Germany is more complex than above; usually, there is 1) a ministerial department in charge of OHS, 2) a Landesamt, and 3) labor inspectorates (for enforcement and advice). In some states, Landesamt and labor inspectorates are part of the same "Executive," in others the inspectorates are regionalized.

research and dissemination, coordinating and cooperating with preventive bodies in regional governments. It also serves as a secretariat to the National Commission (the consultative policymaking body for health and safety at the national level).

In Austria workplace health and safety falls under the authority of the Federal Ministry of Economics and Labour, of which the Labour Inspectorate is part. In addition, the Chemicals Department of the Austrian Federal Environmental Agency (UBA Austria, *Umweltbundesamt*) is the federal government authority for environmental protection and control and provides general information about chemicals, especially concerning notifications and registration procedures, classification of existing and new substances as well as other data in the register for chemicals. The UBA Austria carries out research on selected hazardous substances and produces technical documents for the assessment of chemicals such as the series of technical guidance documents for performing risk assessments (TGDs). The accident insurance companies, principally among them the AUVA, also play a central role in providing OSH advice.

INSPECTION AND ENFORCEMENT AGENCIES

In some countries the roles of other agencies for regulating chemical products may overlap with those dealing with health and safety at work, but it is the health and safety agencies that are of primary concern in this account. Generally they operate through a mixture of advice, education, persuasive approaches and enforcement actions. There are differences in the exact nature of the actions available to inspectorates, the legal frameworks and procedures under which they may be taken, as well in the extent and balance of approaches that are used in different countries. There is also variation in how much such activities are centralized or devolved to state or regional levels, reflecting wider differences in state administration between countries. So for example, where there are federal systems in place such as in Germany, legislation is enforced by the federal states through state health and safety authorities and their inspectorates, and there are considerable variations in the ways in which this is organized, which may in turn lead to differences in inspectorate strategies.

A major difference between Germany and the other countries in the study concerns the additional inspection role of the statutory insurance associations for occupational risks that are part of the so-called dual system in Germany. Under this system, the statutory accident-insurance associations are responsible for a second track of regulation and enforcement of occupational health and safety. Nineteenth-century statutes created the legal basis for accident-insurance funds; they have powers to issue and enforce autonomous rules—the Accident Prevention Orders—at sectoral or regional levels (Schaapman, 2002, pp. 114-115). Their role is therefore not only a major aspect of the infrastructural support for OHS, including chemical risk management, but one that operates with legal support and enforcement powers.

In Austria each federal province has at least one labor inspectorate. Their activities are coordinated at the national level by the Federal Ministry of Economics and Labour, of which the Labour Inspectorate is part. The Inspectorate has around 500 employees, of which in 2004, 308 were field service staff, responsible for the surveillance of health and safety in some 230,000 workplaces with 2.5 million employees. It has special powers in relation to chemical risks. As well as surveillance of workplaces, they include the authority to require information from the manufacturers, suppliers, and importers concerning the health and safety of their products. Provincial governments are responsible for chemical inspection to ensure compliance with legislation on toxic substances and biocides. The Chemicals Department of the Federal Environment Agency (*Umweltbundesant*) provides advice and technical support.

In other countries the primary responsibility for monitoring and enforcing compliance with legislative requirements on chemical risk management within workplaces rests with centrally coordinated regulatory agencies for health and safety at work. Even here however there is considerable delegation of duties. In the UK, for example, while the HSE is the central and supreme regulatory authority for health and safety at work, inspection in large parts of the services sector (such as those concerned with retail, leisure, and hospitality, where most private-sector businesses are small) enforcement of health and safety requirements is devolved to the environmental health department of local authorities. Inspection standards among such local authorities are known to vary and have represented cause for concern in the past (James & Walters, 2005). It is not clear how such inspectorates fare in relation to monitoring and enforcing measures on chemical risk management in small enterprises, but the more general concerns about variation in the adequacy of local authority provision for inspection give little room for complacency.

It is difficult to measure the impact of health and safety inspection and control in relation to chemical risks in small workplaces. Indeed, in many countries, data that might be useful, such as systematic information on enforcement actions and their outcomes in relation to chemical risk management is either not collected routinely or not publicly available. However, as Walters and Grodzki (2006) note, the trend in inspection of the management of chemical risks in small enterprises in most countries is toward integrating it into inspection of health and safety management more generally. Additionally, it is the subject of occasional specific inspection campaigns and, further, enforcement actions tend to be more prominent following the introduction of new regulatory provisions.

For example, in Sweden in 2003 there was a national inspection campaign focusing on hazardous substances. Since that time inspection of the management of hazardous substances at work has been part of the inspection of systematic work environment management more generally. As well as emphasis on the integration of chemical risk management into systematic work environment management, there is at the same time a tradition of more problem-based approaches by the SWEA. As a result, there has been an intensive focus on isocyanates by the Authority. Inspection campaigns in some sectors, measurement of exposures, and research on secondary exposures, have led to revised regulation, its more consistent interpretation by inspectors, the production of guidance, and generally far greater awareness among users of the risks of isocyanates.

In the Netherlands chemical risk management is also inspected as one aspect of systematic health and safety management. The Labour Inspectorate focuses its inspection strategy on the management system for health and safety in organizations. Infringements of specific standards that apply to the work place and work practices are therefore regarded as symptomatic of failure of the management system and used as indicators for correction at this level. In terms of chemical risks, the Dutch approach found in the "Industrial Hygiene Strategy," issued as guidance under the Working Conditions Act, emphasizes control at the source and companies are required to provide evidence of this in the form of risk inventories and evaluations—the risk assessment. Until 2005 such risk assessments were undertaken by the *Arbodienst,* to which companies were required to be affiliated. It appears that the Labour Inspectorate uses the existence of risk assessments as evidence of satisfactory standards of chemical risk management. As Walters and Grodzki (2006, pp. 305-306) discovered by examining unpublished reports of inspection statistics on recorded violations in sectors in which there was a high use of chemical substances (such as metal working and the chemical industry itself), in the year 2000, such violations that could be linked to the use of chemicals formed a significant proportion of infringements.

All this assumes that systematic risk management is widespread; that firms, regardless of their size, have equal and sufficient access to occupational health services; and such services perform risk assessments adequately in relation to chemical hazards. A number of studies on small firms, risk assessment, and occupational health services have questioned such assumptions (Karageorgiou et al., 2000; Popma et al., 2002).

In the UK there is some evidence that shows how inspection of chemical risks featured more prominently following the introduction of new regulations on chemical hazards, when achieving compliance with the regulations is an objective for planned inspection campaigns. For example, during the early 1990s, following the introduction of the COSHH Regulations, there was considerable attention paid to these Regulations in enforcement priorities. Not surprisingly, HSE analysis of its enforcement data for this period shows that certain of the Regulations (such as that requiring risk assessment) featured with great frequency in actions undertaken by its inspectors (HSC, 2002).

Despite the evidence of a strategic approach to inspecting the management of chemical risks, in all of the countries studied the overall picture of the role of inspectors and inspection in securing improved risk management in the use of chemicals in small enterprises is one of relatively limited engagement.

One reason for this is disparity between the human resources available to national inspectorates and the enormous number of small enterprises in which hazardous chemicals are in use. Although there are considerable variations in the ratios of inspectors to the premises under their jurisdiction in different EU countries, in no case is the ratio so favorable as to allow for routine visits more than once in several years. In Sweden for example, on average a small worksite is likely to receive an inspection only once every 14 years. In the UK on average only one in 20 workplaces could expect to receive a visit from an inspector annually.

Limited resources lead inspectorates to set priorities for inspection visits, which may mean that smaller workplaces receive lower prioritization than larger ones. In the UK for example, the HSE prioritization of inspection according to a risk-based approach has become increasingly systematized since the introduction of more process-based regulatory requirements on risk management. It is dependent on good quality intelligence concerning the occurrence, use and scale of use of hazardous substances. As a result it is frequently biased toward larger enterprises where the use of hazardous substances is likely to be both more conspicuous and quantitatively greater than in small enterprises. As a result, large premises feature more prominently in the prioritization of inspection visits than their smaller counterparts.

In Germany, although the state inspectorates have been involved in a range of initiatives implementing strategic approaches to regulating chemical risk management that target small firms, reduced resources for inspection in all states has meant that comprehensive enforcement activities, including regular visits to all workplaces, are no longer feasible. Regular inspection visits are made to large enterprises with a high risk potential (typically industrial production or assembly plants). Additionally, as part of a special activities program, comprehensive visits may be made to a significant number of enterprises in a particular trade or sector of industry, yet in many cases these will take place only in one specific region of the state. Such visits are used not only for enforcement activities but also to offer advice and support. Finally, enterprises are visited as a result of complaints by employees or after an accident. Some states, however, have drastically reduced the number of workplace visits and have shifted the focus of their activities from enforcement to advice. In 2001 a joint strategy paper was agreed upon by ministers to harmonize these various strategies (ASMK, 2001). The role of advice and support was underlined, and enforcement activities were addressed as *ultima ratio* to be pursued if information and advice failed to lead to the results intended. The necessity of developing support tools adequate for practical use, as well as strategies and sector-specific solutions applicable in SMEs, was underlined. The federal states have a special committee (*Länderausschuss für Arbeitsschutz und Sicherheitstechnik—LASI*) to coordinate their various strands of occupational health activities, a working group of which has developed an electronically accessible database on hazardous substances (*Gefahrstoffdatenbank der Länder—GDL*[2]).

Resource-driven shifts in the balance between enforcement and advice are also found in Sweden where, while the SWEA is well aware of the general deficiencies in chemical risk management in small firms, discussion is ongoing concerning the balance between enforcement and advisory roles. Authorities are also anxious to secure engagement of the organizations representing employers and employees in supporting chemical risk management in small firms through their production of guidance and training materials, as well as supervisory and counseling roles.

In Austria there has been increasing emphasis on the role of the Labour Inspectorate in the provision of advice concerning prevention (ZAI, 2004). In 2003 and 2004 about 11% of all enterprises with 1 to 50 workers were subject to full inspection by the Labour Inspectorate (excluding outdoor worksites and construction sites). This percentage does not include campaigns and checks of specific OSH issues. Only just over 1% of the latter focused on chemical substances. By comparison just over 2% of advisory talks provided by the inspectorate for all enterprises focused on chemical substances (Kittel, 2006).

The Labour Inspectorate's approach helps determine the type and frequency of inspections in relation to risk potential and the level of protection existing in the enterprise. Choice of enterprises for routine inspections is determined accordingly, and enforcement practices are linked to observations not only of hazard but also of management practice. In the inspection work plan for the first half of 2006, this approach resulted in an Austria-wide main focus on SMEs, car varnishers, carpenters and explosion-protection documents. Another example of the effects of this approach is seen in the main focus on chemical substances and the organization of labor protection in electro-plating enterprises in upper Austria in 2003 (Kittel, 2006). The Inspectorate places emphasis on particular sectors through pilot projects and compiling specific information materials on, for example, wood dust in wood processing and floor dust and other hazards in bakeries. A Workplace Health Promotion project *Backen wir's* by the bakers' *Landesinnung*, the *AI Linz*, the *OÖGKK*, the *AK OÖ*, and the upper Austrian AUVA was followed by brochures and an Austria-wide campaign on safety and health protection in bakeries from 2000 to 2005.

In contrast, in the Netherlands there was a definite policy shift for the Labour Inspectorate in the last decade, away from an advisory role to that of greater "policing" of occupational health and safety. One significant influence behind

---

[2] At http://www.gefahrstoff-info.de/

this shift was the introduction of inspectorate powers to issue "administrative fines," a second was the role of the *Arbodiensten,* which were supposed to take over the role of providing advice. However, this does not lead to more frequent inspections of small firms, for the other reasons already mentioned that contribute to their low profile in inspection programs.

In Spain a recent study of worker perceptions of chemical risk indicated a level of dissatisfaction with the inspectorate caused by perceptions that inspectors were failing in their duties by, for example, announcing inspection visits in advance and reaching conclusions by common consent with the employer (Gadea, 2006).

Further reasons for the limited influence of inspection are found in the restricted capacity of labor inspectorates to implement risk management strategies that require technical inputs. As Walters and Grodzki (2006) demonstrated in their study on the role of OELs in chemical risk management, regulatory inspectors themselves may lack sufficient skills to enforce legal requirements concerning the evaluation and control of exposures to hazardous substances. Inspectors indicated they were underresourced and insufficiently skilled to undertake these activities in anything more than a highly selective way, even in northern European countries such as Sweden and the Netherlands. In the UK the HSE's own research on the enforcement of the COSHH Regulations demonstrated that inspectors were more likely to initiate actions around requirements on risk assessment than they were on control, because the former were easier to understand and inspectors more confident in using them. In all cases, inspectors reported insufficient technical support for their workplace inspection of chemical risk management, both in terms of instrumentation and skills.

These findings are confirmed by further examples in countries featured in this study. In Sweden, following the SWEA inspection campaign in 2003, inspectors reported to the campaign coordinator that they had appreciated learning more about chemicals and chemical risk management themselves as a result of the concentration on chemicals during their inspections in the campaign. In Spain inspection tends toward enforcement more than advice. However, the Spanish Inspectorate is a general labor inspectorate and not well served with specialist expertise on occupational risk prevention; therefore its activity is focused on checking the application of regulations and proposing sanctions if necessary (Uberti-Bona & Rodrigo, in press).

PREVENTION SERVICES

Framework Directive 89/391 requires employers to use competent advice in discharging their responsibilities on health and safety. This applies to managing chemical risks as much as it does to other aspects of the work environment. There is a variety of approaches to achieving these requirements in different

EU countries.[3] This is partly because of the prior existence of national styles and legislative frameworks governing the structure, coverage, and competence of occupational health and safety support and partly because of differences in conceptualization of the role of support in the delivery of competent health and safety management.

The prior existence of detailed provisions on employers' responsibilities to use occupational physicians and safety engineers according to the number of workers employed in organizations, as well as on the qualifications and competence of such expertise, has been a major influence on the way the Directive has been transposed, for example, in Germany and Austria (and also in other countries not included in this study, such as France). National considerations on the type of preventive service offered played a major role in determining the integrated approaches found in Scandinavian countries and in the Netherlands, as well as in providing certification systems for quality assurance of services in countries like the Netherlands. A complete overhaul of old legislative requirements in Spain has allowed for the introduction of new integrated models.

Conceptual differences are evident between these continental European approaches and those in the UK, where preventive services are not regarded as central to occupational health and safety management but seen rather as a peripheral support. Emphasis has therefore been laid upon employers undertaking their own risk assessments and using advice from competent services to help them do so. Still further differences can be accounted for by the extent to which employers' responsibilities in relation to using preventive expertise were already governed by statutory requirements and therefore a tradition of regulatory intervention prior to the adoption of the Framework Directive. This was the case in most continental EU countries, in contrast to the UK where, with the exception of very specific situations, there was no such tradition. At the time of the transposition of the Directive, the UK regulators were concerned to do as little as possible to change existing regulatory provision and as a result, almost completely ignored the provisions of Article 7 of the Directive (James & Walters, 1999). Even today, following subsequent legislative amendments to rectify this situation, employers' duties in relation to using prevention services as well as the constitution and quality of such services remain the most lightly regulated in Europe.

Some of these differences have resulted in infringement proceedings being started at the European Court of Justice, in turn adding further legal interpretation to requirements. Indeed, 15 years after the deadline for transposition of the Directive's provisions, harmonization of approaches to preventive services throughout the EU remains some way off.

---

[3] Vogel's comprehensive study of preventive systems remains a substantial source of informa- tion on these provisions (Vogel, 1993, 1998). For a more recent account see Westerholm and Walters (2007).

Despite the complexity of the current development of preventive services, there are some features of their form, content and coverage that are generalizable across most EU countries. Some aspects of these are of particular significance for small enterprises and for managing chemical risks within them. It is evident that the integration of multidisciplinary expertise into a single service is seen as desirable in most countries. One reason for this is found in the conceptual shift in the thinking about prevention toward focusing on the work environment rather than on the worker. There are links between this theoretical position and the more holistic and collectivist legislative approaches to prevention that are contained in the "preventive principles" underpinning employers' duties in the Framework Directive. Both internal and external models of delivery of services are also found in most countries. All of this points toward a potentially useful support for chemical risk management in small enterprises.

However, it is equally evident that these approaches, no matter how theoretically desirable, are incompletely achieved in small enterprises. The reasons for this are complex, and hard evidence is limited; but it suggests they are related to a mixture of issues concerning supply and demand. First, the huge number of small enterprises compared with the very few external integrated preventive services that exist means that such services are unlikely to reach more than a small percentage of the total number that might benefit from them. Second, there is a range of financial barriers for both users and providers that limit the role of preventive services in small enterprises. If there is a cost to the small enterprise as a client, they are unlikely to regard paying for such a service as a priority unless they have very convincing reasons for doing so. Even in systems where such costs are borne in other ways and where employers are under an obligation to use available services, the percentage of time allocated to individual small enterprises is such that only a very limited provision of service can be economically offered.

The most significant problem for small enterprises generally in relation to prevention services is one of availability; it seems that in most countries there simply aren't enough services to cover the number and variety of small firms, nor do such firms generally have the resources to use such support. In Sweden, where coverage of preventive services has traditionally been quite high, recent data indicates that 42% of employees in micro-companies and 67% in small companies claim they have access to occupational health services. The distribution according to different sectors is shown in Table 4.2. But these figures are probably overestimates, as sometimes access to a doctor is interpreted as access to an occupational health service. A more reliable estimate is that about 30% of Swedish small companies are affiliated with an occupational health service (Antonsson, 2007). Affiliation is more common among small manufacturing companies than among small trade or service companies.

The issue of access notwithstanding, in market-based systems the range of services that an integrated preventive service is able to offer its clients is

Table 4.2 Company Size and Access to Prevention Services in Sweden[a]

Sector	Size of workplace			
	0-9 empl.	10-49 empl.	50- empl.	**Total**
Agriculture, hunting, forestry and fishing	39	68	89	**45**
Manufacturing, mining and quarrying	40	71	92	**81**
Electricity, gas and water supply	100	92	94	**93**
Construction	49	81	91	**71**
Wholesale and retail trade, repair of motor vehicles, motorcycles and personal and household goods	29	49	74	**47**
Hotels and restaurants	14	23	55	**25**
Transport, storage, and communication	35	67	75	**64**
Financial intermediation	73	85	90	**86**
Real estate, renting and business activities	38	64	79	**62**
Education	64	70	72	**70**
Health care and veterinary activities	47	78	78	**75**
Social work	61	68	66	**66**
Other community, social and personal service activities	35	66	83	**54**
Public administration and defense, compulsory social security	78	90	89	**88**
Total (all sectors)	**42**	**67**	**82**	67

[a]Figures are based on the percentage share of employees in companies in different sectors stating that they have access to occupational health service. Answers are divided according to size of establishment, not size of company.
Source: www.av.se

determined by what clients perceive to be their needs. One of the most significant findings from research among owner/managers in small enterprises on the management of chemical risks concerns the high level of ignorance about chemicals, their hazards and risks, and what to do about them. It is unlikely that help with chemical risk management from a preventive service will be perceived as an obvious need by such owner/managers.[4] Of course, the preventive service could develop its approach to more effective marketing of these aspects to small enterprises. There are some examples of such practices, but they appear to be infrequent (EU OSHA, 2004a).

Messages received from the state are also likely to be relevant to the way in which small firms set their priorities regarding their possible use of preventive services. In most countries in which such services are active or where there is some obligation on small employers to use them, such as in Sweden and the Netherlands, the message from the state concerning its overriding interests and aims is clear: to reduce the costs of sickness absence. The same is true to a greater or lesser extent in other countries in the study. The results of these pressures go some way to help explain the significant use of preventive services in issues concerning medical certification and sickness absence.

In the Netherlands, while the *Arbodiensten* are legally required to offer at least four areas of expertise, including occupational hygiene, as well as to approve risk assessments, it is evident that the primary interests of both the service and their clients are in the areas of medical examinations and the fitness of individuals for work. Despite the theoretical 100% coverage, researchers have found that small enterprises in high-risk sectors regard the *Arbodiensten* of little help in chemical risk management or in risk assessment more generally (Nossent et al., 2003a; Van Heemskerk et al., 2003).

In Sweden a recent survey of what elements provided by occupational health services were used by small companies revealed that small companies mainly used their medical services. About 50% had used some kind of technical service in the recent past, but only a fraction of these concerned chemical risk management. Therefore even if occupational health services are one of the prominent actors within chemical risk management in small companies in Sweden, they service only a fraction of small companies in this way. Because they operate in a free market, they tend to sell only what companies want to buy. If companies do not demand assistance with chemical risk management, the occupational health services do not market or sell that kind of service.

In Spain there is concern that although the preventive services established by the Mutuas are strictly constituted to facilitate an orientation toward

---

[4]For example, as a recent report from IVL in Sweden shows, despite training, many small enterprise owner/managers do not appreciate the need of expert help to evaluate risks and apply appropriate controls for chemical risk management. See http://www.ivl.se/rapporter/pdf/B1668.pdf

prevention, in practice they are commercially driven and therefore tend to be focused on reducing sickness absence (Garcia, 2006). Worker health and safety representatives perceive prevention services offered by Mutuas as oriented toward company interests and hostile toward worker representatives, the Mutuas considering the employers as their sole customers (Garcia & Rodrigo, 2005).

The relationship between supply and demand for services has a further consequence in that over time it affects the kinds of services that organizations are resourced to provide. In spite of legal requirements in some countries and good practice guidance in others, there is evidence that many preventive services are ill-equipped to provide support for chemical risk management. In Sweden occupational health services should in theory be able to provide services relating to chemical risk management. Normally their safety engineer would deliver such provision, but safety engineers are usually not chemists or chemical engineers, and they have limited education on chemical hazards. Additionally, the number of safety engineers with training in, for example, dust sampling, has decreased from about 300 in 1985 to about 100 today. The lack of safety engineers with chemical competence has resulted in poor quality reports on exposure measurements. An investigation made by the Swedish Work Environment Authority showed that only 20% of such reports contained at least half of the information that ought to be included in the report. Safety engineers conduct training related to chemical risk management, they assist with compiling lists, making risk evaluations and suggest control measures. Occasionally they also measure exposure to the most common air contaminants such as different kinds of dust and organic solvents. When it comes to substances requiring more advanced measuring techniques or the use of direct-reading instruments, they usually leave this to other actors, such as departments for occupational and environmental medicine at university hospitals or consultants specializing in measurement.

In the Netherlands there have been requirements that preventive services must approve risk assessments and that occupational hygiene be among the disciplines offered by the service. In theory this should mean that chemical risk management is well covered. However, here too the emphasis on sickness absence and medical care in contracts between them and enterprises, coupled with research evidence showing their limited engagement with risk assessment, suggests at the very least that their occupational hygiene skills are not in high demand. It therefore seems likely that the high degree of market determination that characterizes features of the system would act to lessen this provision by the prevention services in general. In practice, if the dictates of the market are a significant influence, it would be anticipated that resources for technical support for chemical risk management would tend to be concentrated among the *Arbodiensten* that contract with large firms in sectors that are major users of chemical substances, and that small firms in other sectors would be less likely to have access to such provision. There is some support for this supposition in the findings of TNO researchers referred to previously (Nossent et al., 2003a; Van Heemskerk et al., 2003) and also in the evidence of low compliance with risk assessment requirements among small firms. The fact that as well as the *Arbodiensten*, there are a variety of specialist consultants offering occupational hygiene services to firms, suggests that there is a niche in the market for support for technical aspects of chemical risk management that *Arbodeinsten* have not covered (Walters & Grodzki, 2006). The changes to the legal requirements on preventive services that came into force in July 2005 are unlikely to increase the chances of the *Arbodiensten* further developing their role in relation to supporting chemical risk management in small enterprises and indeed, may act to reduce it further.

INSURANCE ASSOCIATIONS AND MANAGING CHEMICAL RISKS

In Austria there appears to be a comparatively strong and well-structured system for support for small enterprises that is provided by prevention services. However, this is made possible largely through the resources of the statutory accident-insurance system and developed from recognition of the failure of the existing provision to address the specific need for support for health and safety management. The history of this development is instructive. The Occupational Safety and Health Act 1994 provided for two legal alternatives for the provision of preventive services (OSH Act, 1994:78b):

- A general model in which the employer contracts with and pays for occupational health and safety experts (in-house, external) or an Occupational Health and Safety Centre (external preventive services, some of which have an occupational medicine orientation, some a safety engineering emphasis, while others are integrated and multidisciplinary)
- An employer model (applying to small establishments only) where the employer himself fulfills the function of a safety engineer after relevant training. He has to ensure and pay for the provision of the other necessary services.

Complaints from small enterprises and lobbying from their representatives about the economic burden of this system resulted in the introduction in 1999 of the AUVAsafe system (*AUVAsicher*) for supporting health and safety in small enterprises. The AUVA is the main social-insurance organization for occupational risks in Austria, covering around 4.25 million workers. Like the German social-insurance system on which it is modeled, it has its own autonomous administration, an income from accident-insurance contributions from enterprises and representation from employers and employee organizations. In addition to its treatment and rehabilitation services, it also has advisory and training services, as well as technical support and engages in a range of preventive projects. In response to the lobbying from small enterprises and their representatives, it established a free preventive support service for worksites with up to 50 employees in enterprises of no more than 250 employees, in which employers in such worksites can, without charge, call upon the services of the OSH personnel of a prevention center run by the AUVA. The program in effect represents a redistribution of financial resources from bigger to smaller companies, since it is supported from the contributions paid by all companies insured against occupational accidents by the AUVA. Its primary objective is to reduce substantially the number of work-related accidents and diseases. It includes all areas of occupational health and safety: informing about relevant requirements, assisting employers in meeting their legal responsibilities (e.g., through assessment and instruction), advising on how to deal with authorities and how to invest in OSH management, and providing information and practical advice (Friedl, 2000). Chemical risk assessment is central to the program. In 2004 the program set its main activities on the 27 economic sectors with the highest accident rates. This led to a focus on sector-specific company visits in which detailed measures on sector-characteristic chemical risks were implemented (Pfoser & Peer, 2004).

One of the main principles of the program is the proximity of prevention centers to the companies involved. The AUVA has set up prevention centers in all nine federal states in Austria. Inspections are performed by prevention experts, and company visits should be performed about every six months (AUVA, 2004). The experts are AUVA employees as well as freelance OSH experts, occupational doctors and private consulting centers, who are well equipped and specially trained.[5] AUVAsafe is strongly promoted by the AUVA, the authorities and the social partners, in particular the economic chambers.

Systematic feedback and evaluation procedures are also established. After the inspection is complete, the enterprise is initially asked to fill in a feedback questionnaire. As a result it was possible to estimate that in 2003, of the SMEs visited, 90% rated their expectations regarding care and advice as fulfilled, and 72% of them said that the company's OSH information was substantially improved by the AUVAsafe assistance. Since 2004 a random sample of enterprises has provided feedback by means of participation in a telephone survey. The recent substantial reduction in accident rates observed in enterprises with fewer than 100 workers is attributed by the AUVA to the success of the AUVAsafe system, although a detailed evaluation has not been undertaken to confirm this, and other factors may have contributed to the improvement (EU OSHA, 2003a).

In the two years after its launch in 1999, the AUVAsafe system had reached about 93,000 enterprises (Müller-Wechselberger, 2002) and about 120,000 by 2003. This represents 41% of companies with fewer than 11 employees, 68% of those with between 11 and 20 employees, and 71% of all companies with 21 to 50 employees; overall, 55% of all companies with fewer than 50 employees. While this success is seen as remarkable, it still means that about 30% of all companies

---

[5] In the year 2003 the staff consisted of 239 AUVA employees and contractual members (AUVA, 2004a).

with 11 to 50 employees and about 60% of all companies with 1 to 10 employees are without any service, since it is unlikely these companies will pay for services themselves or are sufficiently resourced to act competently on health and safety without such support.[6] Moreover, the minimum number of contact hours required of the service is low in companies with fewer than 50 workers, and contact is limited to short visits (mostly only once a year or every two years). The employer is free to purchase additional contact hours, but mostly they do not. Despite these limitations, the AUVAsafe system represents considerable progress in the provision of support for health and safety management, including that on chemical risks, in smaller enterprises.

If the success of the Austrian approach is made possible by the resources and infrastructure provided by the social insurance system for work accidents and ill health, it is interesting to compare it with the situation in Germany, where there is a highly developed infrastructure, largely organized by sector (with an additional regional element in the metal and construction industries, the public sector, and in agriculture). Its legal basis is found in the Social Code, Part VII: Mandatory Accident Insurance (*Sozialgesetzbuch VII—Gesetzliche Unfallversicherung; SGB VII*). The tasks of the insurance associations are the prevention "by all suitable means" of occupational accidents, occupational diseases, and work-related health risks, and the rehabilitation and compensation of their victims (SGB VII, § 1). At present, there are 26 liability insurance associations in the industrial sector, 9 in agriculture, and 34 in the public sector (a merger of the independent regional industrial insurance associations is currently under way). All three sectors have their own federal association, and additionally the industrial insurance associations have a joint structure at the regional level consisting of six associations for different parts of Germany. This creates an autonomous health and safety system operating in parallel with the federal and state systems.

As in Austria, insurance associations for occupational risks are financed by contributions from the enterprises or institutions insured with them, and they are governed by an assembly of an equal number of representatives of both employers and employees of the insured enterprises (*Vertreterversammlung*). For any decision, a majority vote is necessary, as either side can block any decision, so the social partners are always forced to reach a consensus. Autonomous legislation is passed by the assembly and is enforced by the executive of the respective insurance association through its technical inspectorate.

The insurance associations have established standing Expert Committees (*Fachausschüsse*) at the federal level for a number of issues. In mid-2004 there were 34 committees in existence in the industrial sector and 12 in the public sector.

---

[6]Enterprises with 1 to 10 employees are a special problem: many of them have only one or two employees.

The subject of hazardous substances is dedicated to a specific committee in each of these sectors.

Corresponding to the database on hazardous substances established by the federal states, the insurance associations have established their own information system on hazardous substances (*Gefahrstoffinformationssystem der gewerblichen Berufsgenossenschaften—GESTIS*).[7] Currently it contains information on about 8,000 substances and focuses on their safe handling at the workplace (BGIA, 2005a). Additionally, two other databases are made available by the insurance associations: the German version of the International Chemical Safety Cards (ICSC), published as part of the International Programme on Chemical Safety (IPCS) (BGIA, 2005b) and an information center on safety data sheets (*Informationsstelle für Sicherheitsdatenblätter—ISI*), established jointly with the German Chemical Industry Association (*Verband der chemischen Industrie— VCI*) which contains about 650,000 safety data sheets from about 260 companies. The latter is accessible to the enforcement institutions of the federal states, the insurance associations, and to certain emergency services. Only a small selection is accessible to the public, dependent on the explicit consent of the publishing companies (BGIA, 2005c).

The insurance associations offer training courses to their members on a wide range of occupational health-related subjects. Target groups are safety experts (occupational hygienists), employers, and works councillors; they are the largest provider of such courses in Germany.

There is an abundance of printed material available from the insurance associations on most issues regarding occupational health and safety. Traditionally directed to technical concerns, this literature increasingly addresses organizational aspects. However, few publications are adapted to the needs of small enterprises. One exception is a brochure from HVBG (1999) that outlines five building blocks for a well-organized enterprise, including occupational health. At the sector level, in the construction and the quarrying industries, the insurance associations offer OHS management systems for SMEs (AMS BG, 2005; SMS, 2005).

Most insurance associations provide support tools for risk assessment in general, mainly as brochures and checklists. An overview of these tools adapted to the specific conditions of different sectors can be found on the Web site of the Hesse occupational health administration (HESSEN, 2004). A simple introduction to risk assessment is offered on its Web site by the insurance association for the printing industry (BG DRUPA, 2004a). Several insurance associations have developed electronic media-based tools for risk assessment and risk management in relation to hazardous substances; for example in woodworking (HOLZ BG, 2005); mechanical and electrical engineering (BG FE, 2002); the plating industry

---

[7] Available in English at http://www.hvbg.de/bia/gestis-database

(BG FE, 2001, 2004), wholesale and warehousing (GROLA BG, 2003) and in dentistry (BGW, 2002, 2004).

Both specific and generic approaches to the substitution or control of hazardous chemicals are promoted. An overview of sector or process-specific solutions (*Branchenlösungen*) for either substitution of hazardous substances or the establishment of control measures is presented in the annually updated booklet *Hazardous Substances* (*Gefahrstoffe*) (Hamm et al., 2005). Many of these solutions were developed by insurance associations and include various processes in the printing industry (BG DRUPA, 2001, 2002, 2004b, 2005) the cement industry, for labeling man-made mineral fiber products (FMI, 2000); cleaning work in shops, offices and public buildings (HVBG, 2001); the handling and storage of hazardous substances at the premises of public maintenance utilities (BUK, 2004); a variety of tasks involving hazardous substances in the construction industry (GISBAU, 2005a, 2005b); and the chemicals industry (GISCHEM, 2005).

Generic approaches to managing chemical risks include the so-called column model (*Spaltenmodell*), which was developed by the insurance associations through their Institute of Occupational Safety *(Berufsgenossenschaftliches Institut für Arbeitsschutz—BGIA)*.

Overall in Germany, as in Austria, the insurance associations for occupational risks provide a substantial infrastructure for support for health and safety management, and chemical risk management specifically, across the range of sectors in which chemical risks occur. Unlike in Austria there is no single initiative in Germany for which they are responsible that is directed to the needs of small enterprises. Rather there is a diversity of approaches reflecting the extensive expertise and resourcing of support at the sectoral level and the extent and complexity of its industry, which has resulted in the emergence of several initiatives that are relevant to the needs of chemical risk management in small enterprises. In countries such as Germany and Austria, in which social insurance for occupational health and safety is deeply embedded in the system for prevention, they provide a substantial additional dimension to the infrastructure for support for health and safety management in small enterprises.

PREVENTION AND PREVENTIVE SERVICES
IN A REGULATORY VACUUM:
THE UK SITUATION

In contrast with countries like Germany and Austria, in the UK, employers' liability insurance has no direct preventive function. Its role is restricted to the coverage of employers' financial liabilities for occupational accidents and ill health, and its influence on prevention in small enterprises is minimal. In comparison with continental European countries, sectoral infrastructures supporting health and safety are also poorly developed in the UK, where there is a tradition of limited regulatory intervention in economic affairs and a weak presence of corporatist structures. This tradition is deeply embedded in the UK political economy and has received additional reinforcement from the free-market strategies of both Conservative and Labour governments since the late 1970s.

Regulatory measures on employers' responsibilities in relation to the use of preventive services leave them with considerable discretion. Further, the competencies of such services and their personnel hardly feature as subjects of regulation. Indeed, with the exception of special cases involving dangerous trades, the existence of general requirements on competent advice for support for health and safety management is a result of transposition of the EU Framework Directive rather than a UK initiative. A consequence is that although a range of integrated prevention services exist and are staffed by appropriately qualified professionals, estimates suggest that only 8% of private-sector companies are actually using some form of occupational health support and only 5% of small firms have access to any form of occupational health services (Bunt, 1993; Pilkington et al., 2002). Moreover, the largely free-market regulation of the quality and take up of such provisions allows room for many operations that are unable to deliver quality preventive advice (Waterman, 2007).

It is arguably the lightness of the regulatory engagement in these issues coupled with a limited supportive infrastructure that causes the HSE to be in the vanguard of policy development on alternative strategies for securing health and safety improvements in small enterprises. During the second half of the 1990s it developed its "small firms strategy" in which a strong case was made for using various actors and processes in the business environment of small firms as levers to promote and support health and safety management in these firms (see for example Haslam et al., 1998; Haslam & James, 2001; Breakwell & Petts, 2001). As Walters (2001) notes, by the end of the 1990s national policies on these issues were more developed in Britain than in any other European country, and since that time policy development has continued to increasingly embrace alternatives to regulatory inspection and to traditionally constituted occupational health services.

Spurred by governmental recognition that by 2005 over 2.5 million people were on incapacity benefit,[8] there has been a strong effort to link the provision of advice on health and safety matters to improved economic performance and wider governmental approaches to supporting work retention and return to

---

[8] Incapacity benefit is paid to people of working age who have been certified by medical practitioners as unable to work because of an ill-health condition. The largest categories are those incapacitated by mental ill health (most commonly depression) and through musculo-skeletal disorders—these two account for approximately 2/3 of the total.

work; the HSC has directly funded or co-funded several pilot and pre-pilot initiatives that provide occupational health (and safety) advisory services to small and medium-sized enterprises. Building on these pilots, in 2006 it launched a scheme called Workplace Health Connect, which is claimed will cover some 38% of all SMEs in England and Wales between 2005 and 2008, when its state funding ends.

The rationale of these approaches is based on the idea that what many SMEs need in practice is simple, sector-specific guidance on practical measures to reduce exposure to hazardous agents, advice on enabling workers with health problems to continue working, together with information about ways of keeping healthy. It is argued that such advice may be obtainable from a variety of sources, and many workers and their employers in small businesses are likely to remain reliant on nonprofessional sources for advice (OHAC, 2000). At the policy level therefore, while keeping in mind the ideal of an integrated prevention service that provides support that is focused on the work environment, the way such support could be provided has been extended to include many other players that might help employers and workers in small enterprises. In discussion on this at the national level, the challenge has been defined as getting all employers and workers to take responsibility for work-related health standards, rather than creating professional teams that try to do so from outside the workplace.

The current approach envisages an individual employer or worker making contact with an occupational health and safety advisory service by responding to advertisements; through various gatekeepers such as trade associations or trades unions or HSE inspectors; by meeting representatives of advisory services at events such as a trade fairs or local community gatherings; or through meeting people who are already taking advantage of the support available. Once engaged with the advisory service's support team, the worker or employer's representative will be able to get practical assistance in evaluating the risks to health that characterize the workplace and in establishing what the control priorities may be. The final stage of the support, having raised general awareness and specifically drafted an Action Plan for tackling significant health risks, is signposting to other organizations—commercial and public—with the competence to provide longer-term support that might cover training, occupational hygiene, medical and other services, which can be purchased and tailored to identified needs. It is therefore a hub and spoke model, whereby initial core support is provided by the hub support service and the specialist organizations that might help later are represented by the spokes. Advice and guidance on chemical risk management is theoretically within the remit of the delivery of support to small enterprises both at hub and spoke levels.

This approach is still in the early stages of its development. It has been tested by pilot projects in the construction industry and more widely in Scotland. In England and Wales it is being rolled out in a series of regional pilot projects funded with £20 million over two years between 2006 and 2008. Evaluation of the impact of these projects is also underway but not yet completed.

The rationale for this initiative is not without its critics. In parallel with the positive publicity it has received from the HSE and government sources, Workplace Health Connect has been variously portrayed as a weak, privatized substitute for the occupational health inspection services traditionally supplied by the regulatory agency itself, which has been systematically reduced during the same period as Workplace Health Connect has been rolled out; or as lacking any form of compulsion on employers to use the services and as having no provision for direct access for employees without going through their employers. This leads to the further criticism that the scheme is unlikely to reach those situations in which interventions are most needed. It has been condemned by critics as an inadequate substitute for what is really needed first: a meaningful regulatory response to achieve the long overdue, proper transposition of the requirements of preventive services in the Framework Directive 89/391 (James & Walters, 2005). The extensive investment of scarce HSE resources in the scheme has also been criticized and blamed for the financial crisis in which the organization found itself in by mid-2006, during which a moratorium was imposed on any new spending on research and considerable concern expressed over potential reductions in staffing across the organization.

THE ROLES OF OTHER ACTORS
AND PROCESSES

The UK is not alone in its pursuit of alternative solutions for supporting health and safety in small firms. The spread of deregulatory policies in other advanced market economies has also given impetus to discussion of the potential roles of economic actors and processes in stimulating and supporting health and safety in small firms in these countries too. However, a difference between the UK and most other European countries is that in the latter, traditions of regulation and corporatism mean that there are already substantial infrastructures in place that could support initiatives from a range of economic actors. This study found extensive evidence of this in relation to supporting chemical risk management in small firms. It includes the activities of employers' organizations and trade unions at sectoral and sometimes regional levels, both separately and jointly; the role of these organizations in combination with the state and with other bodies such as health and safety practitioner organizations; the activities of education and training institutions; as well as activities of industry associations in which chemicals are produced and used extensively. Some selected examples of particularly significant forms of infrastructural support in different countries are outlined in the following pages.

Legally Mandated Associations

In Austria there is an infrastructure of organizations to which employers and employees are legally required to belong, which is separate from trade unions and voluntary employers organizations. The Austrian Federal Economic Chamber (*Wirtschaftskammer Österreich—WKO*) is the legal representative of Austrian business. Membership includes some 300,000 enterprises. Regarding OSH matters, the Economic Chamber and its regional bodies are mainly concerned with statutory provisions. As well as articulating their political position on topics, they see their task as giving information and support to their members in the implementation of regulations. Apart from providing advisory services, they offer OSH training courses for safety engineers and experts. They compile many OSH-related information materials, develop simplified forms for risk assessment in different sectors for SMEs, as well as support and promote workplace health promotion.

For employees, institutions equivalent to the WKO are the Chambers of Labour (*Arbeiterkammer—AK*), of which membership is compulsory for all employees, and the unemployed, although civil servants and agricultural workers are exempted. The total membership is 2.6 million. The chambers are obliged by law to represent the social, economic, occupational and cultural interests of employees. There is a separate AK in each of the nine federal states, with the Federal Chamber of Labour in Vienna as the umbrella organization. In total they employ a staff of about 2,500 persons and are financed by the AK levy on salaries.

Their role on health and safety includes ensuring observation of legal regulations. They are represented in the Industrial Safety Advisory Board of the BMWA, which serves as an advisory body on occupational health and safety for the ministry, and they have their own departments dealing with OSH matters. Training for workers and their representatives on health and safety, including courses on issues related to the safe use of chemicals, is provided through the educational institution for workers (the bfi), which is owned jointly by the AK and the Austrian Federation of Trade Unions (ÖGB). The AK also provide brochures and leaflets on, for example, risk assessment (including chemical risks), and OSH management systems, as well as developing OHS tools jointly with other main actors such as the Labour Inspectorate, AUVA, WKO, and ÖGB.

In Germany there is an analogous infrastructure of bodies to which employers are obliged to belong. These are the chambers (*Kammern*), which represent the interests of their members in relation to political institutions and public administration at various levels (state, regional, local) and provide advice and services to their members. In the context of this study, the most relevant ones are the chambers of industry and commerce (*Industrie und Handelskammern*) and the chambers of skilled crafts (*Handwerkskammern*). These are regional institutions with their own federal structure, and they help to facilitate structural cooperation between employers' interests on health and safety and those of the insurance associations that have resulted in the development of a range of preventive activities.

An important task of both the chambers of industry and commerce and the chambers of skilled crafts is their responsibility for the training of master craftsmen (*Meister*) and, jointly with state authorities, for the vocational training of apprentices. Thus, the chambers can influence the extent to which the subject of occupational health is included in the training and the teaching methods used. An example of this is the use of guidance documents developed as part of the SGU project in Rhineland-Palatine in the occupational health section of the training courses for master craftsmen (Schulte-Hubbert, 2005a).

In general, the support activities of chambers of skilled crafts and guilds are focused on making products of other institutions available to their members. One approach to achieve this is through cooperation at the regional level with labor inspectorates, occupational health administrations of the federal states, or with mandatory employers' liability insurance associations. An approach of some chambers is the provision of dedicated advisors on technical, environmental, or occupational health matters, that include the issue of hazardous substances in the range of subjects on which they advise.

Institutions in the skilled-craft trades provide advice for newly founded businesses. Specific advice on occupational health issues has been offered; for example, the Düsseldorf Chamber of Skilled Crafts offers information on occupational health on its Web site through a dedicated portal (*InfoManager Sicherheit und Gesundheit im Handwerk*), developed by the Chamber's Centre of Environment and Energy. Support is focused on risk assessment, including risk assessment for tasks with hazardous substances. Similar provisions are also made by some other Chambers of Industry and Commerce, often in collaboration with labor inspectorates (IHK KREFELD, 2000, 2004).

Parallel organizations for employees are not legally mandated in Germany except in two federal states, Bremen and in the Sarre, where a chamber of employees (*Arbeitnehmerkammer*) or a chamber of work (*Arbeiterkammer*) exist. They do not offer any specific help in relation to employees' interests in chemical risk management in small firms.

Voluntary Trade and Employers' Associations

In Germany, in addition to the legally mandated structures previously outlined, there is a plethora of voluntary associations covering business, trade, and employers' interests that provide support for various aspects of the commercial activities of businesses. Some provide health and safety support; for example, in the industry and commerce sector, the Central Association of the German Car Trade (*Zentralverband Deutsches Kraftfahrzeuggewerbe—ZDK*) developed two tools for the management of hazardous substances in 1989 and 1996, a general work instruction for the safe handling of hazardous substances, and as a complement, a brochure: "Hazardous Substances in the Car Trade." They were to be used to support the development of specific work instructions in individual businesses, to compile an inventory of hazardous substances, and to document the employees' participation in the annual verbal instructions on chemicals-related hazards (Steber, 1999). Both tools are still available and have been adapted to changes of the Hazardous Substances Ordinance (Steber, 2005).

In the construction sector, the two employers' associations—the General Association of the German Construction Industry (*Hauptverband der Deutschen Bauindustrie*) and the Central Association of the German Construction Trade (*Zentralverband des Deutschen Baugewerbes*)—have been partners in initiatives by the construction insurance associations, addressing chemicals-related subjects such as the promotion of the use of both chromium-reduced cement and new types of man-made mineral fibers that are not suspected carcinogens. In the printing industry, the Federal Printing Association (*Bundesverband Druck*) has supported an initiative on the reduction of solvent emissions in offset printing that was started by the insurance association for the industry.

In Sweden employers' organizations provide information to member companies through circular letters, e-mail newsletters, and their home pages, in which general questions relating to chemicals are dealt with. Chemical risk management may also be the subject of training courses arranged by the employers' organizations and as part of information campaigns. Small companies sometimes contact employers' organizations to discuss the interpretation of regulatory requirements on chemical risk management and how they should be met. The most frequently occurring topics are how risk evaluation can be conducted simply; how information in SDSs should be interpreted and used; and how specific chemicals such as asbestos, glue, isocyanates, organic solvents, thermosetting plastics and products treated with pesticides should be handled. In general, employers' organizations have relatively few contacts with small companies (Alvarez de Davila et al., 2002).

In the UK, despite its advocacy of the development of working with intermediaries, the HSE has cautioned that the representation of intermediaries varies according to sector; noting for example, that Chambers of Commerce, which are the most common business associations, have limited activity on health and safety; and banks and accountants, which are often the only intermediary encountered by SMEs, do not regard health and safety as a priority (Walters, 2001).

Employee Organizations

There are of course many examples of trade union activities supporting workers' protection from chemical hazards and trade union organizations in most countries regard this as one of their major activities on OHS. In Germany all of the eight sector federations that form the German Trade Union Congress (*Deutscher Gewerkschaftsbund*—DGB) offer advice on occupational health issues but at the federal level. Only the metal workers' union (*Industriegewerkschaft Metall*—IG *Metall*) provides an extended range of brochures and leaflets on the subject. Two brochures address hazardous substances in SMEs: wood dust in the wood sector and hazardous substances in general in car repair shops (IGM, 2002, 2004). In addition, in some districts of this union, campaigns have been pursued since the early 1990s on occupational health issues, in which attention has been directed at hazardous substances, such as coolants, solvents, and cutting oils applied in metal treatment. In the construction industry, the trade union has addressed issues related to hazardous substances, such as using chromium-reduced cement to fight skin diseases among bricklayers and making recommendations for the selection and use of man-made mineral fibers when dust from certain types of these fibers became a suspected carcinogen. Usually these issues were tackled together with the insurance associations in this industry. Similarly, the former union of media workers campaigned in the early 1990s on the issue of substituting volatile solvents in offset printing. The campaign resulted in a sector-based solution on this issue coordinated by the insurance association in the printing industry. Similar actions and campaigns can be found in all of the other countries in the study.

Perhaps the most widespread trade union activity in modern health and safety systems is the support they provide for the employee representation and consultation, arguably one of the cornerstones of the self-regulatory approaches to health and safety management embraced by Framework Directive 89/391. There is substantial international evidence demonstrating the effectiveness of this engagement of employees and the role of trade unions in supporting it (Walters, 2006b). Other studies suggest that this will be no less true in relation to chemicals than for other aspects of OHS, showing that in relation to chemical hazards, trade union representatives are often far better informed than their counterparts in management (Research International, 1997). Part of the reason for this can be found in the major role that trade union organizations play in training worker representatives, which in terms of both its quality and quantity far exceeds that taken up by managers in many countries (Walters & Kirby, 2002). Other prerequisites for effective employee representation are related to workplace size; there is no doubt that larger workplaces are better served in this respect than their smaller counterparts.

Trade union organization is less well developed in smaller enterprises, and in some countries there are size limits placed on employers' duties to facilitate employee representation in their enterprises. As a counter to these challenges in recent years, trade unions and others have become increasingly interested in the role that access to peripatetic forms of trade union representation can play in improving health and safety in small enterprises. Probably the most significant stimulus for this interest has come from the success of the regulatory framework for regional safety representatives appointed by trade unions in Sweden (Lamm & Walters, 2004). This provision and the resulting network of health and safety representation for workers in small enterprises that it has created, is widely recognized as making a major contribution to support for health and safety in small firms (Frick & Walters, 1998). It has served as a model for the introduction of similar approaches in regulatory measures in other countries such as Italy and Norway and is the inspiration for a substantial number of voluntary approaches across a range of countries and sectors (see Walters, 2002, 2004).

In Sweden regional representatives are known to deal with many different kinds of working-environment problems including chemical risks. They provide an important stimulus for employers' efforts to manage chemical risks as well as a powerful socioeconomic determinant of sustainability of such actions. In other countries the specific support from such representatives and their trade unions for chemical risk management is less documented, although it is known to be a prominent part of their activities under statutory schemes in industries in which chemicals are used extensively, such as in construction in Norway and in crafts and construction in Italy (Walters, 2002). It is also an important element in voluntary schemes such as in the construction industry in the UK (Shaw & Turner, 2003).

Joint Employer/Trade Union Initiatives

Most countries have joint or tripartite advisory structures on health and safety that have been established between employer and employee organizations and sometimes with input from the state. Examples of their engagement in activities on chemical risk management can be found at both national and sectoral levels. However, activities focused specifically on addressing the needs of small enterprises are less frequent. Nevertheless, potentially at least, such joint arrangements form an important part of the established supportive infrastructure for health and safety in small firms. This is especially so in countries with a well-established history of corporatism in approaches to employment relations.

In Sweden there is a longstanding practice of joint activities of employers and employee organizations on health and safety, including support for chemical risk management in small firms. The joint employer/trade union body for health and safety information, advice, and training, known as Prevent, handles many activities aimed at supporting health and safety in small firms. The Chemical Guide, produced by the Swedish Environmental Research Institute, was developed by and is marketed with support from Prevent. Examples of other initiatives include:

- a range of courses and study materials on chemical hazards;
- an interactive register of chemical substances with physical data, risk and safety phrases, hazard symbols, instructions for handling and storage,

transport instructions for the sender and the transport organizer, available on CD-ROM and on the Web;
- Web sites developed to spread information about allergies and those at high risk; and
- leaflets about new risks with isocyanates developed by initiatives from the social partners to draw attention to risks with thermal degradation products formed from materials containing polyurethane.

In the Netherlands, with the introduction of *Arboconvenantnen,* the role of employer/trade union joint bodies has been reinforced in current approaches to health and safety at sectoral levels. Although initiated by the Ministry of Social Affairs and Employment, the involvement of employers and trade union representation at sectoral level is fundamental to the operation of these *Arboconvenantnen,* it is significant that 14 of them identify handling hazardous chemicals as one of the issues in their action plans (Jongen et al., 2003).

THE INFRASTRUCTURES OF
CHEMICAL SUPPLY

Before leaving the topic of infrastructural support for chemical risk management, it is important to say a word about supply chains. Modern health and safety policymakers view them as critical to infrastructural support for chemical risk management in small enterprises, and REACH will place new responsibilities on suppliers and users of chemical products that are intended to promote the role of the supply chain in supporting more effective risk communication. Here, concern is with structural aspects of this support, while in Chapters 6 and 7 further issues of current and future operation of supply chains are discussed.

Chemical supply chains are not uniform entities. They vary in breadth, length and in the number of actors they engage. They may be anything from local to global in reach. They are mostly branch specific, and many of their features will be defined by the nature of the use of chemical products, their market dependence and by the kind and extent of technologies involved. Supply chains originate with manufacturers or importers of base chemicals, as well as final or intermediate preparations. These may be purchased directly by users in some cases but in others they will be transformed into different products by formulators that create new preparations from mixtures of substances they have received, before selling these formulations on to end users either directly or through further intermediary traders or distributors. Generally, the SMEs that form the vast majority of end users of chemical products purchase them from distributors. There are estimated to be 1,200 chemical product distributors in the EU. They might purchase substances and preparations from manufacturers inside or outside the EU, and they might store, repackage, or relabel products before selling them to the next link in the supply chain. It is recognized that distributors may represent a significant barrier to risk communication in the chemical-product supply chains since they might have little knowledge of the use to which the substances will be put, and because their role in supply may be limited to identifying a source of a particular product for a customer, obtaining it and passing it on to the customer at a competitive price. At the same time, this is not always the case, and some distributors have a very good market overview and technical knowledge and may even provide consulting and technical support for clients.

There has been some interest in describing the variation in supply chains in research projects undertaken to inform policy in the run-up to the implementation of REACH. For example, in a project concerning the production of technical guidance for downstream users (RIP 3.5.1, 2006), researchers describe supply chains in several different branches of economic activity, including textiles, printing, adhesives and paints, microchip production, detergents and construction.

In each case it is evident that the special characteristics of the economic activity described help to determine the nature of the supply chain. For example, in textile finishing, businesses are critically dependent on the supply of appropriate chemicals. Companies formulating chemicals from products produced elsewhere are an important link in the chain as they prepare and supply many of the products used by the finishing companies. The same formulators may also be the manufacturers of some of the substances they supply. At least half the formulators supplying the European textiles finishing companies are themselves SMEs that purchase most of their chemicals directly from their manufacturers; but they may buy base chemicals from distributors. The textile-finishing companies they supply are also mostly SMEs. Companies in the chain have close ties with research and development in the chemical industry, so development cycles are short and market pressure (consumer demand) is a critical driver of innovation. Therefore communication in the supply chain is quite strong, and although companies are small, there is usually a good technical understanding of the chemistry involved, both because of its critical role in business success and also because of fairly stringent demands of environmental and consumer protection requirements.

At the other extreme, in construction, supply chains are more appropriately described as "supply nets." They are broad and diverse and may include the supply of single substances such as solvents, preparations, raw materials, as well as semi-finished and finished articles. There are bulk chemical products such as cement, concrete and bitumen used in very large quantities and speciality chemicals such as paints and adhesives that are used in smaller amounts. The technical understanding by the users of these products is generally poor and further complications are introduced by the practices of contracting, subcontracting and self-employment on construction sites as well as by the use of migrant and casual workers.

In graphic printing, supply chains are often quite long, involving large international suppliers as the majority of companies supplying chemicals. Formulators play an important role and usually buy directly from the manufacturers of their constituents, although intermediate traders may also be important. They may in turn use distributors of their products to reach the SMEs that make up the vast proportion of users. Here, as with the supply and use of paints, sealants, adhesives and many other chemical products, there may be concern about revealing business-sensitive information on composition and use of products that may affect communication in the supply chain.

Wright et al. (2005) note that clients who make health and safety a pre-condition for supply can have a significant impact on the suppliers, but they further point out that this is more likely to occur within heavily regulated sectors such as the chemicals industry or as a result of actions from larger clients that wield some economic power in the supply/user relationship. Such cases are found among large multinational car producers, as well as some furniture and textile producers, where these users have developed traditions of setting limits on certain dangerous substances for their suppliers. (RIP 3.5.1, 2006, p. 13) The same approach sometimes operates between suppliers and users, such as in Germany, where services provided by major car producers—VW-Audi and DaimlerChrysler—offer their contracted car dealers and garages specific support for the management of hazardous substances.

Generally, there is unlikely to be such support for small firms using chemicals and especially not for those that operate outside tightly controlled chains such as these examples. Nevertheless, in their study of these firms, Briggs and Crumbie (2000) found that the supply end was the most common source for information on the chemical products. Two in three users cited container labels, closely followed by suppliers and sales representatives, while 40% cited safety data sheets as sources of information. They found that the most influential source was the supplier sales representative, (38% of respondents). In a similar vein, the RIP study states (RIP 3.5.1, 2006, p. 14):

> . . . it is interesting to note that none of the chains studied report that SDS is the most important source for information on chemicals. All the chains have supporting information sources from their suppliers, from their customers and/or from their associations.

In anticipation of REACH, new legislation in countries such as Germany (with the most recent revision of Hazardous Substance Ordinance) already makes provision allowing enterprises to use a risk assessment provided by the supplier of a chemical product if the product is used according to the supplier's description and, particularly, by applying the risk management measures recommended. As outlined in Chapter 3, this approach was introduced to complement the obligation of providing exposure scenarios for identified uses of chemicals, foreseen in the draft version of the REACH regulation. In their initial public reactions, representatives of the German chemical industry have expressed scepticism about this approach and stressed that responsibility for risk assessment must remain with the user of chemicals (Bender, 2005). Equally, in the RIP study (RIP 3.5.1, 2006), it is noted that under existing workplace requirements, chemicals information focuses on classification and labeling and on providing substance-specific information if required. Formulators are required to merge information on the substances and preparations they have used in creating a new preparation into a safety data sheet for this preparation. Recommendations on risk management measures are based on the hazards of these products rather than on a risk assessment under REACH.

CONCLUSIONS: THE ROLE OF THE HEALTH AND SAFETY SYSTEM IN IMPROVING CHEMICAL RISK MANAGEMENT

It is widely accepted that small firms need direction and support in order to manage chemical hazards effectively. Traditionally this has been found in the health and safety systems of each country, comprising the national institutions for regulation and control, the providers of information, guidance and training at this level and at sectoral and local levels, the preventive services and the inspection authorities. Supplementing this institutional support in some countries is the parallel provision for prevention that is provided by insurance associations for their members. In addition, trade associations, employers' organizations, and other associations of businesses interests provide a further range of services that in some cases are relevant to chemical risk management. Included or associated with such initiatives are those based around the economic relations between suppliers and users of chemical products, which have been utilized to promote and support best practice on chemical risk management among users. Trades unions are also active in representing the interests of workers in small enterprises in relation to chemical hazards; especially significant among their initiatives is the specific legislative support that they have secured for representing workers in small enterprises in some countries.

However, the common theme that runs through the experiences reported here is that the number, variety and economic situation of small firms and related work scenarios present a significant challenge to the availability of support for chemical risk management from all these sources. At the same time there is substantial evidence that the availability of some elements of this support may be diminishing. This is especially so in relation to the traditional state provision for inspection and control as well as for specialist support from prevention services.

This reduction is an important concern for two reasons. First, research evidence on what are the most effective strategies to influence health and safety in small firms is clear that what works best is face-to-face contact between owner/managers and change agents of the health and safety system, whether they are inspectors, health and safety practitioners, regional health and safety representatives, or others with some degree of health and safety expertise (Walters, 2001). Although it is clear that face-to-face contact will never be completely achieved, the uptake and spread of strategies to promote and develop improved risk management in small firms using chemical products are nevertheless crucially dependent on the presence of elements of traditional infrastructural support. Such initiatives may appear quite successful in the contexts in which they are developed and tested, but rolling them out to wider uptake cannot be taken for granted in situations in which this traditional infrastructure is known to be weak, and may be getting even weaker.

Second, in the UK at least, there is strong evidence that for small firm owner/managers, the threat of a visit from an inspector, no matter how remote the reality of such a visit may be, continues to be a powerful incentive for them to address their health and safety management responsibilities, including those relating to chemical risks (Vickers et al., 2003). This important evidence sits uneasily with the observation, made in many countries in the study, that resources for inspection, already perceived to be insufficient, are subject to further reduction as governments attempt to curb public expenditure. Such reduction helps to place present regulatory strategies in perspective. The moves toward better and more accessible advice and education in relation to chemical risk management, for example, toward generic solutions for the control of exposure and an increased role for the supply chain in securing improved chemical risk management in small firms, are all approaches that take some account of the limitations of regulatory inspection. It needs to be borne in mind that there is no evidence to suggest that any of these approaches will work as alternatives to such inspection or face-to-face contact. Further reduction of inspection and its replacement with more arms-length advisory and persuasive approaches to compliance therefore would seem to fly in the face of the hard evidence of what works in achieving improvement in risk management in small enterprises.

A distinction is required here. The desirability of efficient methods to improve chemical risk management in small enterprises is not in question. Equally, the notion that all workplaces must receive regular inspection visits is untenable. Clearly, appropriate and effective combinations of guidance and deterrence are required to maximize efficient use of inspectorate resources. However, this should not be confused with the neo-liberal agenda pursued by many national governments as well as at the EU level in which regulation and regulatory inspection have a much-reduced role in this essentially business-friendly approach.

Caution is warranted when policymakers at the national and EU levels invoke the supply chain and the business networks of small enterprises as the new locus of control for chemical risk management. The evidence to date is that suppliers of chemical products still have some way to go before the information they supply on the hazards of their products and how to use them safely is adequate for the needs of chemical risk management in small firms. There are economic reasons why the supply of high quality information may not be a priority for suppliers, in the absence of firm regulatory guidance on its provision and accountability for failing to do so. While current approaches toward the manipulation of business relationships to promote chemical risk management, such as envisaged in the REACH regulation, are useful additions to the checks and balances in place to achieve improved chemical risk management, they are not substitutes for either inspection or the engagement of competent advice. Nor are they likely to be effective without the continued and developing presence of a strong infrastructure that is supportive of improved chemical risk management in small firms.

A further important point about the role of the supply chain observed in this study is that where it appears to work most favorably is in situations in which the economic relationships involved are most tightly controlled. For example, within the chemical industry itself, supply-chain initiatives such as "Responsible Care" appear to be operating quite successfully. However, the challenge for managing chemical risks in many small enterprises is found in their remoteness from such situations. Means of addressing this limitation need to be found if manipulating supply-chain relationships is to have a widespread effect on improving chemical risk management.

This study finds empirical evidence for these observations. It seems clear that in countries in which sectoral infrastructures are best developed, such as in Germany and Austria, there are good examples of support for chemical risk management in small firms. This contrasts with countries like the UK in which sectoral infrastructures are considerably less developed and where, in the absence of a preventive role for insurance and a legal requirement for prevention services, specialist support for small enterprises is more limited and the extent of development of sectoral initiatives and cooperation is con-siderably less.

The role of corporatist structures and processes at sectoral levels are also important, as is shown by the example of the Netherlands, where *Arboconvetanen,* providing a structured and targeted approach to improved health and safety including chemical risk management, have been agreed upon and implemented in many sectors. The well-established traditions of social dialogue and joint initiatives in Sweden add another dimension to practical support for cooperative efforts to engage with small firms and improve their approaches to chemical risk management.

Relatedly, the role of trade unions in representing the interests of employees in small firms may be a powerful aid to the uptake of chemical risk management strategies in these firms. There is evidence of this in Sweden. Although trade union organization is undoubtedly weaker in small firms than in larger ones, this does not mean that the trade unions should be dismissed as sources of support for chemical risk management strategies in these firms. The evidence suggests that such support can operate on a number of levels and that it can be enhanced by regulatory provision. Research evidence encourages the idea that employee involvement provides an important dimension to the improvement of the quality of health and safety performance and that trade unions provide the only form of autonomous institutional support for such involvement. There is considerable potential for the further development of their role in most countries.

The ideal model of infrastructural support that emerges from this analysis is a multidimensional one in which mechanisms for both knowledge transfer and the incentives for action are present. It is unlikely that regulatory strategies or tools to improve chemical risk management will be entirely effective in the absence of multi-dimensional support, regardless of how generic or simplified they may be. This is because they address only part of the problem. Generic risk assessment and control solutions, simplified tools and improved dissemination may be important and improved means of *doing* chemical risk management in small firms, but factors affecting their uptake are clearly linked to the broader structures of vulnerability with which small firms are surrounded. Strategies to improve health and safety management (whether in relation to chemical substances or more generally) need to address these issues as well as provide specific tools to support improved practice.

The supply-chain focus of current regulatory approaches is one example of an attempt to do this by exploiting economic dependencies to provide the necessary pressure to ensure cooperative action on chemical risk management between suppliers and users. But such strategies are based around assumptions about interests between actors in business relationships that are at best only partially tested in practice and, at worst, misinterpret the reasons for the spread of networked business relations (James et al., 2007). A better and more in-depth understanding of these issues is required before confidence can be placed in the likely success of these strategies.

In the meantime there are other elements of the support infrastructure already in place that could be further utilized to bring about improved performance. Again, evidence is far from complete, but what seems to represent the most optimistic scenarios are the combinations of mutually supportive actors and actions that engage with small firms to implement approaches to chemical risk management. The success of such approaches is to a large extent determined by the development of the support infrastructure itself, which is the reason why moves to reduce any of its elements should be of concern.

CHAPTER 5

Tools to Improve Chemical
Risk Management in
Small Enterprises

The aim of this chapter is to illustrate something of the richness and diversity of the tools to support chemical risk management that are currently found in different countries and sectors, as well as to provide some concrete examples of their operation. The basis of selection is the extent to which these tools take some account of the nature of the problem of managing chemical risks in small enterprises and are related to current regulatory strategies and the actors and infrastructures that support them. Additionally, attention is paid to tools that seem likely to lend themselves most successfully to operationalizing EU influences such as those promulgated by REACH.

Ideally it would be useful to be able to identify the tools that are most effective in terms of their operation and their effect on health outcomes as well as those that are most transferable. However, limited evaluation of the effectiveness of chemical risk management instruments as well as considerable uncertainty about what features support and promote their transferability mean that this is not possible. Instead, a typology is presented of the more prominent examples of instruments to support small firms in chemical risk management, identifying features they have in common and ones that seem to make certain tools especially useful.

An important finding is that there is a range of instruments to support chemical risk management in small firms, developed and applied at various levels in all the six countries studied. The number of such tools runs into hundreds. In Germany especially, the involvement of sector-based insurance associations, trade organizations, the labor inspectorate and others in different states has resulted in a rich multiplicity of tools, many of which can be applied in small enterprises. Indeed, this development is so much more extensive in

Germany than in other countries in the study that it merits a separate section in the pages that follow.

Many of these tools are in fact similarly constructed and serve the same functions in different countries or sectors. Rather than attempt to catalog them all, their significant characteristics and some prominent examples are outlined by way of illustration. Features that are of particular interest include:

- their relationship to wider regulatory strategies;
- their process orientation—i.e., some tools address only one aspect of chemical risk management, others provide for more comprehensive support;
- intended users—i.e., some tools are designed to assist owner/managers and workers in small enterprise to manage chemical risks, others are focused more on the actors that are involved in supporting small enterprises in this respect, such as OHS practitioners, labor inspectors, trade union representatives and supply-chain actors;
- role—i.e., some tools are designed to support hands-on approaches to chemical risk management while others may have more remote support functions; and
- medium—i.e., traditionally most tools were paper based, or sometimes using video/CD-ROM technology—one-way communication was most frequent—currently, Internet-based tools are increasingly common, and interactive functions are more frequent.

A further consideration is the relationship of tools to other supports and incentives, such as insurance incentives, supply-chain leverage, or the engagement of particular actors and organizations for improving chemical risk management in small firms.

While this approach allows a degree of systematicity, there is some variation in the information available on the operation of many of these support instruments; this is especially true with regard to objective evaluation of their effectiveness, transferability and sustainability. This account is therefore no more than a snapshot of current practices. At the same time it is a useful gauge of the limits of current knowledge and helps to frame important questions for evaluation of support strategies. It begins with a categorization of tools according to the principles evident in regulatory approaches. Thus, examples of tools to support substitution; to aid understanding and use of suppliers' information in risk assessment and control; to inform or train owners, managers and workers about risks to health and safety as well as risk prevention and control measures; and to implement control measures according to an established hierarchy of good practice are outlined. Given the supply-chain focus of future provisions framed by REACH, examples of tools that engage with supply chains are also examined, before turning to consider some of the more prominent examples of German instruments to support chemical risk management.

Following this typology, the chapter concludes with a brief discussion of key features required to integrate instruments to support chemical risk management with national and international strategies to achieve this effect in small firms.

A TYPOLOGY OF TOOLS TO SUPPORT CHEMICAL RISK MANAGEMENT STRATEGIES

There is a plethora of instruments available to support employers in meeting the regulatory requirements of chemical risk management. Although they originate separately in different sectors and different countries, many are very similar to one another. Some deal with support for substitution, but the majority provide support for aspects of risk assessment, management and control of chemical substances in the workplace. Of these, a number are based around providing support with understanding suppliers' information, while others address appropriate means of using this information in assessing and managing risks. Of the latter, some can be regarded as complete tools, inasmuch as they are intended to take the user through several stages in the process of identifying and assessing the risks of chemical substances through to providing appropriate control solutions in use and disposal. There has been a trend toward the increasing development and use of such complete tools in the last decade as well as a move toward more Internet-based instruments. Tools are almost entirely aimed at employers and owner/managers, but some tools may include guidance on the design of written working instructions for employees.

Substitution

There are several instruments to support employers in reviewing their purchasing policies, helping them to consider both whether their use of hazardous chemicals is always necessary and whether substitution with safer alternatives may be possible. In the Netherlands there are well-developed instruments to aid in the calculation of likely exposure scenarios in the use of paints that help to inform the choice of products. In Germany the *Kooperationsstelle Hamburg* has for several years engaged in projects supporting the development of tools for substitution. Its most recent project, *CLEANTOOL*, is outlined in Box 5.1.

Another German example, the *BGIA-Spaltenmodell,* is a well-known scheme for the assessment of substitution, also known as the "column model." The tool allows a comparison of risks posed by different substances or preparations that could be used for the same task (BGIA, 2006). In its latest version, the scheme is based on six parameters, compared separately for the chemicals in question. If a chemical scores better in all six categories, it should be chosen for the task assessed. If a chemical rates better in some categories but worse in others, it is necessary to assess which hazards lead to a lower risk in the particular situation and choose the chemical accordingly. A more user-friendly online version of this

Box 5.1—*CLEANTOOL*

Kooperationsstelle Hamburg (http://www.kooperationsstelle-hh.de/), part of the Department of Science and Health of the State of Hamburg, has supported cooperation between universities and trade unions since the early 1990s. A central theme is occupational health and safety in general and the substitution of hazardous substances in the workplace in particular. It has been especially active on the implementation of solutions for the substitution of volatile solvents in a range of applications. Its projects, several of which were performed as European cooperation initiatives, have been focused on vegetable oils as substitutes for cleaning agents based on volatile solvents in offset printing, in the metal industry; in industrial processes in general and as substitutes for mineral oil-based concrete mold-release agents in the construction sector.

CLEANTOOL is its most recent project and is focused on solutions for the degreasing of metal surfaces. It is intended as an aid to SMEs. Within the EU, about 550,000 SMEs operate in three sectors covering the manufacture of metal products, machinery, and transport equipment. It is estimated that for about a third of them, cleaning tasks constitute an important issue. It is claimed that optimized solutions provided by the project should help to save costs while at the same time improving the quality of cleaning results and taking both environmental and health and safety aspects into account (*CLEANTOOL*, 2004a).

As a result of the project, information on about 260 different cleaning processes has been compiled, including new cleaning processes and new cleaning agents; measurement tools for the assessment of the efficacy of the process; information on the costs of the technology and on the operating time of the cleaning agent; environmental aspects such as energy consumption, waste disposal, and avoidance of emissions; and the assessment of the risk to workers (*KOOPERATIONSSTELLE*, 2003; *CLEANTOOL*, 2004a).

Since 2004 the results, together with pictures and video sequences of the processes have been publicly accessible in an Internet-based database at http://www.cleantool.org/. They address 15 categories of cleaning processes, 23 types of cleaning agents, 33 types of dirt, and 29 types of surface materials with 260 examples (*CLEANTOOL*, 2004b). Guided support is offered to search the database for material, mass, dimensions, geometry and numbers of parts to be cleaned, as well as type of dirt to be removed and treatment after cleaning. The database can also be searched for cleaning processes according to industry (*CLEANTOOL*, 2004c). Links to other databases, electronic expert systems for cleaning processes, and substitution for solvents are also provided on the *CLEANTOOL* Web site (*CLEANTOOL*, 2004d).

In September 2004, at the end of the project jointly pursued in five European countries, an average of 600 visits were registered for the Web site per working day in a five-week period and about 300 visits per working day for the database (*CLEANTOOL*, 2004d). Between one-quarter and one-half of the visits originated from Germany. However, feedback on the application of the tool for the development of alternative solutions for existing metal degreasing processes has been received from only a small number of enterprises. A similar tool for cleaning processes in maintenance operations is under development (Dobernowsky, 2005).

tool is provided by the Institute for Occupational Medicine, Safety Technology, and Ergonomy (*Institut für Arbeitsmedizin, Sicherheitstechnik und Ergonomie e.V.—ASER*) on its Web site.

Similarly, in the Netherlands the research institute TNO has developed a model supporting the substitution of carcinogenic and other dangerous substances (Van Niftrik et al., 2005).

Suppliers' Information, Risk Assessment and Control

Tools to assist small companies in dealing with suppliers' information exist in all the countries studied, since the inadequacies of such information are widely recognized. The various instruments available often provide alternative and fuller sources of information about hazards and risk as well as more accessible instruction and advice on safe use. They also support employers in risk assessment. It follows therefore that many such instruments have been developed by sectorally-based interests with detailed knowledge of conditions at this level.

For example, in Austria a Web-based support tool designed for smaller companies—(www.eval.at)—is available for general risk assessment. This database is derived from a model project about sector-related basic risk assessments (supported by the AUVA and the social partners). The Web site is intended to be useful for SMEs in all sectors. It targets a wide range of risks and includes many chemical-related situations. The database can be searched by workplace or sector and contains around 400 assessment documents for a broad spectrum of working environments, including the description of workplaces, tasks and OSH measures, documents for risk evaluation and the identification of necessary measures. There are complementary materials such as CD-ROMs on risk assessment and videos for specific sectors (e.g., hairdressing, metal sectors, and skin protection). There is a close connection with the AUVAsafe system, in which the (www.eval.at) Web site is used as a support instrument suitable for smaller companies.

In the Netherlands the *Stoffenmanager* (chemicals manager) and the older *Chemiekaartenboek*, an initiative of the former *Veiligheidsinstituut* (Safety Institute) and the Dutch chemicals industry, provide information on the hazards, risk assessment, safe use and storage of a range of substances.

Tools to deal with specific issues such as the choice of personal protective equipment are also numerous. For example, a German tool developed specifically for the printing industry and designed to help small enterprises in the selection of appropriate personal protective equipment for use with chemical substances, was developed with support of the insurance association of the printing industry and aids the selection of protective gloves and skin-care products. Introduced in 2004, the *BASIS-Modul Hand- & Hautschutz* (BASIS module on hand and skin protection) is the first module of BASIS, a sectoral occupational health information system for print shops and paper-processing enterprises (BASIS, 2004).

Of somewhat greater relevance to current regulatory strategies are the "complete tools" that exist in most countries, supporting small enterprises through the whole process of chemical risk management. Perhaps the most well-known is the UK *COSHH Essentials,* which was developed in tandem with the critical review of regulatory strategy on chemical risk management undertaken by the UK authorities in the late 1990s. *COSHH Essentials* represents a comprehensive Web-based approach to chemical risk management in small firms. In response to studies indicating that the single most important source of information used by management in small enterprises is that provided by suppliers, the approach of COSHH Essentials utilizes information used on suppliers' safety data sheets and on labels required by law. Using the steps outlined in Box 5.2, this information helps to establish accessible assessment and control criteria through a simple system of generic assessment based on the suppliers' hazard information (R-phrases, etc.) combined with likely use scenarios. Generic approaches to health hazards and potential exposure are matched by equally generic approaches to control, utilizing three basic control methods: general ventilation, engineering control, and containment; and a fourth approach signaling that special controls needing expert advice are required. Its objective is to provide clear advice on good practice in relation to appropriate controls and their selection. The HSE research on which the guidance was based argued that it was possible to determine a range of adequate control strategies and advice based on analogies with substances with similar hazardous properties (Russell et al., 1998). In essence therefore, the approach represents a process in which hazards and exposure potential (based on the extent of their likely use) are grouped in various combinations that generate appropriate control measures—R-phrases defined under regulations are grouped into bands covering the range of seriousness of health effects resulting from inhalation and skin and eye contact. Each band signifies a different level of control measure required.

The basic scheme, outlined in Box 5.2 is presented as simple step-by-step guidance, with checklists to guide the reader through the process of assessment and a means of identifying the appropriate control guidance sheet for whatever operation the user requires. Although not comprehensive, it is wide-ranging in its coverage. It is intended that access to this guidance be supported by exploiting existing information routes that are used by owner/managers of SMEs, such as suppliers, trade associations, trade union representatives, and OHS professionals.

One criticism, made especially by occupational hygienists, is that the ease of use of the control checklists may result in its users overlooking the more desirable methods of avoiding exposure at the first three levels. Nor does COSHH cover all the legal requirements, such as health surveillance, or all health risks; for example, process-generated hazards, such as solder fumes, are omitted.

Box 5.2—COSHH Essentials

The COSHH Essentials approach is based on a series of tick-boxes that lead the user through each of five steps:

1. Find the material safety data sheet for each chemical used and determine the task to be assessed; for example mixing, weighing, drying, storage.

2. Look at the three factors that identify the control approach;

   – the possible health effects from exposure—a chemical is assigned to a hazard group on the basis of risk phrases. Thus R20—harmful by inhalation would put a chemical into hazard group B. There are six groups—A–E and S for substances causing harm through skin contact based on the risk phrases for chemicals that should be identified by section 15 on the suppliers' data sheet.

   – the amount in use (small, medium, or large). Guidance is given on choosing the appropriate category; and

   – how dusty or volatile the chemical is (low, medium, or high). Guidance is given on choosing the appropriate category.

3. Find the control approach using the information from steps 1 and 2. Risk matrices for each of the hazard groups identify the appropriate control approach:

   – general ventilation;

   – engineering control;

   – containment; or

   – special.

   For each approach there is a general control guidance sheet.

4. Find the task-specific control guidance sheets. In addition to the general advice provided by step 3, further guidance is given in 60 single-page sheets detailing practical control measures depending on: the task, whether the chemical is solid or liquid, and how much is being used.

   The task-specific control guidance sheets have a common format giving advice on access to the work area; design of the process and equipment; maintenance; examination and testing; cleaning and housekeeping; personal protective equipment; training supervision; and sources of further information. The sheets also contain an employee checklist for making the best use of controls.

5. Implement the action and review:

   – assess other chemicals used and tasks;

   – plan the implementation;

   – consider safety and environmental hazards;

   – consider other aspects of COSHH, such as health surveillance and exposure monitoring;

   – implement the control measures; and

   – review the assessment.

An interactive electronic version of COSHH Essentials followed the original paper-based tool in 2002,[1] with the HSE claiming that the electronic version could be used by "anyone." By October 2003 the HSE had completed phase 2 of COSHH Essentials, with the launch of 70 control guidance sheets (HSC/ACTS, 2004). Nearly half the sheets were a response to local authority requests for guidance similar to that already available for industrial processes (i.e., common tasks in the service and retail industries involving chemicals). The remainder fell into two groups: sheets contributing to the HSC's strategy on occupational asthma (flour dust in craft bakeries and flour mills, use of isocyanates in motor vehicle repair, wood dust in woodworking, and health surveillance): and sheets on process dusts and fumes not previously covered by COSHH Essentials (foundries and rubber making).

In 2004 the HSE issued a further tool, Chemical Essentials[2]—a demonstration CD-ROM in the mould of COSHH Essentials—bringing together, for the first time, the regulation of occupational health, safety and the environment. It was developed with the Environment Agency and the Scottish Environment Protection Agency and was intended to eventually be a free online service. However, in 2006 it was announced that resource limitations meant further development of *Chemical Essentials* by HSE would cease.

COSHH Essentials and Chemicals Essentials are closely related to recent British regulatory strategies on chemical risk management. COSHH Essentials was developed in parallel with the changes in British regulation brought about as a direct result of concerns about the extent to which small firms were able to comply with existing arrangements. It was developed at the instigation of the Advisory Committee on Toxic Substances (ACTS) and promulgated in the specialist literature in parallel with discussion on the need to address research findings on the limited understanding of COSHH and its legal requirements by users of chemicals, especially those in smaller enterprises.

Although data is available concerning the extent of visits to the COSHH Essentials Web site, more detailed evaluation of the effectiveness of the scheme and its use in practice is limited and largely based upon opinion rather than objective measurement.

COSHH Essentials has also been adopted as a generic tool elsewhere, as well as influencing the development of further generic approaches, both in the countries included in the present study and at the international level. In Germany, for example, recent initiatives to support the new Hazardous Substance Ordinance include developing generic guidance in programs such as the Easy-to-use Workplace Control Scheme (*Einfaches Maßnahmenkonzept*) at the federal level, which is strongly influenced by the approach of COSHH Essentials.

---

[1] www.coshh-essentials.org.uk
[2] chemical.essentials@hse.gsi.gov.uk

In other countries different generic tools have been developed with an emphasis on their use in small enterprises. In Sweden the *KemiGuiden* (Chemical Guide) and the brochure *Kemitermomteteren* (the Chemical Thermometer) are typical "working materials" providing support for chemical risk management, which are designed for use by any company, regardless of sector, but with a focus on small firms. The *KemiGuiden* is an interactive tool designed to help small companies identify the requirements they need to fulfill concerning chemical risk management and giving advice on how to do so. It is made available through the joint employers/trade union organization, Prevent. It gives tailored advice to companies based on answers to a set of questions investigating in detail: what provisions and requirements the company has to comply, what routines are present in the company, and what control measures are needed. The Guide covers not only requirements related to the work environment but also requirements from other authorities. It is therefore an holistic tool, which in many ways meets the needs of small companies.

As Table 5.1 shows, there is evidence of the uptake of the Guide by small and micro-companies. Here again, there has been little evaluation of its actual use in practice following its uptake.

The tailored advice it presents is kept as short and pertinent as possible. The approach of the Chemical Guide is to encourage "learning by doing," a strategy

Table 5.1 Registered Users of the
Interactive Web Site the
Chemical Guide (Sweden)

Users of the Chemical Guide, distributed by firm size 05-02-2005		
Firm size	Registered users	Percent firms
1–10	279	19%
11–20	187	13%
21–50	301	20%
51–100	214	14%
101–200	170	12%
201–500	161	11%
> 500	164	11%

Note: 963 companies have not registered number of employees.
Source: KemiGuiden Web site: http://www.prevent.se/kemiguiden/

believed to be well suited to small companies (NUTEK, 2000). Despite this, because requirements of the regulations are quite extensive. For companies having few of these required routines in place, the advice needed may be considerable, and this may discourage small companies from starting to work with chemical risk management.

The Pimex (Picture Mixed Exposure) system (see Box 5.3) is a well-known tool, widely regarded as successful (Novak, 2003, p. 139ff; Novak, 2004: p. 2f; Wichtl & Novak, 2002). It visualizes risks at workplaces by video and monitoring, combining video filming and simultaneous measurements of different workplace exposures by fast response real-time reading instruments. One of its primary objectives is to promote participative approaches to health and safety management in small firms. Despite its prominence and the high regard in which it is held, for example by the AUVA in Austria, systematic evaluation of its use has not been carried out.

Box 5.3—PIMEX in Austria

Originating in Sweden, Pimex has been used in Austria for nearly 15 years by the AUVA, which has further developed it to PimexPlus. Originally used only to visualize chemical risks, it is now also possible to use Pimex to visualize other physical or physiological factors (Rosén et al., 2005). One of its main objectives is the reduction of exposure to chemicals in small companies with a high level of manual handling, such as in dealing with plastic reinforcement, including styrene (ski and snowboard production) or screen printing shops (using alcohols and other solvents). This participatory method is used to assist with the risk assessment, to produce OSH measures at workplaces or to qualify and motivate workers by instructional films.

The necessary equipment, including measuring instruments and the Pimex-Software and support (www.pimex.at/) is continually improved upon and readily available. Initially it was promoted mainly by the AUVA, but now there are more promoting institutions, and an international network is underway to strengthen the sustainability of this tool. In the European WISP-project ("Workplace improvement strategy by PIMEX"), partners from Austria, Sweden, Finland, and the United Kingdom tested the effect of PIMEX (Rosén, 1999). Examples showed that it was possible to reduce exposure by more than 90% merely via a more effective use of necessary prerequisites that already existed in the workplace. But it seems that the coverage of the system is still rather small.

That it is transferable is demonstrated by its successful transfer from Sweden to Austria. A project to further transfer the Pimex method as practiced in Austria to Germany and Greece was undertaken recently (Kooperationsstelle Hamburg, 2004) and promoted by the European Agency for Safety and Health at Work. Target sectors were car repair and metal-surface cleaning. The project is intended to be the starting point for an international Pimex network.

Supply-Chain Tools

The increased prominence given to the potential of the supply chain in supporting chemical risk management in small firms has been noted and the structure of such chains described, but to date there are few tools that make extensive use of this potential. In some countries however, there are examples of developments in this direction. To help spread COSHH Essentials in the UK, the HSC/E has used intermediaries known to be important to small firms, such as the Chemical Industries Association (which ran nationwide seminars through its Responsible Care network) and banks (which reached over 300,000 small firms and new businesses with features in their business newsletters) to distribute information on the tool.

The chemical industry utilizes supply chains to promote its programs such as Responsible Care and Product Stewardship. The former is largely focused on environmental matters and participating companies commit themselves to reducing their emissions and to searching for processes that will be less of a burden to the environment. Product stewardship concerns the sound management of safety, health, and environmental effects of a product through continuous improvement during its entire life cycle. It is the products and supply chain-oriented part of the Responsible Care program and extends marketing efforts for a product to environmental effects that take place beyond the sales process, requiring consideration of all phases of the life cycle of products, from starting material to waste. This necessitates cooperation between dealers and users; the program is intended to offer an early warning system for safety, health, or environmental risks of a product, allowing problems to be tackled proactively and in cooperation with other involved parties. In theory it should lead to increased trust between suppliers and customers and greater confidence throughout the whole product chain, as well as acting as a motor for continuous innovation that will enable incorporation of both new regulatory and market developments.

In Germany VW-Audi offers specific support for the management of hazardous substances it supplies to about 2,600 contractual car dealers and garages with an average of 10 employees. About 2,500 different chemical products are available under the VW-Audi label, the use of which is prescribed by them. For those products classified as hazardous or that contain hazardous ingredients, it is determined that no less-hazardous alternatives are available, so the users are relieved of the obligation to check for substitutes. Furthermore, product- or substance-related model work instructions are provided which have to be completed by the garages themselves in agreement with the details of the tasks for which the products are used and with the specific situation found on the premises (BMA, 2002, p. 14; Sul, 2004). An inventory of those hazardous products provided by VW-Audi is also offered. Hazardous substances acquired from other suppliers have to be added by the enterprises (Sul, 2005). Test kits for the measurement of the air concentration of hazardous substances are available from VW-Audi, and advice on the construction of garages with regard to fire protection and environmental obligations is also available (Sul, 2004). The allocation of a protection class (*Schutzstufe*) according to the new Hazardous Substance Ordinance is being considered as an extension of the support system for each of the hazardous products offered. Since the allocated protection class depends not only on the classification of the substance but also on the exposure conditions defined by the task it is used for, this will also require consideration by the company (Sul, 2005). Provision of written work instructions according to the Hazardous Substances Ordinance has also been proposed but not yet implemented (Sul, 2005).

Although this support has not been evaluated, responses from users indicate the relevance of the system, at least with regard to selected issues such as the storage of chemical products. Since safety data sheets are in demand for this purpose, not only are they electronically submitted when a product is purchased but they are also available on the intranet of the company so that the customers do not have to organize their own safety data sheet archives. Two observations corroborate the extent of demand: when the service was first launched, dealers and garages complained that the access was too complicated and not user-friendly, and this triggered an improvement to access. In an instance when the server was inaccessible for a certain time due to technical problems, the department in charge received a significant number of phone calls indicating the need to access the safety data sheets (Sul, 2005).

One reason for these demands is that the contractual dealers and garages are obliged to comply with the quality management system of the company. Under this system, compliance with storage obligations and regular updates of the inventory of hazardous substances are required and checked during annual audits.

A similar offer is provided by DaimlerChrysler for its contractual dealers and garages in Germany. They receive the complete collection of safety data sheets for all chemical products under the DaimlerChrysler label on CD. It also contains the corresponding substance-related model work instructions that have to be completed by the garages and a form that can be used as the basis for an inventory of hazardous substances.

The *Sicherheits Certifikat Contraktoren* (SCC Certificate) that was developed about 15 years ago in the Netherlands to evaluate and certify the OSH and environment management systems of contractors is an example of supply-chain leverage on SMEs that supply larger companies, that may have some potential for influencing chemical risk management practices. It is a means to demonstrate that a contractor works in compliance with fundamental statutory requirements in the national safety, health, and environmental legislation. It was developed as a third-party certification system to evaluate and enhance the contractor's performance on safety and health as well as environmental protection by putting in place agreed-upon, industry-proven best practices in safety, health, and environmental management, specified in a checklist. Significant improvement was reported as a result of its development (EU OSHA, 2002b, p. 30ff). SCC is often a prerequisite/condition for qualifying to submit a tender or to be awarded a contract. There is a simplified system, the limited certification SCC, for enterprises with fewer than 35 workers, which assesses OSH and environmental protection management activities directly at the workplace. SCC is used and accredited in the Netherlands, Belgium, Germany, Switzerland, Austria and a Euro-SCC Platform has been established. In Austria for example, SCC is required of suppliers mainly by large enterprises in the paper and oil industries (Pawlowitsch, 2002). Currently there are about 100 Austrian companies certified with the international SCC certificate (ÖSNE, 2003, 2004); however, most of them are larger companies.

Another example of supply-chain support is found in the OSH networking of car repair shops such as is practiced in the Austrian *Kfz-Werkstättennetzwerk* project, where the Mercedes Wiesenthal group of 11 car repair companies decided, as a result of an analysis, to improve OHS performance, including that on chemical risk management. The group developed a series of training workshops, an OHS manual and checklists for internal reviews. The materials were published within an intranet site and made available to other repair shops by Internet, they included activities focused on dangerous chemicals (EU OSHA, 2004a, pp. 38-39).

A potentially powerful supply-chain lever is found in public-sector purchasing power as well as in spin-offs from environmental protection. Many approaches and instruments developed in relation to eco-efficiency produce indirect positive effects on the OSH situation of the enterprises involved. One example from Austria concerning procurement is the *Beschaffungsservice Austria*. This free service was established in 1997 to give advice and to offer assistance for public purchasers in the form of guidelines and information. Its primary focus is on ecological purchasing, but health- and safety-related considerations are closely linked, as for instance with the main purchasing areas involving cleaning agents, paints and varnishes and chemicals used to maintain machinery and vehicles. *Beschaffungsservice Austria* publishes regularly updated guidelines and a criteria catalog for green procurement (EU OSHA, 2001, p. 5f; Oehme, 2001). While improved safety and health may be only a "side issue" of environmental concerns, such environmental focus provides producers and suppliers with powerful economic incentives to develop products and services in line with the requirements. In Austria, a market emerged for ecologically improved and healthier products, because large purchasers such as public authorities like the city of Vienna[3] changed their procurement policy by legislative means (such as through banning PVC products and requiring environment friendly procurement).

[3] See "Oekokauf Vienna" www.wien.gv.at/wua/2004/oekokauf.htm (since 1999), and also the European Green Public Procurement
http://ec.europa.eu/environment/gpp/guidelines.htm

These moves are thought to have also resulted in positive OHS effects within the producing companies.

Other supply-chain approaches that are primarily environmental in orientation but which are likely to have improved OHS spin-offs include those that use the "chemical leasing" business model and which are already applied in the car, electronic and clothing industries at an international level. In Austria chemical leasing models have been strongly encouraged by the Austrian Ministry for Environment (BMLFUW). Studies it commissioned showed a potential of almost 4,000 Austrian companies cutting the current annual usage of 150,000 tonnes of chemicals by one-third and therefore reducing emissions to air by 10%, emissions to water by 15% and waste by 75%. That this would not only save costs but potentially reduce chemical risks for the workers, makes such strategy, at least in theory, an important contribution to chemical risk management in small firms (BMLFUW, 2002a, 2002b). Currently, the BMLFUW is undertaking a great deal of public relations work in this field, supports pilot projects and is establishing a local center of excellence for metal cleaning in Austria (BMLFUW, 2003; Perthen-Palmisano & Jakl, 2004).

Suppliers' associations also are important actors in supporting leverage. The Supply Association for the Painting Trade in the Lübeck area (*Einkaufsgenossenschaft der Maler zu Lübeck eG—MALEG*) in the federal state of Schleswig-Holstein in Germany is a wholesale association for enterprises in the painting trade with about 8,000 products offered, about 3,100 of which are hazardous substances. In order to support its members in their compliance with the obligations under the Hazardous Substances Ordinance, *MALEG* has set up a specific management system, the Maleg Hazardous Substances Management System (*Maleg-Gefahrstoff-Management—MGM*) (BMA 2002, p. 26). In addition to the obligatory safety data sheets, model work instructions are automatically provided for products for which they are available; also the compilation of an inventory of hazardous substances is offered to the individual enterprise. Based on the inventory, enterprises can also receive personal advice on the replacement of hazardous products by less hazardous ones (MALEG, 2004).

A NATIONAL FOCUS—GERMANY

The developments just outlined notwithstanding, without doubt the most significant array of tools, both complete and specific, is found in Germany. Here, within sectors and federal states, there is a considerable range that provides various forms of support for substitution, for better understanding and using suppliers' information, as well as for undertaking risk assessment and introducing appropriate risk management measures. The highly developed but differentiated structures of federal states, sectoral insurance associations, peak trade and employers' organizations, as well as trade unions mean that in Germany not only are there many initiatives supporting chemical risk management in firms but that there is also considerable duplication and overlap among them. The following cases are not comprehensive but illustrative of the main features and better-known examples.

In the federal state of Rhineland-Palatine, where more than half the workforce is found in enterprises with fewer than 50 employees (SGU, 2000b), sector-specific guidance documents have been developed and aimed at SMEs since 1998. They include checklists and specific examples that allow enterprises in the respective sector to check whether they are conforming with obligations under environmental and occupational health legislation and if they are not, to eliminate deficits and support environmental and occupational health-management systems. Sector-specific guidance documents have been developed jointly by various institutions, including the labor inspectorate, the regional chambers of skilled crafts, the regional chambers of industry and commerce and regional branches of liability insurance associations (Rheinland-Pfalz, 2000a). The instruments include checklists and specific examples that allow enterprises in respective sectors to check whether they are conforming to obligations under environmental and occupational health legislation and, if they are not, to eliminate deficits. Guidance documents for each sector comprises seven modules, one of which deals with hazardous substances (SGU, 2000a). It addresses the inventory of hazardous substances, storage, handling and sector-specific substances. Under "inventory," the obligatory substitution check is also covered (SGU, 2000a). They provided free on CD for the metal sector in 2000 and for the wood and construction sectors in 2003 (Rheinland-Pfalz, 2003a). By mid-2005 about 4,000 CDs had been distributed (Schulte-Hubbert, 2005b). The three guidance documents can also be downloaded from the Internet (Rheinland-Pfalz, 2003b). Guidance to the printing sector is currently under preparation and it is intended that all four documents will be made available on a single CD (Schulte-Hubbert, 2005b).

The module on hazardous substances deals with four issues: the inventory of hazardous substances, their storage, handling and sector-specific substances. Under each, several further subjects are addressed, including for example, the obligatory substitution check; the obligations for storing solvents and lacquers with regard to flammability and explosiveness; protective measures, written work instructions and oral instructions. Measures addressing sector-specific substances include for example, in the metal sector: coolants and metal cutting fluids, welding fumes, diesel motor emissions and lacquers and solvents (SGU, 2000c).

Although systematic evaluation has not been undertaken, in several enterprises it was observed that the guidance document was used as a manual to be consulted when certain problems arise but not as tool that is applied systematically (Schulte-Hubbert, 2005b). While the response to the guidance document in the metal sector was encouraging, in the wood sector and in the construction sector the uptake was more limited. In the wood sector, only about one-fifth of the enterprises in which the guidance document was tried out were willing to continue with its use (Schulte-Hubbert, 2005b). In addition, the guidance documents were used as support tools by external occupational-health experts who provide their services commercially (Schmidt-Jung, 2005), and they were also incorporated into the occupational-health curriculum of the training courses for master craftsmen in the region (Schmidt-Jung, 2005; Schulte-Hubbert, 2005b).

The Pragmatic Management of Health and Safety in Small Enterprises (*Pragmatisches Management von Gesundheit und Sicherheit in kleinen Unternehmen—PragMaGuS*) is an Internet portal providing another example of integrated systems developed at federal state level. It was part of a research project organized by the Social Research Institute Dortmund (*Sozialforschungsstelle Dortmund—SFS*) between 2001 and 2004 and supported by insurance associations, trade bodies, trade unions, and federal state agencies (Landesinstitut Sozialforschungsstelle Dortmund, 2003; Projekt PragMaGuS, 2004a).

The project aimed to establish a health and safety management approach that was simple, yet complied with legal obligations, as well as the evaluation, and the transfer of its results. It was based on previous research on social and organizational processes in SMEs and the role of health and safety in them (Georg, 2004). It includes an Internet-based toolbox and other elements. Chemical products are addressed as one of the 24 thematic building blocks of the project (Projekt PragMaGuS, 2004b). Generic information for employers with regard to the use of chemicals covering relevant issues, such as the definition of hazardous substances, substitution, acquisition, risk management measures for use, storage and disposal are included. In line with the conceptual approach of *PragMaGuS,* support provided on specific obligations is limited to simple explanations; and for additional or more in-depth questions, users are referred to other sources, since the repetition of otherwise available support was not intended (Landesinstitut Sozialforschungsstelle, 2003, p. 33).

Its suppliers report about 60 to 80 visits to its Internet site per day, which include the download of material (Georg, 2005). It is reported that the pilot enterprises in the project performed their risk assessment, sought advice from occupational health experts and included occupational health and safety issues into their technical and organizational routines. Some of the pilot enterprises used the toolbox on an occasional basis, while others used it regularly (Georg, 2005).

Originating in North-Rhine Westphalia, the Hazardous Substances under Control (*Gefahrstoffe im Griff*) Internet portal was established in April 2004 as part of a project "building a support network for SMEs" set up by a consortium of actors including the federal state OHS administration, a university, insurance associations and the chamber of skilled crafts (Institut ASER e.V., 2004; EU OSHA, 2004b; Netzwerk gefahrstoffe-im-griff de, 2004). It provides well-structured access to information supplied by various German institutions (Lang, 2004). Comprehensive information is accessible via four different modes (GiF, 2004a):

- links to support tools for the design of control measures in a number of crafts, branches, or sectors (GiF, 2004b);
- links to a wide range of general management tools (e.g., for substitution, forms for inventories of hazardous chemicals, forms for written work instructions and for verbal instructions (GiF, 2004c);
- a search engine for various issues related to hazardous substances and to their management (GiF, 2004d); and
- access to the KomNet Web site,[4] through which online advice by a network of experts is provided.

A comprehensive collection of links to such tools is available, comprising databases and data collections related to hazardous substances; a database of safety data sheets and tools for both the compilation and interpretation of safety data sheets; tools for substitution checks and databases with solutions for substitution; tools for risk assessment; model forms for inventories of hazardous chemicals; model forms for written work instructions; support tools for verbal instructions; and a collections of legal and statutory texts. The search engine *Info-System Gefahrstoffe* is targeted exclusively at selected Web sites, with dedicated information in German on hazardous and nonhazardous chemicals and on substitution products. More than 5,600 documents are included.

At the end of the nine-month project a survey on short-term effects was performed, in which employers from twelve enterprises in the building and office cleaning services and eight physicians participated. It found that 90% of respondents had been able to relate to its approach on management of hazardous substances. Principal measures they adopted included the collection of safety data sheets and the compilation of written work instructions (Seiler, 2005). According to the evaluation of project promoters, both the gradual process of establishing the management of hazardous substances at the enterprise level and the Internet-based support tools for such an approach could be continuously improved upon by the project-mediated interaction between enterprises and local experts. They also concluded that the majority of company owners prefer direct face-to-face advice and consultation, which can be supplemented but not replaced by Internet-based support (Seiler, 2005).

In early 2005, based on the results of this project, the Occupational Health Administration of North-Rhine Westphalia started a more ambitious program, called Hazardous Substances in the Crafts and Trades (*Gefahrstoffe im*

---

[4] The KomNet online advice system offers the opportunity either to pose questions to experts, electronically or by phone, or to search a database in which problems previously addressed are documented for all areas of health and safety including hazardous substances. Currently, the KomNet database contains nearly 2,400 dialogues. These are questions posed addressing specific problems and the respective responses given. About 250 of these dialogues are related to hazardous substances. There is some evidence that a substantial proportion of these are initiated by small enterprises.

Handwerk), covering the whole of the federal state (NRW, 2004) and targeting SMEs with up to 20 employees in four sectors: building and office cleaning services; car repair shops; the plumbing, heating, and air conditioning trade and woodworking (Seiler, 2004).

Another earlier project with the same name was developed in Aachen by the Labour Inspectorate (*Staatliches Amt für Arbeitsschutz Aachen*) in cooperation with trade bodies and guilds, insurance associations, the regional Centre for Technological Advice and painters belonging to the Painters' and Varnishers' Guild. The original Aachen project comprised a set of Internet-based support tools and their promotion through leaflets and information meetings. The offer of advice was also provided to individual enterprises (EU OSHA, 2003b); it was taken up frequently and simple, effective, support provided (Lynen, 2005). The guidance is characterized by a pragmatic approach in five steps to the management of hazardous substances. Under a single portal, basic support tools designed for the specific needs of five crafts and trades (painting and varnishing, tile fitting, building and office cleaning services, car repair and maintenance, carpentry) address five tasks: the identification of substances as hazardous, acquisition of safety data sheets, introduction of an inventory of hazardous substances, drafting of written work instructions, and verbal instructions to employees (STAFA Aachen, 2003). Information is offered for each task on a separate Web site and is complemented by four model forms in electronic format and by a list of institutions both in the area and in the state, which may be contacted for additional advice. In order to keep the tools simple, issues such as the substitution of hazardous substances and the obligation of controlling the exposure levels in the workplace are not, or only indirectly, addressed.

Although limited resources means that an evaluation of the project has not been published, one of its promoters has observed that its approach was well received and led to encouraging results, raising awareness on chemical risk management tasks in a considerable number of the targeted enterprises. At the same time it was concluded that the project demonstrated that craft and trade enterprises cannot be accessed effectively solely via the Internet. Personal contact is also required, and owner/managers in these enterprises also need access to personal advice structures. As a consequence, the establishment of a permanent support network accessible to interested enterprises is planned (Lynen, 2005).

One of the more internationally known German instruments for supporting chemical risk management is the Hazardous Substance Information System of the insurance association for the construction industry (*Gefahrstoff-Informationssystem der Berufsgenossenschaft der Bauwirtschaft—GISBAU*). A comprehensive system for the management of hazardous substances has been available since 1989 and is targeted primarily at SMEs. The core instrument of GISBAU is the WINGIS database and software package available free on

CD. About 60,000 copies of the latest version 2.5 of WINGIS (published in 2005) including the new Hazardous Substances Ordinance have been distributed (Kluger, 2005). To assess its potential impact, this figure has to be compared to about 300,000 enterprises in the construction industry, that are members of the liability insurance association. Until October 2005 WINGIS was solely provided on CD; complementary tools could be accessed on the Internet (GISBAU, 2005c). In October 2005 an Internet version of WINGIS was launched.

The WINGIS CD is normally distributed to enterprises by the technical inspectors of the insurance association who are trained in the use of the system. WINGIS provides task-specific information on a wide range of chemical products used in the construction industry, differentiated for four different groups of users: employers, occupational physicians, occupational hygienists and works councillors. It is based on both information on the ingredients collated by GISBAU and product information provided by the suppliers via safety data sheets and technical instructions (Kluger, 1997). Issues covered for each product comprise classification and OELs, exposure measurement methods, health hazards, toxicological characteristics, occupational hygiene, information on substitution, technical and organizational control measures, personal protective equipment, first-aid measures, medical examinations, handling of the substance, storage, disposal, spillages and transport. The WINGIS package facilitates the compilation of an inventory of chemicals, and it provides model work instructions in 13 different languages (EU OSHA, 2003c).

The WINGIS system is complemented by product "codes" for up to 13 groups of chemical products widely used in the construction industry, as shown in Table 5.2. For each of the groups or subgroups, categories are defined according to criteria and arranged in such a way that the lower the number of a category within a group or subgroup, the lower the hazards of the products included. Selection of the least hazardous product type necessary for a specific task is facilitated in a straightforward way by this system. For each category, model work instructions are available, sometimes also differentiated according to a variety of tasks if the products in the respective category can be used in various work procedures for which different control measures apply. On the GISBAU Web site, all model instructions are provided in both German and English.

The categorization has been validated by a large number of exposure measurements and analyses of product samples (Kluger, 1997). As the working conditions described represent what is currently technically feasible, enterprises achieving these conditions are in compliance with the Hazardous Substances Ordinance. According to GISBAU experts, large manufacturers of chemical products for the construction industry report that their customers request products for which a product code has been allocated (Kluger, 2005). It is further estimated by the various supply associations for the painting trade that about 80% of

Table 5.2 Chemical Products in the WINGIS System in Germany

Product group	Number of subgroups	Total number of categories
Laminate adhesives	6	25
Epoxy resin coatings	1	11
Surface treatment agents for wooden floors	6	22
Bituminous products for building insulation; low temperature application	1	7
Concrete admixtures	1	3
Cement-containing products	1	2
Paints and lacquers	15	55
Cleaning products	10	65
Wood preservatives	3	23
Concrete release agents	1	7
Methylmethacrylate-containing coatings	1	2
Polyurethane systems	1	8
Anticorrosion products	5	31

Source: Adapted from GISBAU, 2003.

the paints and lacquers they supply exhibit a product code (Rheker, 2005). These observations suggest that at least in the craft part of the construction sector, product codes are a popular tool.

CONCLUSIONS: INTEGRATING TOOLS WITHIN CHEMICAL RISK MANAGEMENT STRATEGIES

As important as all these tools may be, experience in their use demonstrates that a significant feature likely to influence the success with which they are adopted is the extent to which they are integrated into other elements of support in the environment of small enterprises. For example, although the absence of properly conducted evaluations makes it difficult to be certain, it seems quite likely that in Germany the absence of a clear unifying strategy at national level to which tools can be related is an important weakness that may lead to uneven application, especially among small firms in sectors in which infrastructural supports are not well developed. A second limitation, which partially follows from this, is that there is considerable overlap and duplication among German tools. It is partially in recognition of this weakness that current strategies to address the application of the Hazardous Substances Ordinance with the Easy-to-Use Workplace Control Scheme (*Einfaches Maßnahmenkonzept*) has been developed at federal level; but as earlier chapters indicate, the structural complexity of the dual system in Germany means that it cannot be assumed that such federal-level development will be rolled out successfully through federal state structures and insurance-based sectoral organization to the workplace level in the absence of a clear national strategy. Recent moves toward the development of such national strategies for the work environment more generally are encouraging, but it remains to be seen how effective they will prove to be in practice (Kuhn, 2006).

In other countries, partly because national, regional and sectoral organization is simpler, structures supporting preventive approaches to the work environment are in turn less complicated, allowing more direct connection between national strategies and workplace implementation. In the Netherlands the mere existence of tools is recognized as insufficient to guarantee their use by those who need them most. Key elements of the current Dutch strategy, which is exemplified by the *VASt* Programme, include the preparation of sectoral-level action plans in high-risk sectors that identify specific improvement activities; engagement from the business community; and emphasis on supply-chain responsibilities, from producer to user. Alongside the other major Dutch strategy-introducing covenants (*Arboconvenanten*) between employers and trade unions at the sectoral level, setting achievable targets for improvement of health and safety issues, this provides a framework for institutional support in which more specific tools for chemical risk management can be deployed. Especially significant in relation to VASt is the effort to improve chemicals management through a special substances covenant with sectors where the risks of chemicals are regarded as high. Much effort has been put into including MKB Nederland (the national organization representing SMEs in some 170 different parts of industry and commerce) among the signatories to a covenant agreed upon in March 2005. Through these strategic approaches, the considerable array of tools to aid implementation of chemical risk management strategies can be made available at the enterprise level. Indeed, TNO's published inventory of instruments and other supports for chemical risk management in the Netherlands catalogs 146 such tools.[5,6,7,8,9]

In Sweden the *KemiGuiden* (Chemical Guide) was developed with support and financing from trade unions and employers organizations. It is made available through the joint employers/trade union organization, Prevent. Both the Work Environment Authority and the social partners have assisted in marketing, especially of the Chemical Guide; and the Authority and several trade unions and employers' organizations have links to it from their home page. It is therefore delivered with the active institutional support of the regulatory authorities, employers and trade unions.

These observations are important. They indicate that support for chemical risk management in small enterprises is likely to benefit from a coordinated and strategic approach, but that it equally requires engagement of a range of actors and processes in their economic and regulatory environment. In countries such as Germany, Austria and the Netherlands it is noticeable that comparatively highly developed institutional engagement of this sort at the sectoral level comes from bodies such as insurance organizations, trade and employers' organizations, trade unions and regulatory bodies. They are all traditional actors in the health and safety system and their engagement demonstrates the importance of active sectoral infrastructures in supporting chemical risk management. At the same time, it is in countries such as Germany that supply-chain initiatives are also found most frequently. This is likely to be the consequence of the already highly developed institutional support that is a feature of the environment of small firms, especially at the sectoral level in the country. This seems to provide opportunities to mix detailed sectoral- and branch-level understandings together with supply-chain actors and approaches resulting in the most developed examples of support for chemical risk management being found in Germany.

It is not obvious that in the UK and countries in southern Europe with far less developed sectoral infrastructures, there is the same kind of support or motivation for the engagement of intermediary actors and processes in supporting chemical risk management in small firms. While there has been much regulatory rhetoric

[5] Informatiebladen "Effectieven instrumenten" (information leaflets: "Effective Instruments"). Hans Marquart and Sonja Nossent, TNO, 2004.

[6] Technologische innovatie bij het terugdringen van blootstelling aan gevaarlijke stoffen (Technological innovation for the reduction of exposure to hazardous chemicals). Mat Jongen, TNO, 2004.

[7] Werken met stoffen en producten: brancheopleidingen (Handling of chemicals and products: branch schooling systems). Remco Visser, TNO, 2004.

[8] Kennis delen tussen bedrijven over stoffen en producten (Exchange of knowledge between companies on substances and products). Sonja Nossent, TNO, 2004.

[9] Leren communiceren rond stoffen in de keten (Learn how to communicate about substances in the supply chain). Remco Visser, TNO, 2005.

concerning the potential role of the supply chain in the UK, in practice its development is considerably limited in comparison with experiences reported in Germany and the Netherlands. In southern European countries like Spain, the study was able to identify few, if any examples of innovative tools to address chemical risk management in small firms. Strategic approaches seem to be limited to recasting traditional regulatory arrangements, for which weak infrastructural support gives little reason to suggest successful future outcomes.

In summary therefore, it is clear that the challenges of achieving effective management of the risks associated with using chemical products in small enterprises are widely acknowledged in northern European countries. There are both strategies and instruments now in place to address them, but the effectiveness with which they do so is obviously an important question and it is to the issue of evaluation that we turn in the following chapter.

CHAPTER 6

What Works?
Evaluating The Evidence

The safer and healthier use of chemical substances is the desired outcome of chemical risk management. Clearly, it is important to know how successful the strategies and tools described in previous chapters are in helping to achieve and sustain this outcome. There are a limited number of studies measuring the success, sustainability and transferability of current approaches, and this chapter reviews what can be learned from these concerning the factors that seem to promote success in the implementation of support for chemical risk management in small firms. It identifies considerable gaps in current knowledge and suggests a need to gain greater and more systematic understanding of the issues involved.

One of the main arguments throughout this book is that the success of chemical risk management strategies for small firms is conditional upon the wider support of the institutional frameworks and economic contexts in which such strategies are developed and tools deployed. Several elements of the economic and institutional frameworks in which chemical risk management strategies are implemented are identified. It is argued that some of these elements are critical to the success of strategies and tools aimed at supporting small enterprises, while others are substantial barriers, constraining the effectiveness of such approaches. These wider contexts are especially important when attempting to answer important questions of coverage, such as for example, whether chemical risk management strategies are likely to reach a substantial proportion of their target group or whether they are sustainable over long periods of time.

THE ELEMENTS OF SUPPORT FOR CHEMICAL RISK MANAGEMENT

Figure 6.1 illustrates the main elements and orientation of the traditional approach to managing the risks of using chemical substances at work. They involve knowledge transfer through the generation and presentation of various forms of information on hazards, risks and the safe use of chemical products.

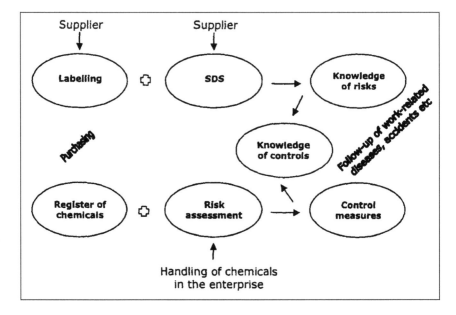

Figure 6.1 Aspects of chemical risk management.
Source: After Antonsson, 2006.

Information on hazards is found in hazard and risk databases and is supplied with products in the form of labels and material-safety data sheets. Many support tools focus on improving this information or making it more accessible for users. Tools further proliferate as aids to the supply of concrete guidance for specific work tasks involving particular chemical products and as guidance on the nature of specific chemicals. For example, there are tools in the form of checklists and sector-specific information as well as those providing advice on possible substitutions, on purchasing policies and on health surveillance. At another level, there is a body of tools addressing risk management according to generic principles.

Tools such as these are intended to achieve their effects by having an impact at various points in the supply and use of chemical products as is illustrated in Figure 6.2.

To evaluate effectively, we need to know whether the use of tools has led to discernable improvements with regard to the health and safety of users, whether they have a particular value in their application to the needs of users in small enterprises and additionally, what factors lead to the effective use of such tools and how widely they are used or have the potential to be used. The integration

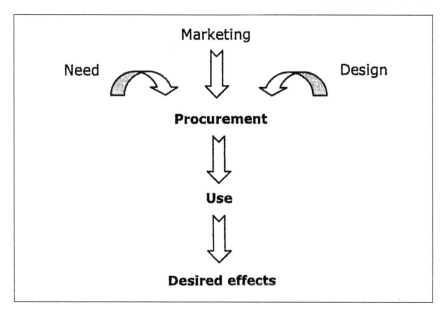

Figure 6.2 How do tools have effect?
Source: After Antonsson, 2006.

of tools into the business and support environment of small enterprises is an important element in this respect and it is therefore necessary to know whether, how and to what extent this is achieved. Research must ask to what extent responsible personnel in small enterprises are aware of their need for such tools, and how their awareness is developed and reinforced. Information on how tools are marketed and what influences their effective uptake is important, as is the extent to which not only the tools but also the marketing strategies are designed to maximize their impact on small enterprises.

Complete answers to these questions are rarely available because there have been relatively few properly conducted attempts to obtain them. To begin with dissemination, the evaluation of sources of information, guidance and advice, other than that involving human interaction, have been limited to counting the quantity of uptake, such as with records of the distribution of paper guidance and CDs, or with counting visits to Internet-based guidance such as the Chemical Guide in Sweden and COSHH Essentials in the UK (Wiseman & Gilbert, 2002), the distribution of inquiries on the *KomNet* database, and the number of visits to the *Gefahrstoffe im Griff* portal in Germany. Where such tools are interactive, inferences are drawn about use from time logged onto a site or following multiple visits of a particular user to the same site. However, apart from such quantitative measures of interest, little is known about the quality of use of the tools.

Recognizing the problems of determining reliable trailing indicators like health outcomes that are practicable to measure, it could be anticipated that leading indicators of improvements such as evidence of chemical risk management systems in place and awareness of them would be used as their proxy. However, this may not be entirely straightforward in small firms in which conventional approaches to management activities do not apply. Whatever the reason, it appears that existing evaluations have been conducted with only limited reference to either forms of indicator. Such evaluation that exists tends to support notions of simplicity, ease of use and relevance to small enterprises needs as central to success.

THE SUCCESS OF GENERIC TOOLS

One area in which some studies exist is in relation to the development and application of generic tools. Since the early 1990s there has been a strand of technically oriented research that models exposure assessment and underpins the development of ideas on more generic approaches to assessment and its role in determining strategies for managing chemical risk at national and EU levels (Cherrie et al., 2003; Money, 2003; Northage, 2005). Some of the more prominent models of exposure assessment, such as EASE (Estimation and Assessment of Substance Exposure), used to assess potential workplace exposures by the HSE, other national regulatory agencies and European Union regulators, as well as being distributed to a substantial number of other users, have been subject to rigorous assessment in terms of their usefulness as predictive tools for risk assessment since their first development (Tickner et al., 2005). In the case of EASE, independent studies have highlighted weaknesses in the model, indicating that in certain cases its estimates of exposure may be ambiguous or incomplete, leading to overestimation or (more worryingly from the perspective of workers' health) underestimation (Bredendiek-Kämper, 2001; Devilliers et al., 1997; Johnston et al., 2005; Vincent et al., 1996). Proposals for improvements have been made as a result of these and other studies (Creely et al., 2005).

Although they are limited in quantity and scope, these comparatively rigorous technical studies on exposure assessment and control have been positive concerning the levels of protection offered by such generic risk exposure assessment and, as a result, both EASE and COSHH Essentials have been developed, first in the UK and then applied more widely (see for example Brooke, 1998; Maidment, 1998; and Russell et al., 1998 in the UK; Tischer et al., 2003 in

Germany; Tijssen & Links, 2002 for the EU; and Jackson, 2002 on the development of the ILO Chemical Control Toolkit, based on COSHH Essentials).

While the new generic tools have their place in the range of instruments that may be brought to bear on supporting improved chemical risk management in small firms, they are not a panacea, and they also have their critics. The accuracy and efficacy of control-banding approaches aimed at small enterprises, such as COSHH Essentials, have been shown to have limitations (ECETOC, 2004; Tischer et al., 2003) For most authors however, such limitations are relatively insignificant in the context of the improved accessibility to appropriate risk control advice that the approaches apparently deliver to small enterprises (Money, 2006).

Exceptionally, and with a different emphasis, American researchers have argued that the high prevalence of control errors found among the subjects of their study on the application of COSHH Essentials in small enterprises warranted provision of more information on exposure bands and on the evaluation of control technology performance to users of COSHH Essentials than is customary. They further suggest that more systematic study of how small-business owners use the approach was required (Jones & Nicas, 2005a). In a separate account based on the same study, the authors argue that while COSHH Essentials and the ILO Chemical Control Toolkit predict exposures consistent with current exposure limits, the use of minimal margins[1] would be a better indicator of the health protection that they afford, since OELs are not health-based limits (Jones & Nicas, 2005b). In emphasizing accessibility and ease of understanding as well as use of readily available hazard information, the scheme is geared to the needs of SMEs. However, even this approach is not without critics and as a recent study conducted in India suggested, COSHH Essentials may be too complicated for many SMEs.[2]

Other researchers have pointed to the need to refine or target strategies for exposure and risk assessment to ensure efficiency in distinguishing between risk and hazard (see for example ECETOC, 2004 for this approach and a review of others). Other studies have shown strengths in using multimedia approaches to reinforce information use and achieve improved control measures Creely et al. (2003).

---

[1] According to Jones and Nicas (2005b, p. 154) "minimal margins" refers to, ". . . the margin between the dose of the chemical substance which produced the critical toxic effect (in humans or in animals) that served as the basis for the exposure limit, and the limit itself."

[2] http://www.saioh.org/ioha2005/Proceedings/Abstracts/SSI/AbstractI1_3.pdf and http://www.saioh.org/ioha2005/Proceedings/PPT/SSI/I1_4PPTweb.pdf

UNDERSTANDING THE PROCESSES
OF INFLUENCE

In the UK some relevant work has also been undertaken concerning the capacity of employers and employees to handle suppliers' information (Briggs & Crumbie, 2000; Creely et al., 2003), as well as on the flow of information between firms and their environment and its effect on the influence of regulatory intervention (John Kingston Associates, 2001).

Attempts have also been made to model the interface between expert and user information on chemicals that the researchers claim aids understanding of risk communication and demonstrates that difficulties in the application of information in chemical risk management in small enterprises are far more complex than merely the poor understanding of information by users (Cox et al., 2000) They point out that risk communication alone will not necessarily overcome strongly embedded practices, and to be effective it needs to be integrated with other approaches including training regimes, regulatory change, and technical innovation (Cox et al., 2003).

Specificity and Transfer

A major consideration that emerges from the evaluation of current experience concerns the question of the specificity of the new approaches to exposure assessment and control. Despite the attraction of the potential widespread use of generic approaches to chemical risk management, the reality of many of the interventions reported in the previous chapter is that both they and the supports for their application are highly sector specific and dependent on this specificity for the preconditions that underpin their success. While there is evidence that some approaches developed for specific sectors are transferred to a wider range of sectors, or that their extension to other trades is intended or under way, if an integral part of the approach in question involves the existence or the installation of a support structure, the issue becomes more complex. Such is the case of the *Gefahrstoffe im Handwerk* approach in Germany, where adaptations to technical or process-related specifics of the sectors or trades to which the approach is to be extended have been shown to be necessary preconditions, while the under-lying methods of the approach may remain the same. Therefore not only do the traditions and the social and organizational conditions in the additionally targeted sectors and trades have to be taken into account but also local or regional specifics have to be considered, as support structures are typically based at the local or regional level.

For some approaches and strategies therefore only the underlying method can be applied, whereas the concrete details have to be adapted to the particulars of the sector or the process. Examples include sector agreements and sector (or process-specific) solutions such as the substitution of volatile organic solvents with vegetable oils in various applications as pursued by the *Kooperationsstelle Hamburg*, or certain elements of the hazardous substance information systems established by German insurance associations.

In this sectoral context, further strategic differences between approaches pursued in different sectors are relevant, such as where there is a background of different levels of technology. Some of the differences between the *GISBAU* system in the construction industry in Germany and branch agreements in the printing industry in the same country can be understood in this way. The chemicals used in the construction industry are mainly applied independently of complex technical equipment, but the situation is different in the printing industry. When considering substitution of chemicals in printing, restrictions imposed by the use or the treatment of highly valuable equipment, such as printing presses, have to be taken into account, and manufacturers have to be involved as additional actors in the development of viable substitution solutions. By contrast, in the construction industry, for many applications such equipment-induced restrictions do not exist and thus, substitution solutions can evolve bilaterally between users of chemicals and their suppliers.

It can be hypothesized that for a setting including only two major actors—users of chemicals and suppliers of chemicals—the introduction of a rather simple tool such as a product code may be sufficient to initiate substitution or other control processes. Whereas for more complex settings that involve three major actors—not only users and suppliers of chemicals but at the same time, users and suppliers of technical equipment—an external promoter, such as the insurance association in the German case, is needed to initiate and moderate the control processes.

In summary, while the evaluations of the usefulness of generic and other tools and the debates they generate in the scientific literature are important, they address only a small part of the problem of the uptake and use of instruments to improve approaches to exposure assessment and control in small enterprises. Implicit in the findings dealing with national strategies and tools is the importance of the dynamics between actors in the small business environments in influencing the effectiveness of the strategies. With few exceptions, the scientific research on the development and implementation of generic tools has barely touched upon these issues, while more sector-specific research has tended to be quite limited in the extent to which its findings can be extrapolated beyond the situations studied. Neither approaches generally address the regulatory, economic, and societal contexts in which they operate, which are also likely to present push-pull influences on their success.

THE INSTITUTIONAL BASIS OF SUPPORT
FOR CHEMICAL RISK MANAGEMENT
IN SMALL FIRMS

The thinking behind the development of generic tools is clear: provide practical and reliable advice to users of chemicals, especially to those without access to developed occupational hygiene skills. Implicit in this thinking is that they will cover a broad range of users and become widespread in their application. However, while not absolutely contradicting conclusions about the usefulness of generic approaches, the evidence of this study points to some tensions between this thinking and what occurs in practice in many sectors and countries.

The findings reported in Chapter 5 conclude that what happens in many cases of support for chemical risk management in small enterprises is not the independent and unsupported use of generic tools by small enterprise owner/managers, but the application of concrete and sector-specific advice under the influence of institutional mediation and customs and practices that are already operational in particular small business environments. The German experience seems especially relevant here. Small firms have potential access to a range of tools mainly as a result of the diversity of institutionally mediated support for chemical risk management, as well as the size and economic significance of the industries in which the production and use of chemicals is substantial. For example, in construction and printing the involvement of the statutory insurance associations has enabled small firms to have access to quite well-developed support tools that are branch specific, such as *GISBAU* in construction and supports specifically developed with the manufacturers of printing machinery. Small firms in these and other sectors may also have access to Internet portals such as *Gefahstoffe im Griff*, provided through the federal states, and at the same time they may access advice from the Chambers of Skilled Crafts to which they belong. Superimposed on this diverse pattern of institutional support is the more recent development of generic instruments such as the Easy-to-Use Workplace Control Scheme provided by the *BauA*.

While there is little critical evaluation of the effectiveness of these various forms of support available in Germany, it seems apparent that their extent and diversity has both positive and problematic aspects. On one level, they clearly represent a rich resource for small enterprises; on another, their very diversity and that of the actors providing them risks overlap and duplication, creating potential difficulties for the creation of general strategies. Evaluation of the challenge for chemical risk management in small firms in Germany points to the existence of similar problems to those found elsewhere. It has shown that the measurement of exposure to chemical substances takes place in less than 1% of all enterprises (Bartels, 1998); the weakest compliance with risk assessment is found in small enterprises; and great deficiencies are known to exist among small enterprises concerning the understanding of the management of chemical risks, leading one federal state to estimate that 70% of all commercial users of hazardous substances in Germany did not (or could not) observe the appropriate statutory requirements for employee protection (Ministry of Social Affairs, Hesse, 2000). Although it is not possible to make direct comparison of such evaluations with those from other countries, it is nevertheless clear that their nature is the same and that the provision of multiple tools and sources of information supporting chemical risk management is insufficient to ensure their effective use.

In studies on health and safety arrangements for small enterprises more generally, actors and processes in the economic, social and regulatory environment of small enterprises are highlighted as significant levers in improving health and safety management. Face-to-face contact with change agents is regarded as the most important influence on the behavior of employers and workers in small enterprises, whether such agents are the conventional actors of the health and safety system such as inspectors, statutory insurance associations, worker safety representatives, OHS practitioners and consultants, or less conventional intermediaries such as supply-chain actors bearing health and safety messages or institutional actors such as the various statutory or voluntary associations for businesses, trades and workers (Walters, 2001). There has been little evaluation of this aspect of promoting new approaches to chemical risk management in small enterprises, nor has there been a systematic study of the resource implications of the engagement of these actors and processes in support of instruments to improve chemical risk management. Studies that have addressed the dynamics of interaction between actors within small workplaces or between them and the wider sources of influence in the social, economic and regulatory frameworks in which they operate offer only fragmentary indications of the importance of such contexts. The following sections summarize what little is known about the engagement of small firms with mainstream actors of the OHS system in dealing with chemical risk management issues.

The Role of Inspection and Control

There are few recent studies on the role of regulatory inspection and control in relation to chemical risk management and those that exist reach inconsistent conclusions. In the UK the HSE has collated some information on enforcement of the COSHH Regulations. Although not analyzed by enterprise size, they show that between 1997 and 2000 from 12% to 21% of enforcement notices concerned these regulations, indicating that a substantial amount of the regulatory agency's time and resources were taken up with addressing compliance with chemical risk management (HSC, 2002).

A more recent study concerning the compliance of small enterprises with *inter alia* the COSHH Regulations demonstrated that the influence of regulatory inspectors was positively associated with compliance with prescriptive regulatory requirements, while compliance with those involving process-based risk assessment and control activities were more influenced by the requirements of economically significant clients (Fairman & Yapp, 2005). However, other research on the compliance behavior of small enterprises more generally has emphasized the importance of the threat of inspection and the influence of the regulatory agency in perceptions concerning reasons for compliance among small businesses (Vickers et al., 2003). In contrast, research on the inspection of small firms in Sweden indicates that they do little to prepare themselves for inspection. Rather, they wait until they are told what to do as the result of an inspection and usually they are allowed several months in which to implement these reforms (Antonsson et al., 2005).

Nevertheless, in Sweden, while inspection campaigns that focused on chemicals revealed considerable levels of non-compliance with legal requirements on such matters as risk assessment, the regulatory agencies responsible regard these campaigns as powerful influences to secure future compliance. In so doing they identify the temporary increased presence of labor inspectors in the field of chemical regulation during campaigns and the attendant raised profile of the subject of the campaign as important influences on prioritizing chemical risk by owner/managers. However, it is not clear for how long such effects last after an inspection campaign.

Largely anecdotal material presented by inspectors in Italy emphasized the importance of advisory approaches by inspectors and regional and sectoral level cooperation between inspectors, small-firm trade associations and trade unions in securing better chemical risk management in certain sectors in northern Italy. Similar experiences occurring in the Netherlands and Sweden were reported in the same study (Walters et al., 2003).

Preventive Services and OHS Practitioners

Generally, research on the role and activities of preventive services and OHS practitioners indicates they are little used by small enterprises, for obvious reasons of cost. Even when they have a legal entitlement to them as was formerly the case in the Netherlands, it seems that the level of engagement is fairly minimal (Walters, 2001) While there is some evidence from Scandinavian countries and especially from Sweden that occupational health services and consultants do sometimes act as change agents in small enterprises (Antonsson et al., 2002), there is little specific information concerning their role in relation to chemical risk management. Observers suggest this role is likely to be quite limited; in countries such as the Netherlands and Sweden there is evidence that they are less well equipped to undertake sophisticated chemical risk assessment currently than was previously the case, as stronger market demands for other aspects of their services have led to a reduction in their capacity to deliver occupational hygiene (Antonsson & Schmidt, 2003). They also have limited understanding or interest in the needs of small enterprises.

In Germany and Austria the statutory accident-insurance system provides for a high level of technical support for health and safety. In Austria this includes a special service for small enterprises: the AUVASafe system, which involves access to prevention advice from specialists and appears to have achieved some success in accident reduction. In Germany there is a well-developed sectoral provision of specialized accident insurance associations. The *Berufsgenossenschaften* have extensive involvement in supporting preventive OHS activities including a considerable engagement with chemical risk management. In addition, they are substantial providers of training for occupational hygienists and safety engineers as well as employers and trade union representatives. However, despite this widespread and substantial role in preventive OHS (or perhaps because of it), there is little in the way of published concrete evaluation of their effectiveness in relation to small enterprises.

In the UK most occupational health and safety practitioners are employed in large organizations in a largely unregulated market-driven approach toward preventive OHS. While the chemical risk management needs of small enterprises are well recognized, there has been little in the way of institutionally mediated support for them. The recently implemented occupational health and safety advice scheme, focused especially on small enterprises and aimed to cover 38% of them by 2008, is therefore interesting; but although the HSE has commissioned an evaluation of this initiative, no findings have yet been published.[3]

Workers' Representation

As the victims of chemical exposure, as well as the beneficiaries of measures to prevent it, workers stand to gain most from effective strategies and tools to manage the risks of working with chemicals. There is therefore a strong ethical case for the representation of their interests in chemical risk management in

[3] The evaluation is being undertaken by the Institute for Employment Studies, a commercial research organization, specializing in OHS and other employment-related research, mainly for Government bodies, based at the University of Sussex.

all situations in which there is the potential of harmful exposures. Representation of employees in small enterprises is known to be problematic for reasons of size and access. In countries such as Sweden (and to a lesser extent in Italy and Norway) where there are statutory requirements covering them, the role of trade union regional health and safety representatives is linked with the provision of effective advice and awareness raising on health and safety in small enterprises. Researchers reviewing their activities point to their effectiveness generally in small enterprises, but there are no studies of their role in relation to chemical risk management specifically (Frick & Walters, 1998; Walters, 2004).

The role of trade unions and worker representation in supporting the implementation of chemical risk management strategies for small firms in other countries in the study is less clear. Where there is no statutory support for schemes to introduce regional and territorial representation for workers in small enterprises, these schemes are far less developed than in situations where such support exists. In the UK for example, despite significant government financial support and considerable publicity, the voluntary Worker Safety Adviser initiative reached only a tiny minority of small firms with the provision of advice and interventions on health and safety. None of the activities supported by the scheme focused especially on chemical risk management, and there are major questions concerning their sustainability in the absence of continued government support (Walters, 2006a).

Some trade unions, organizing in industrial sectors in which there is a high use of hazardous substances and a large proportion of small firms, have had a significant presence in the development of chemical risk management strategies at sectoral levels. At the same time, in such sectors, traditional models of trade union workplace organization are sometimes highly developed despite the predominance of small-to-medium-sized firms. Parts of the printing industry in the UK provide an illustration of these phenomena, where for many years the antecedents of the present-day trade union for print workers[4] organized workers in small firms in a sector in which 99% of firms have fewer than 50 employees. Historically, the use of the "closed shop" was widespread in the sector, affecting employment even in small firms. Its legacy makes union membership still a significant tradition in many small printing enterprises, and owner/managers

---

[4] The recent history of trade unionism in printing is one of amalgamations and mergers. Historically the National Graphical Association (renamed the Graphical, Media and Printing Union (GMPU), following mergers with other print unions) was the main trade union representing the interests of print workers in these small firms. This more recently has become part of AMICUS, a large conglomerate of previously separate trade unions for engineering and other trades as well as technical and managerial employees.

are frequently members or ex-members themselves. Union workplace representatives are therefore not uncommon in many small enterprises. Where such representatives exist, they are an important source of health and safety information for both employees and the employer. Since working with chemicals is a major aspect of printing, the union and its representatives are a significant source of advice on their safe use. Communication is enhanced in several ways: for example, informal industrial relations structures of such firms increase the direct communication between workplace representatives and the employer (Walters, 1987). The source of much health and safety information for workers and employers is therefore either the trade union itself or the tripartite HSC Printing Industry Advisory Committee (in which the trade union is a proactive participant). This leads to a general acceptance of the role of the trade union in health and safety and means that its activities in areas such as chemical safety is promulgated as a benefit to both employers and employees.

Another example from the UK can be found in the activities of the representatives of construction trade unions on some large construction sites, where there are multiple small employers engaged in contracting and subcontracting. Again there is limited direct evidence of their role in chemical risk management, but a positive role in such activity may be surmised from what is known about their role in training and especially in improving communication between the principal contractor and contractor and subcontractor workforces more generally (see Walters et al., 2005; Walters & Nichols, 2007).

Other Institutional Support

The major form of additional institutional support for chemical risk management is found in those countries in which the development of the legal system for regulating the work environment has allowed a substantial role for statutory accident insurance as in Austria and Germany. As already noted, in its most highly developed form such as is found in Germany, the sectoral distribution of the *Bgen* provides not only an infrastructure for additional information, advice, inspection and control of the work environment, but in many sectors has allowed for the development of particular technical specialization on chemical risks.

Despite the absence of evaluation, the framework of institutional support at the sectoral level found in these countries (and in others based on similar models for the role of social insurance) represents a significant difference in institutionally mediated supports for chemical risk management strategies aimed at small firms in these countries and those such as the UK, in which such institutional frameworks are absent.

In Germany and Austria there are various organizations to which businesses are obliged to belong, including Regional Chambers of Industry and Commerce and Chambers of Skilled Crafts. In Austria there is a well-developed national- and state-level infrastructure of Chambers of Labour. Such organizations form part of the wider structural support that underpins employment in all enterprises in these countries and constitutes a further difference in this respect between them and countries like the UK.

In addition to the traditional actors of the health and safety system, other players may have the potential to act as support to small firms in the implementation of chemical risk management. The important role of the manufacturers of equipment in which chemical substances are used has already been mentioned, and there is some evidence of their role in several of the countries in the study. It is likely that other actors in the support structures for small enterprises such as education and training providers have opportunities to exert influence on chemical risk management practices. Limited examples of the contributions of such agencies, usually the combined efforts of several agencies working together on chemical risk management interventions were identified, but none appeared to be subject to properly conducted evaluation. Further sources of influence from the economic and social environment of small enterprises could include financial institutions, business start-up agencies, as well as various public-interest organizations in local communities providing advice and support on environmental issues. Once again, while there is some potential for the intervention of such agencies, there has been little attempt to evaluate its extent or effect.

To inform evidence-based policy, a more systematic approach to evaluation of the factors that support chemical risk management in small enterprises is desirable, in which underlying principles can be distinguished and institutional as well as infrastructural influences that help to determine outcomes are more clearly determined. Implicit here is the need to know more about the scale and coverage of new initiatives to improve chemical risk management in small enterprises. A major weakness of previous approaches is the limitations of their coverage. Indeed one of the reasons why newer approaches have been proposed is the idea that they will extend improved chemical risk management to situations that are hard to reach by traditional means. The arguments for this are theoretically persuasive, but to date the evidence for their achievement has not been convincingly presented. Moreover, for good reasons, already outlined, there are situations in which the sectoral specificity of successful interventions will militate against their transferability.

At the core of support for chemical risk management is the relationship between the suppliers of chemical products and their downstream users. A key concern in this relationship is risk communication and the dissemination of control strategies through the supply chain. The chemical industry is itself a major influence on good practice concerning the management of the risks associated with its products. The industry initiatives such as Responsible Care and Product Stewardship acknowledge its responsibilities. However, in most countries there appear to be continuing problems of quality and access to suppliers' information. Opinions of users (and to some extent of regulators too) are that there remain differences between the quality of experiences within the chemical industry and those of downstream users outside it. In many interventions to improve chemical risk management, mediation between the information from the industry and the delivery of risk management within the small enterprise is the major focus, there may be ways in which the chemical industry can engage further in this process through improved risk communication and through working more closely with intermediary organizations. A more structured and targeted strategy on the part of the industry may be required in relation to the dissemination of information on hazardous substances in which greater attention is paid, not only to the needs and capacities of downstream users, but also to the production networks in which they operate, the institutional supports on which they draw for the implementation of chemical risk management and the dynamics of the social and economic interactions that are their basis.

INSTITUTIONAL SUPPORT FOR CHEMICAL RISK MANAGEMENT AND THE ROLE OF SUPPLY CHAINS

It is no coincidence that in current policy thinking in market-based economies, influences that can be brought to bear on supply chains are held to be crucial means of effecting change. In the case of the work environment, there has been a growing recognition that the command and control model of regulation can never be effected in anything like all workplaces solely through the intervention of regulatory inspection—there will always be too few inspectors to undertake the task. Additional strategies are clearly necessary to bring about changes that are thought to be desirable to improve the work environment. At the same time the pressures of economic liberalism have acted to downgrade the direct role of regulation in economic affairs in most advanced market economies. As a consequence, dependent relationships within supply chains have come to be regarded as a potential way of achieving desired outcomes through the leverage they provide.

Influences that can be brought to bear on the actors within supply chains are not solely economic; even in liberal market-based economies, suppliers and supply chains do not operate entirely in isolation from regulatory requirements or public interest. These too may play important roles in determining outcomes.

Moreover, influences on supply chains do not operate singly and outcomes may be the product of the interactive effects of constellations of forces acting on and within the supply chain.

Similar conclusions were reached in a recent German study on the sustainable development of strategies to improve aspects of chemical safety through substitution (Ahrens et al., 2006). This research was concerned with understanding two problems: first the ability to be innovative with regard to the substitution of hazardous substances and second, the uncertainties surrounding the direction of innovation in risk reduction. Of special relevance to this study was that to understand these two issues, the objective of the research was to discover "under which framework conditions and in which constellations of actors, substitution of hazardous substances is encouraged or is impeded." In so doing the researchers took into account "specific regulatory systems, conditions on the markets (for chemical products) as well as ongoing public debates." In other words, Ahrens et al. attempted to take into account the same constellation of social, economic and regulatory factors surrounding the supply and use of chemical as are proposed here. They state (2006, pp. 5-6):

> In order to gain an appropriate comprehension of the ability (and not just willingness) for hazardous substance substitution (the ability to be innovative), we therefore must not solely look at individual participants in a supply chain, their interests and opportunities for influence. It is more important to have an overall view of the, in some cases, highly complex "constellations of actors" including the "framework conditions," which have either an encouraging or preventive effect on the substitution process, as legislation, competitive conditions and public debates. . . .

Applying the same logic to the present study and focusing on risk management of hazardous substances in small enterprises, rather than "hazardous substance substitution," the argument is expressed schematically in Figure 6.3.

As in the case of Ahrens et al. (2006), whose model of an innovation system is based on that of Hemmelskamp (1999), the supply chain of chemical products to small enterprise downstream users lies at the heart of the illustration. Its role in improving the safe use of chemicals in small enterprises is affected by various "driving forces" that act to support or hinder the process of communication of good practice and its implementation at the level of the small firm. They include the effects of regulation, both in the form of "push" effects resulting from legislation regulating the introduction of chemicals in to the market and "pull" factors resulting from worker (and environmental) protection measures and regulatory inspection and control. Further driving forces are found in the push of technological change in which new and safer products and processes are

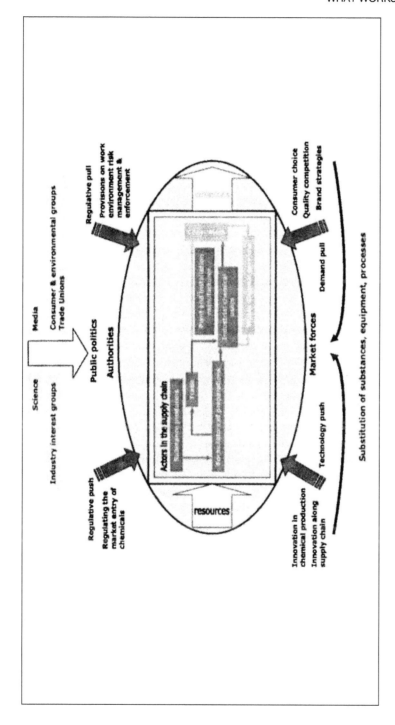

Figure 6.3 Modeling the influences on the supply chain with potential to improve the safe use of chemical products in small enterprises. **Source**: Modified from Ahrens et al. (2006) with kind permission of Springer Science and Business Media.

introduced and in the pull of market demands that might lead to safer usage through, for example, compliance with OHS and environmental quality standards demanded by the market and which are in turn influenced by public opinion and the factors that shape it.

Downstream users of chemicals in small enterprises are also influenced by a variety of actors involved in and around the health and safety system and in representing the interests of labor. However, as Fig. 6.3 demonstrates, their influence is not limited to acting on small enterprises. Many have potential to influence other actors within the supply chain. In addition, the influences on these actors may further include representations of civil society in the form of the media, non-governmental organizations with interests in the environment, and in quality standards, local environmental pressure groups and so on. The ramifications of such sources and routes of influence may be diffuse and diffi-cult to chart, but the important point is that processes of influence on supply chains include not only formal and institutional mediation but also informal and possibly hidden processes. As Ahrens et al. also make clear, actors and driving forces of influence on supply chains do not act in isolation, rather they operate in concert.

Previous chapters have demonstrated that implicit in current strategic thinking is the notion that somehow the economic environment of the small enterprise can be utilized to support and sustain the implementation and effective operation of approaches to chemical risk management in ways that will enhance the traditional roles of regulation, inspection and control, pro-fessional advice and of organized labor. Thus it is supposed that there is a set of relevant institutional supports in the business environment of small enterprises, largely based around the supply-chain relationships between the enterprise and its suppliers and clients as well as their wider social economic and regulatory contexts with the potential to be brought to bear as levers and supports to ensure the implementation and operation of chemical risk management at the level of the enterprise. But as has been observed, there is limited evaluation of how they actually work and what they achieve in practice.

The question for policymakers and regulators concerned with supporting the improvement of chemical risk management in small enterprises, in the absence of such evaluation, is *how* to harness effectively these constellations of forces and their interactions on and within supply chains in order to achieve and sustain improvement. Current regulatory thinking supports these efforts, with REACH placing much emphasis on the role of the supply chain in risk communication between suppliers and the downstream users of their products. Indeed it develops traditional uni-directional notions of risk communication on chemical safety through supply chains to embrace requirements for two-way exchanges between suppliers and users in the processes involved in regulating the safe use of substances in downstream workplaces. However, improving the effectiveness of these developments will need the parallel supportive development of relationships between suppliers and users in new directions. To date there is little evidence on which to predict the success of what amounts to major departures from previous practice.

Current limits of regulatory intervention in chemical risk management, especially in relation to small enterprises, mean that many questions remain asking *how* this might be done. It is important to understand what might be the enabling prerequisites for more effective harnessing of the actors and processes involved in influencing the relationships between supply and use to support improved risk management of chemical substances in small enterprises. It is equally important to know what are the costs of such engagement, both to the actors involved and to the bodies that are seeking to involve them and to determine if such approaches are really as cost-effective as they are supposed to be.

Finally, it is important to acknowledge that these requirements of REACH do not replace those found in the strand of protective legislation on chemicals and carcinogens at EU and national levels; rather, they exist alongside these measures. This coexistence raises further challenges for clarity and consistency in the development and implementation of chemical risk management strategies aimed at small enterprises that policymakers and inspectorates need to consider carefully if such parallel measures are to complement one another effectively in practice at sectoral and workplace levels.

CONCLUSIONS:
WHERE ARE THE KNOWLEDGE GAPS?

The primary conclusion concerning the evaluation of strategies to support chemical risk management in small enterprises is that evaluation itself is very limited and in many cases nonexistent.

There has been some properly conducted research on the technical aspects of exposure assessment modeling, generic risk assessment and control of chemical hazards, which has been used to inform policy development. There has been far less properly undertaken evaluation of initiatives to effect such assessment and control in practice in relation to small enterprises. Such evaluation that exists is often limited to self-evaluation in which participants with vested interests in the success of such schemes find them to be successful. These evaluations are frequently restricted to the narrow circumstances of the application of a particular initiative and rarely seriously consider supports and constraints relevant to its wider use. There remain important questions concerning how evaluation should be undertaken and what should be evaluated. Clearly it is important to determine the extent to which programs and tools work effectively in implementing improved chemical risk management at the level of the workplace. For example, how reliable are they? Do the generic approaches they utilize always provide for safe and cost-effective management of chemical risks? What safeguards are there to ensure the correct use of such approaches? Are there conditions in which their use would be inappropriate? How common are such situations?

Most evaluation undertaken so far has focused on some, but not all, of these aspects. More than this however, there is a demonstrable need to consider the dynamics of the social processes at work in small enterprises and the networks of production in which they are located, that determine the uptake and application of such approaches and their instruments. It is also necessary to understand more of the supports for their sustainability and transferability. In so doing it is important to acknowledge that small enterprises are not a homogenous group of organizations sharing a similar set of features; it is extremely unlikely that in the case of strategies for chemical risk management "one size fits all." Therefore properly structured and targeted approaches that account for such differences are likely to be required.

Finally, it is important that elements of evaluation are connected. The present study has found few cases where this is so. Its reports on the national situations conclude that while in each country it is possible to identify relevant broad regulatory principles on the management of hazardous substances and, in most cases, principles governing improving OHS management in small enterprises, it is less easy to demonstrate clear or explicit relationships between the two. They all identify accounts of the methods and tools used to support chemical risk management in small enterprises and report some evidence of their effectiveness in particular situations. However, such evidence is often not generalizable beyond the situation to which it applies. There are no substantial evaluations of support from other institutions and processes in the economic and regulatory environment of the small firm, even though it is quite clear that the operation of chemical risk management methods and tools are ultimately dependent on their engagement for long-term success. Therefore there is relatively little evidence of effective transferability of these methods and tools beyond the case studies in which they are currently used, or of strategies to achieve and sustain such practice. Nor is there much evidence of the development of the necessary systematic approaches to tackling these issues at the level of the EU, which are necessary if the approaches envisaged in the regulatory discourse surrounding REACH are to be implemented successfully in the future.

It is clear that there is much duplication of effort among the various relevant approaches and the instruments employed. In some countries and in some sectors there are cases of good communication allowing the development and promulgation of practices across regions and sectors, but with these few exceptions the overall profile of chemical risk management initiatives for small enterprises remains low. Information about the many individual cases of good practice that are in existence in northern European countries remains largely specialist knowledge and general access to it is limited. Indeed, complaints concerning inaccessibility of such information by small enterprise owner/ managers appear to be almost as significant an element of current research findings as they were in the studies that led to the current generic strategies on exposure assessment and control. While it is by no means a panacea to resolve such problems, perhaps some steps could be taken in this direction through better information access and dissemination at the EU level and greater attention to this matter by agencies such as the European Agency for Safety and Health at Work as well as for actors within the European chemical industry. Here again, the implementation of REACH, with its emphasis on supply-chain relationships and EU-wide networks involving manufacturers, suppliers and users, creates a need to provide small firms with a far more coordinated and conspicuous information service to support good practice than appears to be the case at present.

In reviewing the little that is known about what works in stimulating and supporting chemical risk management in small firms, discussion in this chapter has returned time and again to questions of motivation and support. It has described an emerging model for understanding the underlying push/pull factors in the environment of small firms that might be utilized to stimulate and sustain improvements in chemical risk management in these firms. It has further noted that such an understanding is evident at least in part in the direction in which the recent development of the regulation of chemical risks has moved at the EU level.

CHAPTER 7

Implementing Inclusive Strategies for Improving the Management of Chemical Risks at Work

Working with hazardous chemicals involves significant risks to health. That much is clear. At the same time, manufactured chemical substances are a fact of everyday life and have contributed substantially to the technological advancement and economy of modern societies. These observations reflect some of the tensions of modernity. From the second half of the twentieth century onward, ways of dealing with them have preoccupied not only regulators and specialists in occupational health and environmental protection but have also held the wider public interest. In the 1980s the social theorist Ulrich Beck coined the now well-aired concept of "manufactured uncertainty" to describe the societal risks of modernization. The unknown risks associated with certain manufactured substances were among the examples he chose to illustrate his thesis (Beck, 1992).

Although Beck and his contemporaries were engaged in a more generalized societal concern about the consequences of modernity than with the subject of this book, a social-science perspective is relevant. Central to the analysis presented here has been the idea that to understand what works in implementing risk management strategies in small enterprises, an understanding of the economic sociology of the people who own, manage and work in them is also required. While it is advisable to be wary of generalizations when discussing small enterprises—because they take many different forms and functions at practically all levels and sectors of the economy—it is widely acknowledged that a large majority struggle for survival, often at the lower end of markets and supply chains. The low skills, poor education and limited training of many of their owner/managers and employees, the low unionization and precarious job security, coupled with their remoteness from specialist advice, inspection and control of their work environments all contribute to the well-documented, multifaceted lack of resources with which this majority are characterized. This further contributes to the vulnerability of workers in these enterprises; such features together help explain why it is that most systematic approaches to management, including those focused on the work environment, are hard to apply, not relevant and fail to work in these enterprises (Nichols, 1997; Walters, 2001).

All this is well established and applies to huge numbers of enterprises; yet, until relatively recently such workplaces were assumed to be simply smaller versions of the larger ones that were generally the main focus of regulatory strategies; this was certainly so in the case of the traditional regulatory approaches to protect workers from exposure to hazardous substances. Their focus on exposure standards and environmental monitoring was developed with the experience of large enterprises in mind. It failed to take into account that the multifaceted absence of resources described above would mean that the majority of small enterprises would not possess the capacity to comply with such requirements and in the absence of extensive inspection and control, would simply ignore them. The regulatory provisions consequently failed to have a significant impact on improving practices on chemical risk management in these enterprises.

In recognition of this failure, and in response to the growing profile of small enterprises in the economy and in economic and regulatory policies, more recent efforts to develop strategic approaches to addressing chemical risk management at work have refocused their approach in an attempt to be more relevant to what is perceived to be achievable in these workplaces. There have been two main elements to this process. One has involved the development of tools and strategies to support better compliance with existing regulatory requirements. The second has been the introduction of changes in the requirements themselves that, it is argued, will make them more relevant to the situation of small enterprises. Of course these two elements are not entirely unconnected and recent changes for example in the UK COSHH Regulations and the introduction of the new Hazardous Substances Ordinance in Germany are closely related to the development of instruments to improve compliance in small enterprises; but the most prominent recent regulatory change has been at the EU level, with the introduction of REACH. Although REACH is an attempt at a comprehensive regulatory strategy embracing the supply, use and disposal of chemicals and aimed not only at occupational exposures but also at consumers and the environment, it has a number of specific features that are orientated toward ensuring greater attention to chemical risk management in small enterprises.

This chapter presents a discussion of the likely impact of the new regulatory approaches to securing improved risk management in small firms in the light of what our findings suggest are the main supports and constraints to achieving such improvement. In particular it looks at the specific features of REACH that it is claimed will have an impact most significantly on improvements in risk management in small-firm downstream users of chemical substances and considers the extent to which the evidence of the study supports these claims. It further discusses the findings of the present study that point to some of the likely limitations of the impact of the REACH approach in relation to small enterprises and identifies additional supports and actions than may be necessary. This chapter also offers some reflections on those hazardous exposures commonly experienced by workers in some small enterprises but which are outside the immediate focus of the risk communication and supply chain strategies envisaged in REACH and asks what is required to enable safe work in these situations too.

WORK, HEALTH, AND MANAGING THE RISKS OF CHEMICALS

Significant Occupational Exposure in Small Enterprises

Chapter 1 showed that there are major gaps in knowledge about the scale and consequences of exposure to chemical substances in small enterprises. It demonstrated that despite uncertainties about the precise toll of morbidity and mortality linked to occupational exposure to hazardous chemicals in these enterprises, enough is known to warrant concern. The nature of the relationship between working with hazardous substances and subsequent morbidity or mortality is particularly difficult to establish for a host of reasons, to do with the long time lags between exposure and the onset of disease coupled with the volatile nature of employment in small firms. The short life span of many small firms, the extent of temporary employment in them, as well as the high incidence of unregistered firms and undocumented employment all contribute to the inadequacy and unreliability of the sources of information that are necessary to determine links between work and ill-health outcomes. Workplace exposure data is extremely limited for the same reasons and also because of the remoteness of most small firms from professionals competent to undertake such measurement. Nevertheless, there are sufficient good reasons to believe that a substantial proportion of the overall burden of work-related ill health and mortality linked to working with hazardous chemicals can be attributed to exposures in small enterprises.

In summary, these reasons include some evidence (from countries such as the Netherlands) that workers in small enterprises may be more exposed to chemical hazards than their counterparts working in larger enterprises; analogous findings on occupational accidents, which demonstrate that workers in small enterprises face considerably greater risk of suffering a serious or fatal injury than those in larger enterprises; and widespread observation that systematic approaches to occupational health and safety management are seldom developed in small enterprises to the extent that they are in larger ones. While at the same time these small enterprises are often quite remote from inspection and control and cannot access professional advice.

Policy and Regulatory Responses

There are several important policy implications that follow from these observations. First, is the fact that most of the unwanted health consequences from chemical use are preventable and it is possible to avoid the exposures that cause them. Second, faced with uncertainties concerning the nature and extent of possible ill health associated with exposure to chemical substances, there is a degree of choice. Traditionally preventive action has been sought when there is sufficient evidence of a link between the exposure and disease; however, the many disasters that were allowed to occur as a result of this approach has led to the application of the so-called "precautionary principle" in relation to such uncertainties. This principle requires that action be taken to manage uncertainties as well as to address known risks.

The implications of these two issues leads to a third: regulatory strategies are required to address the risks and uncertainties surrounding the use of chemicals. Such strategies have been in use since the 1980s and are based around a prioritization of action in which the responsibility for prevention of unwanted exposure has been sought at increasingly higher levels in chemical supply, while at the same time a hierarchy of approaches to minimizing downstream exposures has developed. In other words, regulatory approaches have increasingly emphasized the responsibility of manufacturers for assessing the health risks of the substances they produce and insuring their minimization. At the same time, the law has further required the prohibition of the manufacture or supply of certain substances. Principles of safe substitution are encouraged both in the manufacture and use of chemical substances, and concepts of risk management have developed in which suppliers, having complied with their obligations to assess and minimize the risks of their products, are additionally required to provide sufficient information for users to manage residual risks adequately according to a hierarchy of exposure control.

National and EU Regulatory Strategies

Chapters 2 and 3 drew attention to the regulatory frameworks governing chemical risk management at work, both from the immediate past as well as those of the future—at least those that can be foreseen in relation to the introduction of REACH. They demonstrate how a hierarchy of good practice is intended to help users in their risk management tasks. Again, substitution and risk assessment are emphasized and followed by an approach to prevention or control that prioritizes engineering controls such as enclosure and LEV, working through further controls such as other forms of ventilation, systems of work and proper use of personal protection. However, as in all systems, there are structural pre-requisites that are necessary to support effective operation. In the case of chemical risk management, REACH will fundamentally shift the burden of responsi-bilities to ensure the safety of chemical substances from the state to industry, through its requirements on manufacturers to assess the risks of their products and to manage them safely by providing better information on hazards, risks and how to manage them and passing it down the supply chain. In turn, it places new responsibilities on users to comply with manufacturers' information and to inform them if their products are being used in ways different from those intended by the manufacturer. While this seems like a rational development for risk communication, there are nevertheless some questions it raises concerning the prerequisites that will need to be in place, both in supply chains and at the level of the downstream user, to ensure its effective operation as a system for managing chemical risks. In the case of small firms, with their well-established poor record of compliance with chemical regulation regimes, it is important that such prerequisites are properly understood.

Prerequisites for Effective Implementation: Institutional Mediation and the Impact of REACH

Chapter 4 established the identity of the major institutional actors that have an impact in various ways in supporting chemical risk management in small firms in the countries studied. In Chapter 5 a typology of the tools that have been developed to help implement this support was outlined and in Chapter 6 the available evidence of the effectiveness of these tools and the involvement of the institutional actors that have helped create them was reviewed. As noted, the most striking feature about this evidence is how limited it is. Despite this, however, several conclusions are apparent.

First, it is clear that various forms of institutional mediation have been necessary prerequisites supporting chemical risk management in small firms in all the countries studied. Without such support there are clear problems of compliance with statutory requirements concerning the use of hazardous chemicals that are mainly ascribed to lack of knowledge and resources on the part of small firms.

Second, there is considerable variety in the nature of the institutions providing support in different countries. There would seem to be the greatest differences between countries in which there are sectoral level infrastructures that actively promote a range of tools to support chemical risk management as is evident in Germany and in countries such as the UK where sectoral infrastructures are particularly weak.

Third, and more negatively, although in countries like Germany highly developed sectoral infrastructures have facilitated the growth of a rich collection of tools that are intended to help small firms better manage chemical risk, there is little sign of the emergence of a national strategic direction for this development. As a result there is little if any coordination of development, there may be considerable duplication and there are poor opportunities for knowledge transfer. Conversely, but with equally negative consequences, in the UK where there is a well-developed strategic position at the national level on the use of generic approaches to exposure assessment and chemical risk management resulting in the development of both the EASE model and COSHH Essentials, the weak infrastructural support at the sectoral level leaves the delivery of this strategy to small firms without any significant support.

Countries such as the Netherlands also have highly developed sectoral level infrastructures, although for different reasons than Germany. Also in the Netherlands the Dutch *poldermodel* tradition in the approach to social and economic life may be a further significant factor in promoting the developments observed there. Acting in concert, these two features seem to have provided for the emergence of a coherent strategic approach at the national level. In it, a combination of covenants and the VASt program perhaps comes closer to a strategically coordinated, sectorally based chemicals strategy that is potentially of help to small firms and one that could also be helpful in providing some of the necessary prerequisites to support the role of supply-chain communications as envisaged in REACH. In a less formalized way, the development and dissemination of support tools in Sweden seems to have at least in part been facilitated by the strong traditions of social dialogue and the existence of joint industry and trade union structures that support both the development and delivery of tools. In Austria the combination of a strong and legally mandated sectoral infrastructure, with a well-developed social insurance provision, has allowed for the development of a targeted strategy specifically helping small firms with risk management.

A More Complex Understanding of Role of the Supply Chain

A fourth relevant feature that emerges from the findings of previous chapters is that many of the most prominent institutional actors helping small firms to manage the risks of the chemical substances are not direct actors in the supply chain. Most examples of supply chains in chemicals follow the model shown in Figure 6.3. There is some evidence for the idea that small firm owner/managers rely most on their suppliers for their information on the chemicals they use. But equally, there is considerable evidence of problems with the quality of such material as well as with the capacity of small firms to use it properly, without support. In this review, based on published sources and interviews in several countries, the actors that emerged as the most significant supporters of interventions to *help* small firms manage the risks of the chemicals they use, were outside the direct supply chain; for example, regulatory agencies and their inspectors, statutory accident insurance associations, OHS practitioners and preventive services and trade union regional health and safety representatives. They are most likely to operate, or have the potential to operate, as part of the "constellation of actors" (to borrow the term used to describe them by Ahrens et al., 2006), that apply leverage to supply chains rather than as part of the supply chain itself. Some further strategic thought needs to be given to the role of these actors in the future, if the supply chain is to assume such central importance under REACH.

SIGNIFICANCE OF THE FINDINGS FOR THE IMPLEMENTATION OF REACH

There are several assumptions in the thinking behind the reliance on supply-chain relationships as the basis for improved chemical risk management among downstream users that could bear some closer scrutiny in the light of the findings of this study.

As detailed in Chapter 2, in cases where manufacturers and importers of chemicals will be responsible for providing risk management measures to downstream users that go beyond information in safety data sheets and labels, they are expected to attach "exposure scenarios" to the safety data sheets. Compliance with REACH will mean that the exposure scenarios will need to cover all the identified uses of the substance: the conditions for use, including process descriptions and the frequency and duration of specified operations; risk management measures, including controls of processes and emissions, PPE, etc. factors that might affect exposure levels; and they must address health issues including those for workers, as well as environmental issues. This approach clearly has antecedents in the exposure assessment modeling as well as the generic tools for chemical risk management discussed in the previous chapter and in many ways can be regarded as a logical development, integrating these approaches into a regulatory framework. But volume qualifications on supply before such measures apply will mean that, in practice, they are unlikely to affect most chemical use in small firms. Moreover, it remains to be seen whether small enterprises using such substances have the will and capacity to use such information appropriately, or what other incentives or interventions may be necessary to encourage them to do so. It is far from clear whether this process of risk communication through the supply chain will be of any relevance to the needs of workers in small enterprises at the more remote ends of supply chains.

According to a spokesperson for the Commission (Karhu, 2006), exposure scenarios "may cover a range of processes, uses and/or be applicable to many substances" they "shall be as detailed as needed to ensure that risks are adequately controlled . . . proportional to the risk," which is all very well, but this catch-all approach leaves many practical questions unanswered concerning both the willingness of management to produce such documentation as well as the support that users in small enterprises might need to understand and use it appropriately. Downstream users will be required under REACH to do these things. They must ensure that the use they make of substances are covered by the exposure scenario and implement risk management measures and operational conditions that are at least as effective as those detailed in the exposure scenario. Alternatively, if the use is different, the downstream users must inform the supplier so that it can be made an identified use in the chemical safety assessment, or else they must conduct their own chemical safety assessment for this use themselves (Christensen et al., 2003, pp. 10-13). While there are unlikely to be many small enterprises that are faced with the latter obligation, upward communication in the supply chain is likely to require a degree of confidence and technical understanding of the relevant issues concerning chemical risk management that, it has been well established, are not possessed by many owner/managers in small enterprises.

Despite the existence of sophisticated legislative frameworks and their considerable institutional support for ensuring the protection of workers from unhealthy exposure to hazardous substances, evidence of operation has pointed to major gaps between policy and practice. Such gaps are known to be especially evident in relation to users in small firms, where major problems have been identified with regard to the knowledge and understanding of the requirements for safe use, the quality of the supply of information concerning such requirements and its dissemination to workers, as well as the absence of required environmental monitoring where hazardous substances are in use; all of which indicates that to expect such firms to engage in a new form of risk communication, involving them in a proactive approach, solely on the basis of a EU Regulation, is optimistic. If this approach is to be effective, it will require considerable support. Agencies that can supply such support are likely to be from among those already identified, but the kind of support needed may be different from that currently supplied.

Some confirmation that these kinds of issues may be important is beginning to emerge from findings of work currently undertaken on behalf of the European Commission. Not surprisingly, in the run up to REACH, it took steps to commission a number of studies to investigate the feasibility of the proposed requirements and to anticipate some of the challenges prior to their implementation. These projects are known as REACH Implementation Projects (RIPs).

Two strands are particularly relevant. One concerns the development of guidance for manufacturers, importers, and downstream users on how to carry out the chemical safety assessment covering workers, consumers and the environment. This includes documenting appropriate risk management measures in exposure scenarios and communicating information to downstream users with safety data sheets according to REACH (RIP 3.2.1, 2006). The second strand concerns providing downstream users with guidance on their obligations under REACH regarding the use of substances, exposure scenarios and what information they should expect to be communicated up and down the supply chain (RIP 3.5.1, 2006). At the time of writing, the projects commissioned in both these RIPs are still in progress, and only a limited amount of information on them has so far been published.[1] Nevertheless they note a number of potential problem areas for small enterprises concerning risk communication in the supply chain, many of which echo those addressed here. Moreover they identify several additional barriers to risk communication that are found in some chemical product supply chains. They include issues of economic confidentiality, where revealing detailed information on processes and substances, deemed necessary under requirements for exposure scenarios and those for changed use, may be perceived to conflict with notions of business advantage, especially among firms competing in quality-driven markets.

Although requirements on safety data sheets and on REACH specify information to be available in national languages, existing research has shown this to be frequently not the case in practice. RIP 3.5.1 further suggests that requesting and obtaining additional specific information will be particularly difficult for small enterprises operating within global product chains because of limited language skills. Further reasons include their position in the supply chain and their limited resources. Many small enterprise downstream users obtain their chemical products from distributors rather than their original manufacturers and have most contact with such distributors, whose own understanding of health and safety issues may be limited, but who act as a potential barrier between small enterprises and the primary supplier and manufacturer. It is also noted that exposure scenarios that are broadly defined may in fact require some expertise in deciding whether they cover the uses that a downstream user intends for a particular product, or whether the downstream user needs to inform the supplier of

---

[1] The Web site http://europa.eu.int/comm/enterprise/reach/index.htm provides full European Commission documentation of REACH. For a list of current published documents for all of the RIPs, see http://ecb.jrc.it/REACH/>Documents>public access?RIP final reports.

a different use. Again small enterprises are unlikely to possess such expertise or the resources with which to obtain it.

All this also assumes that small enterprise owner/managers are motivated to seek this information and that suppliers are equally motivated to provide it. However, since research has tended to establish that achievement of legal obligations on managing chemical risks is not a priority in the majority of SMEs, the perceived relevance of the service offered by suppliers to help with this task is questionable and it is unclear how much it is likely to be a significant influence on the choice of the purchase of chemical product by the user. Taking into account that in many cases the costs for such an information service will not be met by the gains from the sales of the product, it may be further the case that suppliers who, in principle, provide that service on request may not be keen to increase the demand for it. Against such a background it becomes clear that the examples mentioned in the last few chapters concerning the positive engagement of supply-chain actors in are indications of good practice rather than a measure of how widespread is their use.

In short, these findings add further support to the conclusion that there is little sign that under REACH, despite its greater regulatory acknowledgment of the role of supply chains, small enterprises will require any less support to implement their approaches to chemical risk management than they do under existing provisions. However, there are some indications that the quality and focus of this support may need to be somewhat different under the new regulatory framework. There are therefore some issues that the actors and agencies involved will need to take into account.

WAYS FORWARD

Some of the issues that require further exploration if improvement in the effectiveness of chemical risk management in small enterprises is to be achieved include the following:

Inspection and Control

Even though it is quite clear that direct experience of inspection is never going to apply to more than a tiny percentage of small enterprises, previous research shows its possibility remains a powerful stimulus for compliance in small firms. However, since it is the capacity rather than will to comply that seems to be the major barrier for most small firms, the first question for inspection agencies is how do they maintain the strength of the incentive represented by the possibility of enforcement, while at the same time helping small firms acquire the necessary capacity for compliance. Of course, how they achieve this in a regulatory environment in which their own resources are likely to diminish and where the role of regulation is increasingly viewed politically as a barrier to the operation of neoliberal market economies is a major challenge. In addition, the impact of REACH suggests that further reorientation of the approach of inspectorates may be required. As Figure 6.3 illustrates, traditional regulatory inspection can operate as one of the elements of regulative pull on the supply chain, requiring evidence of properly constituted information supplied to downstream users being put to proper use in workplaces, but it also has a potential role at other nodes within chemical product supply chains from supplier through to final downstream use.

Additionally, inspectors may be required to provide clarity in cases of possible conflicts between requirements of REACH and those under other measures concerning the safe use of chemical substances at work. The most significant challenge for inspectorates is likely to be found in the implicit notion of REACH as a self-regulating system for a mature industry. The extent to which such a concept will apply to small enterprises is highly debatable and therefore there will remain a role for inspection in these cases; but how this role can be best delivered and balanced within the broader support for self-regulation through supply-chain relationships will need considerable strategic thinking on the part of regulatory agencies. It is also likely to demand a degree of reorientation of inspectors themselves; there are therefore significant implications in this for the future organization and training of inspectorates.

A related issue concerns the extent to which the program for coordinating and sharing experiences, including those of national inspectorates, provided for under REACH will operate in practice. It has been indicated that a "forum for the exchange of information on enforcement" at the European level, under the aegis of the European Chemicals Agency is to be set up under REACH.[2] Its tasks include:

- spreading good practice and highlighting problems at the community level;
- proposing, coordinating and evaluating harmonized enforcement projects and joint inspections;
- coordinating exchanges of inspectors;
- identifying enforcement strategies and best practice;
- developing working methods and tools for local inspectors;
- developing an electronic information exchange procedure;
- liaising with industry and other stakeholders; and
- examining proposals for restrictions with a view to advising on their enforceability.

---

[2] According to Parts IX and XIII of the REACH Proposal.

Potentially therefore, an important mechanism may exist for sharing under-standings of what works in regulating chemical risk management in small enter-prises and what makes it work. However current experience suggests this may be optimistic. Information about the many individual cases of good practice that exist in northern European countries remains largely specialist knowledge and general access to it is limited. Greater steps could already have been taken in the direction of information sharing through better access and dissemination at the EU level. There are agencies such as the European Agency for Safety and Health at Work already in place to achieve this, as well as actors within the European chemical industry that could play similar roles. However, as demon-strated, access to information remains problematic and duplication of efforts in supporting chemical risk management in small firms is also a frequent occurrence. On the basis of this evidence therefore, there is little to suggest that such a "forum" as is proposed in REACH would achieve any more than existing structures have done.

Infrastructural Supports, Specificity and Transfer

This study has identified a range of infrastructural supports that are shown to be necessary prerequisites for better risk management of hazardous substances in small enterprises. It also demonstrated considerable variation in the extent of such support, reflecting different regulatory and economic infrastructures in different countries. There are obvious implications here for national-level policymakers contemplating effective strategies for improving the management of risks of chemical substances in small enterprises. However, the study has also pointed out that there is limited evaluation of the effectiveness of these supports or what aspects of their engagement it is that makes them effective.

A related major consideration that emerges from the evaluation of experiences to date concerns the question of the specificity of new approaches to exposure assessment and control. Despite the attraction of the potential widespread use of generic approaches to chemical risk management, the reality is that supports for application are often highly sector specific and dependent on this specificity for the preconditions that underpin their success. While there is evidence that some approaches developed in one sector are transferable to others, or their extension to other trades is intended or underway, if an integral part of the approach in question involves the existence or the installation of a support structure, the issue becomes more complex. Yet as we have seen, other than to acknowledge the existence of sectoral and regional social and organizational conditions, little attention has been paid to the effects of such factors in evalu-ations to date. Indeed, few evaluations take explicit account of the regulatory, social and economic contexts in which such transfer or its support occurs or directly address the consequences of these contexts for the effectiveness, transferability and sustainability of improvements. This absence provides a significant and immediate challenge for future research. The findings from such work would be especially apposite in relation to the likely implementation of approaches to deliver REACH at national levels in the near future.

REACH and the Hard to Reach:
Where Leverage in Supply Chains May Not Be Sufficient

Users themselves have contributed to complicating the logistics of supply in recent decades. The organization of work has become more fragmented, with a rise in outsourcing and subcontracting as well as in the use of agency workers. Much work involving chemical substances, such as cleaning and maintenance operations, once undertaken by large end-user organizations, is now subcontracted to smaller firms and individuals. In all these developments, use of chemicals by workers in small firms has become increasingly remote from the organizations supplying the chemicals. That there are sometimes serious problems of exposure experienced by such workers that are not properly managed is well documented.

This is an aspect of the failure of wider approaches to systematic health and safety management under fragmented organizational-management structures, in which poor risk communication is an important element. Further thought needs to be given concerning ways in which employers' responsibilities can be effectively delivered for example in multiemployer worksites.

One of the reasons why newer approaches to chemical risk management are proposed is the idea that they will extend improved practices to situations that are hard to reach by traditional means. The extent to which these developments will effect improved risk management in situations in which exposures to hazardous substances may be experienced by workers that are quite remote from relations between suppliers and users, needs to be addressed realistically. Outsourcing, subcontracting and the fragmented management arrangements that are frequently a feature of multiemployer worksites create situations in which many workers are ill-equipped to deal with the risk of hazardous exposures. They may be poorly trained, inadequately informed, have limited access to protective equipment and be in unfamiliar work environments or ones that have not been subject to risk assessment, while at the same time being quite remote from the safety management system theoretically in place at a particular worksite. They may be in these situations as a direct result of large organizations outsourcing their risks to smaller concerns. In all such situations, it is important to ensure that safety management systems are in place in which adequate risk communication and risk assessment are assured for such work and the workers involved.

Experiences in industries like construction show it is possible to achieve this through the greater involvement of trade union health and safety representatives in representing the interests of workers other than those of their employer. Ways of more effectively promoting and supporting such representation could be considered (Walters & Nichols, 2007; also Walters, 2001). However, trade union membership has been in decline for decades in most EU countries and the presence of trade union representatives in many sectors in which small enterprises dominate cannot be taken for granted. Providing regulatory requirements for those at the head of supply chains and linking such requirements with others on intermediaries and end users in supply chains is no doubt helpful—here again REACH is a step in the right direction—but there remains room for considerable further study of the possible ways in which such regulatory initiatives can better support risk management in hard-to-reach scenarios.

The Role of the Polity

The point has been made that supply chains are not isolated from their wider regulatory and socioeconomic milieu but the same point applies to chemical risk management more generally. This implies that ultimately the role of wider societal organization and awareness of the risks of working with chemical substances, and its preparedness to tolerate such risks, will condition the extent of the standards of safety that are required. Thus, attitudes expressed in the media, decisions taken in the courts, the prominence of work-based issues on the agendas of environmental groups, the question of consumer tolerance of chemicals used in the production of consumer goods all have a bearing on what is deemed to be acceptable in workplace exposure to chemicals and, as Ahrens et al. (2006) have pointed out, will help to determine both the extent of regulatory intervention and market influence on chemical risk management strategies of both suppliers and users.

In most advanced economies, societal concerns over environmental consequences of chemical production, use and waste and about the presence of chemical substances in foods and consumer goods acknowledge the universality of perceived risks. Moreover, the level of public concern and the demands for action it engenders are significant enough to be taken seriously by regulators and industry. They are also sufficiently significant to merit the attention of businesses to issues of brand confidence and corporate social responsibility; not for reasons of altruism on the part of business, but because they are issues that are regarded as important influences on business performance and profits. All this creates pressure for change in the nature of chemicals produced and for the stewardship of such products from "cradle to cradle."

It is curious therefore that within this heightened awareness of the consequences of chemical production for the environment and the public, the position concerning the use of chemicals at the workplace has changed relatively little.

The traditional separation of the ways in which risks of the work environment are addressed from the ways in which engagement takes place with risks to the wider public and environment is evident in the features of workplace chemical risk management, whether they concern technical, regulatory, or organizational aspects. As work becomes more and more characterized by open networks for production and services, occupational risks become increasingly less bounded by traditional constructions of the employment relationship. Traditional separations between work, public and environmental risk are less relevant and less useful ways of understanding risk and its control in these situations. The supply-chain elements of REACH, its coverage of production, use and disposal of chemicals, and their consequences for workers, consumers and the environment are in part a regulatory acknowledgment of this changed world. As such it presents an opportunity to review the continued usefulness of traditional separations and to move toward a more all-embracing framework for regulating the management of chemical risks, including those faced in small enterprises and other hard-to-reach scenarios. However this study confirms that the challenges of so doing should not be underestimated, especially with regard to the necessary preconditions for these new approaches and the supports required for their effectiveness in small enterprises.

The Need for Better Evidence

Examples have demonstrated the limitations of existing evaluation of the success of support strategies and tools. The conclusions reached are important enough to bear repetition here. Properly structured and targeted research that accounts for such differences in its evaluation of the supports and constraints to chemical risk management in small enterprises is urgently required, and this is no less so under REACH than previously. The RIP series is a start in this direction, but so far their products are as indicative of the long way still to go in terms of analytical research addressing these issues as they are of any substantial findings.

*   *   *

The risk of harmful effects from working with chemicals in small enterprises remains high and there is much to suggest that as a result of the limitations of risk management it is proportionally higher within them than in larger enterprises faced with similar hazards. While previous chapters showed there is a lot that can be done to support risk management in small enterprises, in the end it is unlikely that such a focus on risk assessment and management on the part of users in these enterprises will alone provide a solution to the problem. For this reason, and because of the continuing uncertainties concerning the nature and extent of the manufactured risks associated with chemical production and use, it is imperative that overall strategies on risk management are conditioned by the use of precautionary principles and that "end of pipe" solutions are not allowed to dominate the approach. This means that further strategic thinking about the role of substitution is required and applied throughout supply chains, focused not only on the notion of safer products, but also safer machinery, equipment and processes. In this sense, substitution should be understood as a much wider concept than merely *the replacement of substances* with those thought to be safer. It must also be recognized that product supply chains do not exist in isolation from the effects of wider public, regulatory, market and consumer interests. Economic relations between individual suppliers and the users of their products are important points of leverage for improved risk management; but in a wider view of the location of supply chains in society and the economy, it becomes clear they are not the only points at which influences to achieve safer and healthier workplaces may be applied. At the same time, the issue of cost-effectiveness and practicability of strategic support for chemical risk management in small firms needs to be borne in mind.

Thinking along these lines is already evident in some recent treatments of the subject (see for example Ahrens et al., 2006). It is also possible that the supply-chain focus of REACH will support the further development of the approach in practice. However, as previously argued, before this can occur there are many prerequisites that need to be in place.

Above all else, it should be apparent from the evidence presented here that small enterprises are not homogenous. Apart from size, they often they have little in common, and they represent a multiplicity of challenges for risk management in which unitary prescriptions to address them are unlikely to be wholly successful. What is required are multiple strategies and instruments that are capable of addressing the multifactorial features of these enterprises that lead to increased vulnerability of their workers. In the case of chemical risk management, this means that a regulatory framework, even combined with a provision of support tools is on its own, insufficient to motivate owner/ managers in small enterprises sufficiently to ensure the widespread or effective operation.

As with health and safety support for small enterprises generally, face-to-face contact with change agents is generally indicated to produce more effective and sustainable results than other forms of support. However, achieving such contact is not straightforward and the existing literature is able to demonstrate only limited examples of success, transferability and sustainability in this respect. The effectiveness of approaches that use existing infrastructures and processes to support implementation therefore requires further examination. This is also why, at the very least, a more reflexive approach is required to understanding chemical risks and their substitution. Multidimensional strategies to ensure improved risk management in small enterprises and the preconditions to support their effectiveness are required; but they need to be developed and applied as one element within this wider reflexive approach, while acknowledging that a more innovative approach to the safer use of chemical substances in small enterprises needs innovation not only in relation to chemical production, but also with regard to its regulation and in making the most effective use of regulatory supports.

Overall, REACH provides some steps in the direction of a more comprehensive framework for chemical risk regulation in which the challenges of chemical use in small enterprises could be addressed. However, many structural supports are still required and most of all, considerable ingenuity is needed on the part of regulators, industry, trade unions and wider society to ensure such support is harnessed effectively. It remains to be seen whether in present economic and political climates there is sufficient will or capacity to ensure this occurs.

References

Ahrens, A., Braun, A., von Gleich, A., Heitman, K., & Lissner, L. (2006). *Hazardous chemicals in products and processes: Substitution as an innovative process.* Heidlberg: Physica-Verlag.

AK Wien (Ed.). (2001). *Arbeitsbedingungen. Zusammenfassung der Ergebnisse des Mikrozensus Juni 1999.* Vienna: Chamber of Labour of Vienna.

Allen, B. (2004). COSHH Essentials: A blunt tool. *Occupational Health Review, 112,* pp. 9-10.

Alvarez de Davila, E., Antonsson, A-B., & Frostling, H. (2002). *What support do companies and organisations need regarding chemicals? A pilot study.* IVL-report B1511, available at: www.ivl.se, http://www.ivl.se/rapporter/pdf/B1511.pdf (in Swedish).

Alvarez de Davila, E., & Cerne, O. (1999). *Substitutionsarbete vid svenska företag* [Substitution of chemicals—How is it done in Swedish companies?] IVL report B 1316.

AMS BG (Berufsgenossenschaft der Bauwirtschaft). (Ed.). (2005). Die Berufsgenossenschaft der Bauwirtschaft stellt AMS BAU vor: AMS BAU—Arbeitsschutz mit System. Berlin. Electronically available at: http://www.ams-bau.de

Antonsson, A-B. (2006). *Tools to support chemical risk management in small enterprises.* Swedish Environmental Research Institute, PowerPoint Presentation at: The International Workshop on Chemical Risk Management in SME, TNO, Amsterdam, May 12, 2006.

Antonsson, A-B. (2007). *Strategies for success? Managing chemical risks in small workplaces: A review of Swedish practice*, IVL report 1717, IVL, available at: http://www.ivl.se/rapporter/pdf/B1717.pdf

Antonsson, A-B., Axelsson, U., Birgersdotter, L., & Cerin, P. (2005). Miljö och arbetsmiljötillsyn i småföretag. En inledande studie. (Environmental and working environment inspections in small companies. An introductory study) IVL-report B1638) http://www.ivl.se/rapporter/pdf/B1638.pdf (In Swedish, English summary).

Antonsson, A-B., Birgersdotter, L., & Bornberger-Dankvardt, S. (2002). Small enterprises in Sweden—Health and safety and the significance of intermediaries in preventive health and safety. *Arbetet och Hälsa, 1.*

Antonsson A-B., & Schmidt, L. (2003). *Småföretag och företagshälsovård—Ska berget komma till Muhammed eller Muhammed till berget?* IVL report B 1542, available at: www.ivl.se, http://www.ivl.se/rapporter/pdf/B1542.pdf

AOK (Allgemeine Ortskrankenkasse Die Gesundheitskasse). (Ed.). (2005). Werkzeugkasten Gesunde Unternehmen. Electronically available at: http://www.aok-business.de/service/pragmagus/index.php?buland=0&buland2-0

ASMK (Konferenz der Arbeits- und Sozialminister). (Ed.). (2001). Handlungskonzept: Gesundheit bei der Arbeit—Notwendigkeit, Ziele, Strategien. Entwurfsfassung. In Behörde für Umwelt und Gesundheit, Amt für Arbeitsschutz (Ed.), *Arbeit & Gesundheit* (pp. 97-110). Tagungsdokumentation des Workshops am 19./20.6.2001 in Hamburg.

AUVA. (Ed.). (2002). *Gefährliche Arbeitsstoffe.* Merkblatt M 390. Vienna: Austrian Social Insurance for Occupational Risks. Download: www.auva.at/mediaDB/112448.PDF

AUVA. (Ed.). (2003a). *Auszug aus der Statistik 2002.* Vienna: Austrian Social Insurance for Occupational Risks. Download: www.auva.at/medialDB/49153.PDF

AUVA. (Ed.). (2003b). *Staub. Evaluierung—Gefahren ermitteln & beseitigen, E 9.* Vienna: Austrian Social Insurance for Occupational Risks. Download: www.auva.at/mediaDB/48829.PDF

AUVA. (Ed.). (2004a). *Auszug aus der Statistik 2003.* Vienna: Austrian Social Insurance for Occupational Risks. Download: www.auva.at/mediaDB/49157.PDF

AUVA. (Ed.). (2005a). *Auszug aus der Statistik 2004.* Vienna: Austrian Social Insurance for Occupational Risks. Download: www.auva.at/mediaDB/93185.PDF

AUVA. (J. Püringer, Ed.). (2005b). *CD-ROM ArbeitnehmerInnenschutz expert. Informationssystem ArbeitnehmerInnenschutz.* Vienna: Verlag Jusline.

AUVA. (Ed.). (2005c). *Gefahrenermittlung (Evaluierung).* Merkblatt M 040. Vienna: Austrian Social Insurance for Occupational Risks. Download: www.auva.at/mediaDB/118475.PDF

AUVA. (Ed.). (2006). *Chemische Arbeitsstoffe. Evaluierung—Gefahren ermitteln & beseitigen, E 4.* Vienna: Austrian Social Insurance for Occupational Risks. Download: www.auva.at/mediaDB/118581.PDF

Bartels, K. (1998). Grenzwertunabhängige Konzeptionen. In BIA-Report 4/98; *Symposium, Grenzwerte für chemische Einwirkungen an Arbeitsplätzen*'; Hauptverband der gewerblichen Berufsgenossenschaften (HVBG); Sankt Augustin, 199 pp.

Barth, C. (2000). *Betriebsärztliche Kleinbetriebsbetreuung, Bedarfsabschätzung, Strategien, zeitgemäße Betreuungsmodelle.* Schriftenreihe der BAuA—Forschung—Fb 904; Dortmund/Berlin, 356 pp.

BASIS (Branchen-und Arbeitsschutz-Informations-System der Berufsgenossenschaft Druck und Papierverarbeitung). (Ed.). (2004). Modul Hand- & Hautschutz. Wiesbaden 2004 (last update: 15.10.2005). Electronically available at: http://www.basis-dp.de/als/index.html

Batzdorfer, L., & Schwanitz, H. J. (2004). Ökonomische Folgen berufsbedingter Hauterkrankungen. In *Die BG 2004,* pp. 278-280.

BAuA (Bundesanstalt für Arbeitsschutz und Arbeitsmedizin). (Ed.). (1999). Europäische Woche für Sicherheit und Gesundheit bei der Arbeit. Von der Werkstattplanung bis zur Führung des Betriebes. Informationstagung für das Kfz-Handwerk am 30. Oktober 1998. Schriftenreihe der BAuA—Forschungsanwendung—Fa 44; Dortmund/Berlin, 229 pp.

BAuA (Bundesanstalt für Arbeitsschutz und Arbeitsmedizin). (Ed.). (2005). Einfaches Maßnahmenkonzept Gefahrstoffe. Eine Handlungshilfe für die Anwendung der Gefahrstoffverordnung in Klein- und Mittelbetrieben bei Gefahrstoffen ohne Arbeitsplatzgrenzwert. Dortmund 2005, 40 pp.

BAuA (Bundesanstalt für Arbeitsschutz und Arbeitsmedizin) et al. (Ed.). (2004a). Checkliste für staubarme Arbeitsbereiche in Tischlereien, bei Möbelherstellern und

Holzverarbeitern. Dortmund, 2 pp. Electronically available at:
http://www.baua.de/nn_12322/de/Themen-von-A-Z/Gefahrstoffe/Arbeiten-mit-
Gefahrstoffen/pdf/Checkliste-Holzstaub.pdf

BAuA (Bundesanstalt für Arbeitsschutz und Arbeitsmedizin) et al. (Ed.). (2004b).
Checkliste "Gefahrstoffe" zur Einsparung von Arbeitsplatzmessungen in Kfz-
Recycling-Betrieben. Dortmund 2004, 3 pp. Eelectronically available at:
http://www.baua.de/nn_12322/de/Themen-von-A-Z/Gefahrstoffe/Arbeiten-mit-
Gefahrstoffen/pdf/Checkliste-Kfz-Recycling.pdf

BAYERN (Bayerisches Staatsministerium für Arbeit und Sozialordnung, Familie, Frauen
und Gesundheit). (Ed.). (2001). *Schriftenreihe Managementsysteme für Arbeitsschutz
und Anlagensicherheit; Occupational Health- and Risk-Managementsystem* (Bd. 4):
Handlungsanleitung für kleine und mittlere Unternehmen. München 2001, 140 pp.
Electronically available at:
http://www.umweltministerium.bayer.de/application/eshop000008?APPL=ESHOP&
FRAMEPAGE=applstart.htm&DIR=eshop&ACTIONxSETVAL(index.htm,USERx
BODYURL:artlist1.htm,APGxNODENR:1349).

Beck, U. (1992). *Risk society: Towards a new modernity.* London: Sage.

BG DRUPA (Berufsgenossenschaft Druck und Papierverarbeitung). (Ed.). (2001).
*Offsetdruck: Gesundheitsschutz im Offsetdruck. Feuchtmittelzusätze für Akzidenz-
rotationen und Bogendruckmaschinen.* Wiesbaden.

BG DRUPA (Berufsgenossenschaft Druck und Papierverarbeitung). (Ed.). (2002).
*Offsetdruck: Bogendruck ohne Alkohol im Feuchtwerk—Erfolgreiches Vorgehen
beim Ersatz von Isopropylalkohol (IPA).* Wiesbaden 2001. Electronically available at:
http://www.bgdp.de/pages/arbeitssicherheit/brancheninfo/offsetdruck/tft-2002-6-S22.htm

BG DRUPA (Berufsgenossenschaft Druck und Papierverarbeitung). (Ed.). (2004a).
Arbeitssicherheit und Gesundheitsschutz. Gefährdungsbeurteilung. Wiesbaden o.J.
Electronically available at:
http://www.bgdp.de/pages/arbeitssicherheit/grundinfo/gefaehrdungsbeurteilung.htm

BG DRUPA (Berufsgenossenschaft Druck und Papierverarbeitung). (Ed.). (2004b). *Rasch
und komfortabel Schutzhandschuhe und Hautschutzmittel finden.* Wiesbaden 2004.

BG DRUPA (Berufsgenossenschaft Druck und Papierverarbeitung). (Ed.). (2005).
Washing and Cleaning Agents for the Offset Printing Industry—Admissible Products.
01/2005 edition. Wiesbaden 2005.

BG FE (Berufsgenossenschaft der Feinmechanik und Elektrotechnik). (Ed.). (2001).
*Gefahrstoffe in der Galvanotechnik und der Oberflächenveredlung. Eine
Handlungshilfe als Grundlage zur Gefährdungsermittlung und -beurteilung nach dem
Arbeitsschutzgesetz.* Köln, 68 pp. plus CD-ROM.

BG FE (Berufsgenossenschaft der Feinmechanik und Elektrotechnik). (Ed.). (2002).
*Gefahrstoffe im Elektromaschinenbau. Eine Handlungshilfe zur Gefährdungsermittlung
und -beurteilung durch Gefahrstoffe nach dem Arbeitsschutzgesetz.* Köln, 23 pp.

BG FE (Berufsgenossenschaft der Feinmechanik und Elektrotechnik). (Ed.). (2004).
Informationsmaterial 2004/2005. Sicherheit in Schrift, Bild und Ton. Köln 2002,
72 pp. electronically available at:
http://www.bgfe.de/bilder/pdf/d_17_a08-2004klein.pdf

BGIA (Berufsgenossenschaftliches Institut für Arbeitsschutz). (Ed.). (2005a). *GESTIS—
Database on hazardous substances.* Sankt Augustin. English version electronically
available at: http://www.hvbg.de/e/bia/fac/stoffdb/index.html

BGIA (Berufsgenossenschaftliches Institut für Arbeitsschutz). (Ed.). (2005b). *International Chemical Safety Cards (ICSC)—Deutsche Version*. Sankt Augustin. Electronically available at: http://www.hvbg.de/d/bia/fac/icsc/index.html

BGIA (Berufsgenossenschaftliches Institut für Arbeitsschutz). (Ed.). (2005c). *ISI—Informationsstelle für Sicherheitsdatenblätter*. Sankt Augustin 2005. Electronically available at: http://www.hvbg.de/d/bia/fac/isi-db/index.html

BGIA (Berufsgenossenschaftliches Institut für Arbeitsschutz) (Ed.). (2006). *Spaltenmodell zur Suche nach Ersatzstoffen*. Electronically available at: http://www.hvbg.de/d/bia/pra/spalte/index.html English version: Column pattern for chemical substitiutes. Electronically available at: http://www.hvbg.de/e/bia/pra/spalte/index.html

BGW (Berufsgenossenschaft für Gesundheitsdienst und Wohlfahrtspflege). (Ed.). (2002). Neues Internetangebot der BGW: „Virtuelle Praxis"; in: *Die Berufsgenossenschaft, 487.*

BGW (Berufsgenossenschaft für Gesundheitsdienst und Wohlfahrtspflege). (Ed.). (2004). *Virtuelle Praxis. Hamburg o.J.*, electronically available at: http://www.bgw-online.de/internet/generator/Navi-bgw-online/NavigationLinks/Virtuelle_20Praxis/navi.html

Bender, H. F. (2005). *Mitgelieferte Gefährdungsbeurteilung. Vortrag auf der BAuA-Tagung 'Neue Gefahrstoffverordnung.'* Dortmund. Download: http://download.baua.de/prax/gefahrstoffe/gefahrstofflagung2005-06.pdf

Bieneck, H.-J., & Rückert, A. (1992). Das Unternehmermodell. *Bundesarbeitsblatt 9,* 18-20.

Birchall, S., & Finlayson H. (1996). The application of European derived safety management regulations to the UK construction industry. In L. Alves Dias, L., Alves Dias, L. M., & R. J. Coble (Eds.), *Implementation of safety and health on construction sites*. Rotterdam: Balkema.

Blank, V., Andersson, R., Linden, A., & Nilsson, B. (1995). Hidden accident rates and patterns in the Swedish mining industry due to the involvement of contract workers. *Safety Science, 21,* 23-25.

BMA (Bundesministerium für Arbeit und Sozialordnung). (Ed.). (1992). Arbeitssicherheitsgesetz. Betriebsärztliche Betreuung von Kleinbetrieben. Schreiben des BMA vom 9 Juni. *Bundesarbeitsblatt, 7(8),* 66-69.

BMA (Bundesministerium für Arbeit und Sozialordnung). (Ed.). (2002). *Neue Ideen gesucht—Hervorragende Lösungen gefunden: 5mal Gefahrstoffschutzpreis*. Berlin 2002, 40 pp. Electronically available at: http://www.baua.de/down/gefahrstoffschutzpreis.pdf

BMAGS. (Ed.). (1999). *Die Tätigkeit der Arbeitsinspektion im Jahr 1998*. Vienna: Federal Ministry of Labour, Health and Social Affairs.

BMLFUW. (Ed.). (2002a). Chemikalien-Leasing. Modell für eine nachhaltige Stoffwirtschaft. *BMLFUW Schriftenreihe* Bd. 13/2002. Vienna: Federal Ministry of Agriculture, Forestry, Environment and Water Management. Download: www.umweltnet.at/filemanager/download/7939/

BMLFUW. (Ed.). (2002b, August). Chemical leasing. A model for sustainable businesses in the chemicals area. English abstract. *BMLFUW Schriftenreihe, 13.* Vienna: Federal Ministry of Agriculture, Forestry, Environment and Water Management. Download: www.umweltnet.at/filemanager/download/7941/

BMLFUW. (Ed.). (2003). Konferenz "Experiences and Perspectives of Service-Oriented Strategies in the Chemicals Industry and in Related Areas." In *Kooperation mit der OECD—Präsentationsunterlagen*. Vienna: Federal Ministry of Agriculture, Forestry, Environment and Water Management. Download: www.umweltnet.at/article/articleview/26848/1/7043

BMWA. (Ed.). (2003). Leitfaden für Arbeitsschutzmanagementsysteme des Bundesministeriums für Wirtschaft und Arbeit (BMWA), der obersten Arbeitsschutzbehörden der Bundesländer, der Träger der gesetzlichen Unfallversicherung und der Sozialpartner. In *Bundesarbeitsblatt, 1*, 101-109. Electronically available at: http://www.baua.de/prax/ams/leitfaden_ams.pdf

BMWA. (Ed.). (2004a). *Arbeitsstoffe—Ein Leitfaden für den sicheren Umgang mit Arbeitsstoffen*. Vienna: Federal Ministry of Economics and Labour. Download: www.arbeitsinspektion.gv.at/NR/rdonlyres/2B8BC7E5-3FFD-42A9-B533-5DA5883 8F6F3/0/asto_br.pdf

BMWA. (Ed.). (2004b). *Grenzwerte und krebserzeugende Arbeitsstoffe*. Vienna: Federal Ministry of Economics and Labour. Download: www.arbeitsinspektion.gv.at/NR/rdonlyres/96913C39-5A93-4CAA-8823-3D0F7391 2A97/0/gkv.pdf

BMWA. (Ed.). (2004c). *Die Tätigkeit der Arbeitsinspektion im Jahr 2003*. Vienna: Federal Ministry of Economics and Labour. Download: http://www.arbeitsinspektion.gv.at/NR/rdonlyres/4EAA3C47-9390-49F9-BC48-723 C01D3ECB4/0/jb2003.pdf

BMWA. (Ed.). (2005). *Die Tätigkeit der Arbeitsinspektion im Jahr 2004*. Vienna: Federal Ministry of Economics and Labour. Download: www.arbeitsinspektion.gv.at/NR/rdonlyres/FF6F8C9E-1521-40B1-B37C-BE25530A77A1/0/jb2004.pdf

Bochmann, F., Hartlieb, D., Meffert, K., Mur, J. M., Nold, A., Pils, P., & Stamm, R. (2004). *Work-related health risks: Research and company practice,* ISSA Prevention Series n0.2049. Paris: INRS (International Social Security Assocation). Download: research.prevention.issa.int/PDF/GTBoch_En.pdf

Boldt, U. (1997). Arbeitsmedizinische Information, Motivation und Beratung von Handwerkern (Schlussbericht). Schriftenreihe der BAuA—Forschung—Fb 766; Dortmund/Berlin 1997, 51 pp.

Breakwell, G. M., & Petts, J. (2001). *Stakeholder participation methods: A scoping study.* Sudbury, UK: HSE Contract Research Report, HSE Books.

Bredendiek-Kämper, S. (2001). Do EASE scenarios fit workplace reality? A validation study of the EASE model. *Applied Occupational and Environmental Hygiene, 16,* 182-187.

Briggs, D., & Crumbie, N. (2000). *Characteristics of people working with chemical products in small firms*. WS Atkins, CRR278/2000. Sudbury, UK: HSE Books.

Brooke I. (1998). A UK scheme to help small firms control health risks from chemicals: Toxicological considerations. *Annals of Occupational Hygiene, 42*(6), 377-390.

Brown, T., & Rushton, L. (2003). *The development of risk reduction strategies for the prevention of dermatitis in the UK printing industry*. Sudbury, UK: HSE research report 158, HSE Books.

BUK (Bundesverband der Unfallkassen). (Ed.). (2004). Umgang mit Gefahrstoffen auf dem Bauhof. GUV-Informationen GUV-I 8561. *Theorie und Praxis der Prävention.* München, 76 pp.

Bunt, K. (1993). *Occupational health provision at work.* Sudbury, UK: HSE Books.

Castillo, D., Landen, D., & Layne, L. (1994). Occupational injury deaths of 16 and 17 year olds in the United States of America. *American Journal of Public Health, 84*(4), 646-648.

Commission of the European Communities (EC). (1998). Commission Working Document (SEC) 1986 final. European Commission, Brussels.

CEFIC (European Chemical Industry). (2003, July 8). *Occupational diseases in the European chemical industry—Impact of REACH.* CEFIC Comments. Brussels: CEFIC.

CEFIC (European Chemical Industry). (2004a). www.cefic.org/factsandfigures/level02/downloads_index.html

CEFIC (European Chemical Industry). (2004b). *SMEs in the EU chemicals industry,* Download: www.cefic.org/files/Publications/SMEs-in-Cl.pdf

Chemical Industries Association (CIA). (1993). *Safe handling of colourants 2: Hazard classification and selection of occupational hygiene strategies.* London: Chemical Industries Association.

Chemical Industries Association (CIA). (1997). *Control of substances hazardous to health—Guidance on allocating occupational exposure bands (Regulation 7).* London: Chemical Industries Association.

Cherrie, J., McIntosh, C., Ritchie, P., & Sewell, C. (1999). *Voluntary reporting by UK industry of occupational exposure data on chemicals—A feasibility study.* Institute of Occupational Medicine, CRR 227/1999.

Cherrie, J., Tickner, J., Friar, J., Creely, K., Soutar, A., Hughson, G., Rae, R., Warrn, N., & Pryde, D. (2003). *Evaluation and further development of the EASE model 2.0.* Institute of Occupational Medicine. Sudbury, UK: HSE Books.

Christensen, F. M., de Bruijn, J. H. M., Hansen, B. G., Munn, S., Sokull-Klttgen, B., & Pedersen, F. (2003). Assessment tools under the new European Union Chemicals Policy. *GMI, 41,* 5-19.

Clapp, R., Howe, G., & Lefevre, M. J. (2005). *Environmental and occupational causes of cancer: A review of recent scientific literature.* Lowell Centre for Sustainable Production, University of Massachusetts, Lowell. Electronically available at: www.sustainableproduction.org

CLEANTOOL Consortium. (Ed.). (2004a). *CLEANTOOL. Innovative evaluation and design of industrial surface cleaning processes. Project Summary. Extract from the Final report.* Hamburg, electronically available at: http://www.cleantool.org/xct/downloads/summary_finalversion_041018.pdf

CLEANTOOL Consortium. (Ed.). (2004b). *CLEANTOOL. Optimierte Beurteilung und Planung von Metall-Oberflächenreinigung.* Hamburg o.J. Electronically available at: http://cleantool.org/lang/dt/start_d.htm English version: *CLEANTOOL.* Innovative Evaluation and Design of Metal Surface Cleaning Processes. Electronically available at: http://cleantool.org/lang/en/start_e.htm

CLEANTOOL Consortium. (Ed.). (2004c). *CLEANTOOL. Assistenten starten.* Hamburg, o.J. Electronically available at: http://www.cleantool.org/lang/dt/easy_datenabfrage.htm. English version: *CLEANTOOL. Start the Assistant.* Electronically available at: http://www.cleantool.org/lang/en/easy_datenabfrage.htm

CLEANTOOL Consortium. (Ed.). (2004d). *CLEANTOOL.* Forum, Magazine, Links, Literatur, Hamburg o.J. Electronically available at: http://www.cleantool.org/lang/dt/start_d.htm English version: *CLEANTOOL.* Fora,

Magazines, Links, Literature. Electronically available at:
http://www.cleantool.org/lang/en/start_e.htm

CLEEN (Chemical Legislation European Enforcement Network). (2004). *ECLIPS (European classification and labelling inspections of preparations including safety data sheets), Final report*:
http://www.umweltbundesamt.at/fileadmin/site/umweltthemen/chemikalien/ECLIPS _Final_Report.pdf.

Cox, P., Fischhoff, B., & Gerrard, S. (2000). *Developing a methodology for designing messages about chemical risks in the workplace using the mental models approach.* Report no. RSU 4048/R64.061. London: HSE Books.

Cox, P., Niewohner, J., Pidgeon, N., Gerrard, S., Fischhoff, B., & Riley, D. (2003). The use of mental models in chemical risk protection: Developing a generic workplace methodology. *Risk Analysis, 23*(2).

Creely, K., Leith, S., Graham, M., Cowie, H., Hughes, J., George, P. & Cherrie, J. W. (2003). *Effective communication of chemical hazard and risk information using a multimedia safety data sheet.* University of Aberdeen, RR 72, Sudbury, UK: HSE Books.

Creely, K. S., Tickner, J., Soutar, A. J. Hughson, G. W., Pryde, D. E., Warren, N. D., Rae, R., Money, C., Phillips, A., & Cherrie, J. W. (2005). Evaluation and further development of EASE model 2.0. *Annals of Occupational Hygiene, 49*(2), 135-145.

DARES (Direction del'Animation de la Reserche, des Etudes et des statistiques). (2005). Les expositions aux produits carcinogens. *Premiere Syntheses Informations, 28*(1).

Davis, D. L. (1990). Trends in cancer mortality in industrial countries. Report of an international workshop, Carpi, Italy, October 21-22, 1989. *Annals of the New York Academy of Sciences, 609*, 4.

Devilliers, J., Domine, D., Bintein, S., & Karcher, W. (1997). Occupational modelling with EASE, SAR, QSAR. *Environmental Research, 6*, 121-134.

Diekershoff, K. H. (1989). Alternativen untersucht. Modellversuch zur sicherheitstech-nischen Betreuung von Klein- und Mittelbetrieben. *Humane Produktion, 8*, 32-35.

Dobernowsky, M. (2005). Kooperationsstelle Hamburg, Hamburg: e-mail correspondence, 9.11.2005.

Doll, R., & Peto, R. (1981). The causes of cancer: Quantitative estimates of avoidable risks of cancer in the United States today. *Journal of the National Cancer Institute, 66* (6), 1191-1308.

Dutch Labour Inspectorate. (2003). *Arbomonitor 2002.*The Hague (in Dutch).

Dutch Labour Inspectorate. (2004). *Arbomonitor 2003.*The Hague (in Dutch).

Dutch Ministry of Social Affairs and Employment. (2004). *ArboBalans 2003— Arbeidsrisico's, effecten en maatregelen in Nederland.* The Hague (in Dutch).

ECETOC. (2004). *Targeted risk assessment.* Technical Report No. 93, European Centre for Ecotoxicology and Toxicology of Chemicals, Brussels.

Epstein, S. (2005). *Cancer gate. How to win the losing cancer war.* Amityville, NY: Baywood.

European Commission (EC). (2000). *Communication from the Commission on the Pre-cautionary Principle.* COM, 1, Brussels.

European Commission (EC). (2001, February 27). *White paper: Strategy for a future chemicals policy.* COM 88 final.

European Commission (EC). (2004). *SMEs in Europe 2003.* Observatory of European SMEs Report, 2003/7, European Commission, Brussels.

European Commission (EC). (2006). *REACH in brief.* Enterprise and Industry Directorate General and Environment Directorate General, European Commission, Brussels.

European Environment Agency. (2001). *Late lessons from early warnings: The precautionary principle 1896-2000.* Environmental Issue Report 22, EEA, Copenhagen.

European Foundation for the Improvement of Living and Working Conditions. (2001). *Third European Working Conditions Survey.* Luxembourg: Office for Official Publications of the European Community.

Eurostat. (2004). *Occupational diseases in Europe in 2001.* Statistics in Focus, Population and Social Conditions No 15. Download:
http://europa.eu.int/comm.eurostat>Publications

EU OSHA (European Agency for Safety and Health at Work). (Ed.). (2001). Quality of work. New approaches and strategies in occupational safety and health. Summary of workshops in Düsseldorf (May 15, 2001) and Bilbao (May 29-30, 2001), *Forum 12.* European Agency for Safety and Health at Work, Bilbao: Austria. Download:
http://agency.osha.eu.int/publications/forum/2/en/forum2_en.pdf

EU OSHA (European Agency for Safety and Health at Work). (Ed.). (2002a). *Dangerous substances—Handle with care.* Magazine 6. European Agency for Safety and Health at Work, Bilbao. Download:
http://osha.europa.eu/publications/magazine/6/magazine6-en.pdf

EU OSHA (European Agency for Safety and Health at Work). (Ed.). (2002b). *Recognition schemes in occupational safety and health.* Report no. 308. EU OSHA. European Agency for Safety and Health at Work, Bilbao. Download:
http://osha.europa.eu/publications/reports/308/recognition_en.pdf

EU OSHA (European Agency for Safety and Health at Work). (Ed.). (2003a). AUVAsicher: A programme to provide OSH assistance to SMEs—Austria. In *Improving occupational safety and health in SMEs: Examples of effective assistance* (pp. 20-26). Bilbao: European Agency for Safety and Health at Work. Download:
http://sme.osha.eu.int/publications/assistancescheme/2002/en/ReportSME_EN1342.PDF

EU OSHA (European Agency for Safety and Health at Work). (Ed.). (2003b). European Week for Safety and Health at Work 2003 Staatliches Amt für Arbeitsschutz Aachen (Ed.) 2003 Electronic risk prevention tool for craft trade. In *The practical prevention of risks from dangerous substances at work.* European Agency for Safety and Health at Work, Bilbao. Electronically available at:
http://agency.osha.eu/int/publications/reports/106/index_15.htm

EU OSHA (European Agency for Safety and Health at Work). (Ed). (2003c). Gefahrstoff-Informationssystem der Berufsgenossenschaft der Bauwirtschaft GISBAU—An information system for small companies in construction; European Week for Safety and Health at Work. *The practical prevention of risks from dangerous substances at work.* European Agency for Safety and Health at Work, Bilbao. Electronically available at: http://agency.osha.eu/int/publications/reports/106/index_14.htm

EU OSHA (European Agency for Safety and Health at Work). (Ed.). (2004a). *Funding scheme 2003/2004. National projects. Dangerous substances under control.* Download: http://sme.osha.eu.int/publications/fs2003/2004/en/index_15.htm

EU OSHA (European Agency for Safety and Health at Work). (Ed.). (2004b). *Promoting health and safety in European small and medium-sized enterprises (SMEs).* Bilbao, Austria: European Agency for Safety and Health at Work. Download:
http://sme.osha.eu.int/publications/fs2002/2003/en/2004-0641_SME_Scheme_EN.PDF

Fairman, R., & Yapp, C. (2005). *Making an impact on SME compliance behaviour: An evaluation of the effect of interventions upon compliance with health and safety legislation in small and medium sized enterprises.* HSE Research Report 366. Sudbury, UK: HSE Books.

Fischer, M. et al. (1998). Burns from undisclosed acids in a liquid used by temporary workers. *Dutch Med. Wochenschr., 123*(6), 151-154.

FMI (Fachvereinigung Mineralfaserindustrie eV) (Ed.). (2000). Ungang mit Mineralwolle-Dammstoffen (Glaswolle, Steinwolle), Handlungsanleitung. Franfurt/Main.

Frick, K., & Walters, D. R. (1998). Worker representation on health and safety in small enterprises: Lessons from a Swedish approach. *International Labour Review, 137*(3), 367-389. International Labour Office, Geneva.

Friedl, W. (2000). Occupational safety and health protection in small and medium-sized enterprises in Austria. In *FORUM News (Bulletin of the European FORUM of Insurance against accidents at work and occpational diseases)* No. 16 (pp. 13-15). Vienna: Austrian Workers' Compensation Board, Download: www.europeanforum.org/pdf/forumnews_nr16_ed.PDF

Gadea, R. (2006). *Necesidades de información sobre medio ambiente para trabajadores de PYME. Percepciones sobre el riesgo químico en las empresas.* Valencia: ISTAS.

García, J. (2006). Mirando al mutualismo alemán. Controversia sobre el presente y el futuro de las mutuas españolas. *Por Experiencia, 31,* 12-13.

García, A. M., & Rodrigo, F. (2005). *Los Delegados de Prevención en España: Estado de situación.* Valencia: ISTAS.

Gardner, L. J., & Oldershaw, P. J. (1991). Development of pragmatic exposure control concentrations based on packaging risk regulation phrases. *Annals of Occupational Hygiene, 35,* 158-163.

Georg, A. (2004). Klein, gesund und wettbewerbsfähig—Rahmenbedingungen und Strategien für Gesundheit und Sicherheit in Kleinbetrieben. Vortrag auf der 1. Tagung des Forums „Kleine und mittlere Unternehmen" am 18.10.2004 in Bad Honnef. Electronically available at: http://www.dnbgf.org/_upload/dokumente/1113_VortragArnoGeorgForumstagung KMU.pdf?PHPSESSID=d320504f4e5d5728af92999d43f94455

Georg, A. (2005). Landesinstitut Sozialforschungsstelle Dortmund—SFS: e-mail correspondence, 6.10.2005.

Geyer, A., & Kittel, G. (1999). *Beurteilung der Verwendung und Brauchbarkeit von Sicherheitsdatenblättern für Klein- und Mittelbetriebe.* Endbericht Österreich. Linz/Austria: ppm research + consulting. Download: www.ppm.at/ppm/downloads/sds_austria.pdf

Geyer, A., Kittel, G., Vollebregt, L., Westra, J., & Wriedt, H. (1999). *Assessment of the Usefulness of Material Safety Data Sheets (SDS) for SMEs.* Final project report. Linz/Austria: ppm research + consulting. Download: www.ppm.at/ppm/downloads/sds_international.pdf

GiF (Gemeinschaftsinitiative Gesünder Arbeiten e.V.). (Ed.). (2004a). *Gesünder Arbeiten—Auch mit Gefahrstoffen.* Düsseldorf. Electronically available at: http://www.gefahrstoffe-im-griff.de/pdf_files/Gefahrstoff-im-Griff-GiGA-Folder.pdf.

GiF (Netzwerk gefahrstoffe-im-griff.de). (Ed.). (2004b). *Berufe/Branchen.* Wuppertal. Electronically available at: http://www.gefahrstoffe-im-griff.de/4.htm

GiF (Netzwerk gefahrstoffe-im-griff.de). (Ed.). (2004c). *Nützliche Instrumente*. Wuppertal. Electronically available at: http://www.gefahrstoffe-im-griff.de/7.htm

GiF (Netzwerk gefahrstoffe-im-griff.de). (Ed.). (2004d). *Info-System Gefahrstoffe*. Wuppertal. Electronically available at: http://132.195.14.44/cgi-bin/gef/asinfo.cgi

GISBAU (Gefahrstoff-Informationssystem der Berufsgenossenschaft der Bauwirtschaft). (Ed.). (2003b). *Übersicht der GISCODES und Produkt-Codes*. Frankfurt/Main. Electronically available at: http://www.gisbau.de/giscodes/GISCODES.rtf

GISBAU (Gefahrstoff-Informationssystem der Berufsgenossenschaft der Bauwirtschaft). (Ed.). (2005a). *Schwerpunktbereiche*. Frankfurt/Main. Electronically available at: http://www.gisbau.de/home.html

GISBAU (Gefahrstoff-Informationssystem der Berufsgenossenschaft der Bauwirtschaft). (Ed.). (2005b). *Übersicht über GISCODES und Produkt-Codes*. Frankfurt/Main. Electronically available at: http://www.gisbau.de/home.html

GISBAU (Gefahrstoff-Informationssystem der Berufsgenossenschaft der Bauwirtschaft). (Ed.). (2005c). *Service. Broschüren. GISBAU—Eine Kurzvorstellung*. Frankfurt/Main. Electronically available at: http://www.gisbau.de/service/brosch/kurzvors.pdf

GISCHEM (Branchenspezifisches Gefahrstoffinformationssystem der Berufsgenossenschaft der chemischen Industrie). (Ed.). (2005). *Inhalte*. Heidelberg. Electronically available at: http://www.gischem.de/e1_allgm/inhalte.htm

Greenberg, R. S., Mandel, J. S., Pastides, H., Britton, N., Rudenko, L., & Starr, T. B. (2001). A meta analysis of cohort studies describing mortality and cancer incidence among chemical workers in the United States and Western Europe. *Epidemiology, 12*(6), 727-740.

GROLA BG (Großhandels- und Lagerei-Berufsgenossenschaft). (Ed.). (2003). Gefahrstoff-Check. Die Mulimedia-Selbstlern-Station zum Thema: '*Gefahrstoffe in Handel und Lagerei.'* Mannheim. Electronically available at: http://www.gefahrstoff-check.de/

Grünewald, O. (1989). Modellversuch der Süddeutschen Eisen- und Stahl-Berufsgenossenschaft zur sicherheitstechnischen Betreuung kleiner Betriebe. Gründe, organisatorische Umsetzung, Schlussfolgerungen. *Die BG, 10,* 687-688.

Guest, I. (1998). The Chemical Industries Association guidance on allocating occupational exposure. *Annals of Occupational Hygiene, 42*(6), 407-411.

Hamm, G. et al. (2005). Branchenregelungen—Hilfen beim Gefahrstoffmanagement. In *Gefahrstoffe*. Wiesbaden, 208 pp.

Haslam, S., & James, J. (2001). *Working with local intermediaries: An evaluation of HSE's Field Operations Directorate pilot project*. Contract Research Report 389. Sudbury, UK: HSE Books.

Haslam, S., James, J., & Bennet, D. (1998). Developing proposals on how to work with intermediaries. HSE Contract Research Report 185. Sudbury, UK: HSE Books.

Heeg, F. J. et al. (2002). Kooperation von Betriebsärzten und Sicherheitsfachkräften—Untersuchung und Umsetzungskonzept für Kleinbetriebe. Schriftenreihe der BAuA—Forschung—Fb 945. Dortmund/Berlin, 136 pp.

Heider, A. (2003). *Einführung in den Arbeitnehmerschutz. Arbeit darf nicht krank machen*. Vienna: Chamber of Labour of Vienna. Download: www.arbeiterkammer.at/pictures/d4/arbeitnehmerschutz.pdf?PHPSESSID=9f2e708d 789411bd763fa6d8bce9cd58

Hemmelskamp, J. (1999). *Umweltpolitik und technischer Fortschritt*. Heidelberg: Physica Verlag.

Hery, M., Diebold, F., & Hecht, G. (1996). Exposure of contractors to chemical pollutants during the maintenance shut down of a chemical plant. *Risk Analysis, 16*(5), 645-655.

HESSEN (Hessisches Sozialministerium). (Ed.). (2004). *Erstellung der Gefährdungsbeurteilung. Handlungshilfen für verschiedene Branchen.* Wiesbaden o.J. Electronically available at: http://www.sozialnetz-hessen.de/ca/ud/zwf/

Hillage, J., Bates, P., & Rick, J. (1998). *Economic influences on occupational health and safety.* The Institute for Employment Studies, University of Sussex, United Kingdom.

HOLZ BG (Holz-Berufsgenossenschaft). (Ed.). (2005). HOLZmultimedia. Die neue CD-ROM HOLZmultimedia—Arbeitsschutzinformationen für die Holzwirtschaft neu aufbereitet. München. Electronically available at: http://www.holz.bg.de/pages/aktuell/theme/premecdl.htm

HSC (Health and Safety Executive). (2002). COSHH enforcement and the role of OELs, Annex 4. *Discussion Document on Occupational Exposure Limits (OEL) Framework.* Chemical Risk Assessment Unit, HSE, London.

HSC/ACTS (Health and Safety Executive/Advisory Committee on Toxic Substances). (2004). *Annual report on the work of COSHH essentials working group.* Advisory Committee on Toxic Substances, paper no. ACTS/15/2004. HSC London.

HSE (Health and Safety Executive). (2005a). *Occupational asthma.* SWI03/04 Table 3. Download: www.hse.gov.uk/statistics/causdis/asthma.htm

HSE (Health and Safety Executive). (2005b). *Control of substances hazardous to health (5th ed.). The COSHH Regulations 2002 (as amended), ACoP and guidance,* L5 (5th ed.), Sudbury, UK: HSE Books.

HSE (Health and Safety Executive). (2006). *Self-reported work related illness in 2001/02: Results from a household survey.* HSE, Bootle. Download: www.hse.gov.uk/statistics.causdis/swi0102.pdf.

Hudspith, B., & Hay, A. W. M. (1998). Information needs of workers. *Annals of Occupational Hygiene, 42*(6), 377-390.

HVBG (Hauptverband der gewerblichen Berufsgenossenschaften). (Ed.). (1999). *5 Bausteine für einen gut organisierten Betrieb—Auch in Sachen Arbeitsschutz.* Sankt Augustin, 37 pp.

HVBG (Hauptverband der gewerblichen Berufsgenossenschaften). (2001). Fachausschuss 'Bau' der BGHZ (Ed.), *Umgang mit Reinigungs- und Pflegemitteln.* BGR 209. Sankt Augustin, 37 pp.

HVBG (Hauptverband der gewerblichen Berufsgenossenschaften). (Ed.). (2003). *Geschäfts und Rechnungsergebnisse der gewerblichen Berufsgenossenschaften 2002.* Sankt Augustin, 144 pp.

IGM (Industriegewerkschaft Metall). (Ed.). (2002). Holzstaub? Nein Danke! Reihe „Gesünder @rbeiten." *Arbeitshilfe, 13.* Frankfurt am Main, 64 pp.

IGM (Industriegewerkschaft Metall). (Ed.). (2004). Gute Arbeit im KFZ-Handwerk: Wissen wo es lang geht. Reihe „Gesünder @rbeiten." *Arbeitshilfe, 18.* Frankfurt am Main, 71 pp.

IHK KREFELD (Industrie- und Handelskammer Mittlerer Niederrhein Krefeld—Mönchengladbach—Neuss; Staatliches Amt für Arbeitsschutz Mönchengladbach). (Eds.). (2000). Gefahrstoffmanagement im Betrieb. Teil 1: Wegweiser mit Sammlung von Mustervordrucken und Musterschreiben zur Umsetzung der Grundanforderungen der Gefahrstoffverordnung. Mönchengladbach, 10 pp. Electronically available at:

http://www.mittlerer-niederrhein.ihk.de/download/innovation_umwelt/innovation_umwelt/arbeitsschutz/broschuere_gfestoffv.pdf

IHK KREFELD (Industrie- und Handelskammer Mittlerer Niederrhein Krefeld— Mönchengladbach—Neuss; Niederrheinische Industrie- und Handelskammer Duisburg—Wesel—Kleve zu Duisburg). (2004). Staatliches Amt für Arbeitsschutz Mönchengladbach (Eds.), In *siebzehn Schritten zum Arbeitsschutzmanagement.* Krefeld, 49 pp. Electronically available at: http://www.mittlerer-niederrhein.ihk.de/download/innovation_umwelt/innovation_umwelt/asm/broschuere_asm.pdf

INSHT (Instituto Nacional de Seguridad e Higiene ene Trabajo). (2004). *Encuesta Nacional de Condiciones de Trabajo—5th National Survey on Working Conditions.* Available in Spanish at: http://www.mtas.es/insht/statistics/enct_5.htm

Institut ASER e.V. (Ed.). (2004). KMU-Netzwerk "Gefahrstoffe im Griff"—Umsetzung und Verankerung eines pragmatischen Gefahrstoffmanagements in KMU. Wuppertal. Electronically available at: http://www.aser.uniwuppertal.de/pdf_files/projekte/3/lfd/314.pdf

Jackson, H. (2002). Control banding—Practical tools for controlling exposure to chemicals. *Asian Pacific Newsletter on Occupational Health and Safety, 9,* 62-63.

James, P., Johnstone, R., Quinlan, M., & Walters, D. R. (in press). Regulating supply chains to improve health and safety. *Industrial Law Journal.*

James, P., & Walters, D. R. (1999). *Regulating health and safety at work: The way forward.* London: Institute of Employment Rights.

James, P., & Walters, D. R. (2005). *Regulating health and safety at work: An agenda for change?* London: Institute of Employment Rights.

John Kingston Associates. (2001). *Development of an information-based approach to self-regulation of health and safety in small firms.* CRR 330/2001. Sudbury, UK: HSE Books. Download: www.hse.gov.uk/research/content/crr/index.htm

Johnston, K. L., Phillips, M. L., Esmen, N. A., & Hall, T. A. (2005). Evaluation of an artificial intelligence program for estimating occupational exposures. *Annals of Occupational Hygiene, 49*(2), 147-153.

Jones, J., Huxtable, C., Hodgson, J., & Price, M. (2004). *Self-reported work-related illness in 2001/02. Results from a household survey.* Sudbury, UK: Epidemiology and Medical Statistics Unit, HSE. Download: www.hse.gov.uk/statistics/causdis/swi0102.pdf

Jones, R. M., & Nicas, M. (2005a). Evaluation of COSHH Essentials for vapour degreasing and bag filling operations. *Annals of Occupational Hygiene, 49*(2), 137-147.

Jones, R. M., & Nicas, M. (2005b). Margins of safety provided by COSHH Essentials and the ILO Chemical Control Toolkit. *Annals of Occupational Hygiene, 49*(2), 149-156.

Jongen, M., Marquart, H., Nossent, S., & Visser. R. (2003). *Prioritering van branches en ketens voor de versterking van arboleid rond gevaarlijke stoffen* [Prioritisation of branches and chains for the enhancement of the OSH policy concerning hazardous chemicals] (p. 16). Amsterdam: TNO.

Karageorgiou, A., Jensen, P. L., Walters, D. R., & Wilthagen, T. (2000). Risk assessment in four member states of the European Union. In K. Frick, P. L. Jensen, M. Quinlan, & T. Wilthagen (Eds.), *Systematic occupational health and safety management* (pp. 251-284). Oxford: Pergamon.

Karhu, E. (2006). *REACH exposure scenarios and exposure assessment,* Powerpoint presentation at REACH and Worker Protection Legislation Conference, Brussels: ETUC September 19. Available at: http://hesa.etui-rehs.org/uk/newsevents/eventsfiche.asp?pk=689

Kauppinen, T. et al. (2000). Occupational exposure to carcinogens in the European Union. *Occupational and Environmental Medicine, 57,* 10-18.

Kinney, J. (1993). Health hazards to children in service industries. *American Journal of Industrtial Medicine, 24,* 291-300.

Kittel, G. (2006). *Strategies for success? Managing chemical risks in small workplaces: A review of European practice, National Report Austria.* Linz/Austria: ppm research + consulting. Download: www.ppm.at/

Kliemt, G., & Voullaire, E. (1999). Gefahrstoffe im Kraftfahrzeuggewerbe *Läßt sich überbetriebliche Unterstützung mobilisieren? Schriftenreihe der Bundesanstalt für Arbeitsschutz und Arbeitsmedizin*—Forschung—Fb 857. Dortmund/Berlin, 228 pp.

Kliemt, G. et al. (2003). Effektivität und Effizienz der betriebsärztlichen Betreuung in Klein- und Mittelbetrieben. Vergleichende Bewertung von alternativen Betreuungs-strategien und Regelbetreuung. Schriftenreihe der BAuA—Forschung—Fb 998. Dortmund/Berlin, 608 pp.

Kluger, N. (1997). Gefahrstoffe in der Bauwirtschaft. *Sichere Arbeit, 1,* 16-20.

Kluger, N. (2005). Gefahrstoff-Informationssystem der Berufsgenossenschaft der Bauwirt-schaft, Frankfurt/Main. Personal communication, 31.10.2005.

KOOPERATIONSSTELLE (Kooperationsstelle Hamburg). (Ed.). (2003). *CLEANTOOL. Optimierte Beurteilung und Planung industrieller Oberflächenreinigung.* Hamburg o.J. Electronically available at: http://www.rrz.uni-hamburg.de/kooperationsstelle-hh/content/arbeitsgebiete/ersatzst offe/informationen/cleantool/setcleantool.htm English version: *CLEANTOOL. Inno-vative evaluation and design of industrial surface cleaning processes.* Electronically available at: http://www.rrz.uni-hamburg.de/kooperationsstelle-hh/content-engl/arbeitsgebiete/ers atzstoffe/informationen/cleantool/setcleantool.htm

Kooperationsstelle Hamburg. (2004). *PimexPro—A project coordinated by Kooperations-stelle Hamburg.* Hamburg: Kooperationsstelle Hamburg. Download: www.pimexpro.org/html/pimex_en.html

Körber, S. (1998). Staatliche Steuerung und gesellschaftliche Selbstregulierung in der Chemikalienkontrolle. Eine sozialwissenschaftliche Untersuchung halbstaatlicher Normierung durch den Ausschuß für Gefahrstoffe. Schriftenreihe der Bundesanstalt für Arbeitsschutz und Arbeitsmedizin—Forschung—Fb 810. Dortmund/Berlin, 310 pp.

Kranvogel, E., Sperr, H., Bautzmann, A., Pochobradsky, E., & Schleicher, B. (2000). *Managementsysteme für den Sicherheits- und Gesundheitsschutz in Kleinbetrieben.* Vienna: ÖBIG (Austrian Health Institute). Download: http://at.osha.eu.int/good_practice/oebig-kmu.pdf

Kremer, A. M. (2005). *Gevaarlijke stoffen op de werkplek. Deelresultaten van de Nationale Enquête Arbeidsomstandigheden 2003* [Hazardous substances. Part of the results of the National Survey on Working Conditions—NEA, 2003]. TNO, Hoofddorp/Zeist.

Kromhout, H., & Vermeulen, R. (2000). Long term trends in occupational exposure: Are they real? What causes them? What shall we do with them? *Annals of Occupational Hygiene, 44,* 325-327.

Kuhn, K. (2006). Powerpoint presentation at the Colloquium on External Services for Occupational Safety and Health: An EU Perspective, Prevent, December 2006, Brussels.

Laflamme, L. (1997). Age-related injuries among male and female assembly workers— A study in the Swedish automomile industry. *Relations Industrielles, 52*(3), 608-619.

Lamm, F., & Walters, D. R. (2004). Regulating occupational health and safety in small businesses. In L. Bluff, N. Gunningham, & R. Johnstone (Eds.), *OHS regulation for a changing world of work.* Sydney: Federation Press.

Landesinstitut Sozialforschungsstelle Dortmund (SFS). (Ed.). (2003). PragMaGuS. Praktisches Management von Gesundheit und Sicherheit in kleinen Unternehmen. Dokumentation der PragMaGuS-Tagung: „Qualität der Arbeit in Kleinbetrieben—Ein Verbundmodell in der Region Dortmund stellt sich vor." Beiträge aus der Forschung, Band 140. Dortmund, 63 pp.

Landrigan, P. J., Baker, D. B. (1995). Clinical recognition of occupational and environmental disease. *Mt Sinai Journal of Medicine, 62*(5), 406-411.

Landrigan, P. J., Markowitz, S. B., Nicholson, W. J., & Baker, D. B. (1995). Cancer prevention in the workplace. In P. Greenwald, B. S. Kramer, & D. L. Weed (Eds.), *Cancer prevention and control* (pp. 393-410). New York: Marcel Dekker, Inc.

Lang, K. H. (2004). KMU-Netzwerk-Portal 'Gefahrstoffe im Griff,' Sicher ist sicher. *Arbeitsschutz aktuell, 55,* 344-347.

LASI (Länderausschuss für Arbeitsschutz und Sicherheitstechnik). (Ed.). (2001). Arbeitsschutzmanagementsysteme. Handlungshilfe zur freiwilligen Einführung und Anwendung von Arbeitsschutzmanagementsystemen (AMS) für kleine und mittlere Unternehmen (KMU). Heft LV 22. Saarbrücken 2001, 104 pp. Electronically available at: http://lasi.osha.de/de/gfx/publications/publications.php

LASI. (2003). *Sicherheitsdatenblatt—Instrument des Arbeitsschutzes. Abschlussbericht zur Schwerpunktaktion.* Saarbrücken 2003, 137 pp. Electronically available at: http://lasi.osha.de/docs/sidatenbl.pdf

Leigh, J., Macaskill, P., Kuosma, E., & Mandryk, J. (1999). Global burden of disease due to occupational factors. *Epidemiology, 10*(5), 626.

Leleu, I. (2003). Occupational diseases in Europe: Four new research reports. In *FORUM News (Bulletin of the European FORUM of Insurance against accidents at work and occupational diseases)* No. 20. August 03, pp. 11-14. Download: www.europeanforum.org/pdf/F_News_ED_20.pdf

Livesley, E., & Rushton, L. (2000). *The prevalence of occupational dermatitis amongst printers in the Midlands.* CRR no.307/2000. Sudbury, UK: HSE Books.

Lofstedt, R. E. (2003). Swedish chemical regulation: An overview and analysis. *Risk Analysis, 23*(2), 411-421.

Lynen, E. (2005). Staatliches Amt für Arbeitsschutz Aachen. Personal communication, 4.1.2005.

Maidment, S. (1998). Occupational hygiene considerations in the development of a structured approach to select chemical control strategies. *Annals of Occupational Hygiene, 36,* 601-607.

MALEG (Einkaufsgenossenschaft der Maler zu Lübeck e.V.). (Ed.). (2004). *MGM—Maleg-Gefahrstoff-Management*. Powerpoint presentation (unpublished). Lübeck.

Mark, D. (1999). *Validation of the EASE model. Report on HSE contract No. R51.172*. Institute of Occupational Health, University of Birmingham, UK.

Mayhew, C., & Quinlan, M. (1998). *Outsourcing and occupatonal health and safety: A comparative study of factory based and outworkers in the Australian TCF industry*. Industrial Relations Research Centre Monograph, University of New South Wales, Sydney.

Mcknight, A., Elias, P., & Wilson, L. (1999). *Workplace injuries and workforce trends*. Coventry, UK: University of Warwick.

McCracken, J. (2006). *REACH: Opportunities and challenges*. Paper presented at the Senior Labour Inspectors' Committee Plenary 28 March Vienna. (HSE, unpublished).

Ministry of Social Affairs and Employment. (2005). *Jaarrapportage arboconvenanten 2004*. Ministry of Social Affairs and Employment, The Hague. (Annual report 2004 OSH covenants), March 2005.

Ministry of Social Affairs, Hesse. (2000). *Status report and future of ASCA—Evaluation of the results of 670 corporate studies on the organisation of occupational health and safety and implementation of occupational health and safety regulations*, cited in Ahrens et al. (2006, p. 34).

Money, C. D. (1992). A structured approach to occupational hygiene in the design and operation of fine chemical plant. *Annals of Occupational Hygiene, 42*(6), 391-400.

Money, C. (2003). European approaches in the development of approaches for the successful control of workplace health risks. *Annals of Occupational Hygiene, 47*, 533-540.

Money, C. (2006). Evaluation of the utility and reliability of COSHH Essentials. *Annals of Occupational Hygiene, 50*(6), 642-644.

Morrell, S., Kerr, C., Driscoll, T., Taylor, R., Salkeld, G., & Corbett, S. (1998). Best estimate of the magnitude of mortality due to occupational exposure to hazardous substances. *Occupational and Environmental Medicine, 55*, 634-641.

Müller-Wechselberger, C. (2002). AUVAsicher Österreich—Netzwerk Arbeitsmedizin. In *Proceedings of the XVIIth World Congress on Safety and Health at Work*, Vienna, 26-31 May 2002. Vienna: Austrian Social Insurance for Occupational Risks.

Musu, T. (2004). *REACHing the workplace. How workers stand to benefit from the new European policy on chemical agents*, Brussels: TUTB. Available from: http://hesa.etui-rehs.org/uk/publications/publications.asp.

Naumann, B. D., Sargent, E. V., Fraser, W. J., Becker, G. T., & Kirt, G. D. (1996). Performance based exposure control limits for pharmaceutical active ingredients. *American Industrial Hygiene Journal, 57*, 33-42.

Netzwerk gefahrstoffe-im-griff.de. (Ed.). (2004). *KMU-Gefahrstoffportal*. Wuppertal. Electronically available at: http://www.gefahrstoffe-im-griff.de/.

Nichols, T. (1997). *The sociology of industrial injury*. London: Mansell.

Nordiska ministerrådets miljörapport. (1986). *Förstår forbrugerna—Advarselmaerkningen af husholdningskemikalier*. Köpenhamn: Produktkontrollgruppen.

Norrby, C. (1997). *Hur ska vi nå de minsta företagen? Kemikaliearbete* [How shall we reach the smallest companies. Chemical management]. IVF report 97850, IVF.

Northage, C. (2005). Commentary: EASEing into the future. *Annals of Occupational Hygiene, 49*(2), 99-101.

Nossent, S., Jongen, M., Visser, R., & Marquart, J. (2003a). *Chemie in branches en ketens. Een onderzoek als opstap naar sterker stoffenbeleid.* TNO, Hoofddorp/Zeist.

Nossent, S., Jongen, M., Visser, R., & Marquart, H. (2003b). *Prioritering van branches en ketens voor de versterking van arboleid rond gevaarlijke stoffen* [Prioritisation of branches and chains for the enhancement of the OSH policy concerning hazardous chemicals]. TNO, Hoofddorp/Zeist.

Novak, H. (2003). PIMEX—Picture mixed exposure (Austria). In *How to convey OSH information effectively: The case of dangerous substances.* EU OSHA Report no. 312 (pp. 139-143). Bilbao: European Agency for Safety and Health at Work. Download: http://osha.europa.eu/publications/reports/312/howtoconvey-en_en.pdf

Novak, H. (2004). PIMEX—Visualising risks at workplaces by video and monitoring. In *Working with dangerous substances: The European policy challenge, Forum 12* (pp. 2-3). Bilbao: European Agency for Safety and Health at Work. Download: http://agency.osha.eu.int/publications/forum/12/en/FORUM12-en.pdf

NRW (Ministerium für Wirtschaft und Arbeit des Landes Nordrhein-Westfalen). (Ed.). (2004). Programme der Arbeitsschutzverwaltung. Gefahrstoffe im Handwerk (GSH). Weitere Infos. Düsseldorf. Electronically available at: http://www.arbeitsschutz.nrw.de/bp/research/programme/GefstoffeHandwerk/weitereInfos.html

NUTEK. (2000). *Företag i förändring. Sammanfattning och benchmarking av lärandestrategier för ökad konkurrenskraft.* [Companies in transition. Summary and benchmarking of strategies for learning and increased competitiveness]. NUTEK. Available at: www.nutek.se

Oehme, I. (2001). Stimulating OSH Procurement—Beschaffungsservice Austria. In *Occupational safety and health in marketing and procurement* (pp. 112-117). EU OSHA Report 304. Bilbao: European Agency for Safety and Health at Work. Download: http://agency.osha.eu.int/publications/reports/304/en/Occup_safety_market_EN.pdf

O'Neill, R. (2005). Burying the evidence. *Hazards, 92,* 4-5.

OHAC (Occupational Health Advisory Committee). (2000). *Report and recommendations on improving access to occupational health support, Section 3.* Occupational Health Advisory Committee (OHAC). London: HSE Books.

ÖNBG. (Ed.). (undated). *Health at the workplace in small and medium-sized companies.* Linz/Austria: Österreichisches Netzwerk Betriebliche Gesundheitsförderung.

ÖSNE. (Ed.). (2003, February). *Corporate Social Responsibility (CSR). Die gesellschaftliche Verantwortung von Unternehmen.* Wien: Website Österreichische Strategie zur Nachhaltigen Entwicklung. Download: www.nachhaltigkeit.at/reportagen.php3?id=42

ÖSNE. (Ed.). (2004, June). *Nachhaltigkeitsmanagement: Systeme und programme.* Wien: Website Österreichische Strategie zur Nachhaltigen Entwicklung. Download: www.nachhaltigkeit.at/reportagen.php3?id=28

Pawlowitsch, F. (2002). Sicherheits Certifikat Contraktoren—SCC. In *Proceedings of the XVIIth World Congress on Safety and Health at Work*, Vienna 26-31 May 2002. Vienna: Austrian Social Insurance for Occupational Risks.

Perthen-Palmisano, B., & Jakl, T. (2004). *Chemical leasing—The Austrian approach. Proceedings of the Workshop Sustainable Chemistry*, 27.-29.01.04, Dessau. Berlin: Federal Environmental Agency. Download: www.sustainable-chemistry.com/download/TAGUNGSUNTERLAGEN-FINAL.pdf

Pfoser, W., & Peer, H. (2004). Beratungsschwerpunkte—Betreuung AUVAsicher. In *AUVA intern ASQS-Sondernummer*, Oktober 04, pp. 12-14. Download: www.auva.at/mediaDB/75242.PDF

Pickvance, S., Karnon, J., Peters, J., & El Arifi, K. (2005). *The impact of REACH on occupational health.* Brussels: ETUI-REHS.

Pilkington, A., Graham, M. K, Cowie, H. A, Mulholland, R. E., Dempsey, S., Melrose, A. S., & Hutchinson, P. A. (2002). *Survey of use of occupational health support.* Contract Research Report 445/2002. Sudbury, UK: HSE Books.

Popma, J., Schaapman, M., & Wiltagen, T. (2002). The Netherlands: Implementation within wider regulatory reform. In D. R. Walters (Ed.), *Regulating health and safety management in the European Union* (pp. 177-209). Brussels: Peter Lang.

Postle, M., Vernon, J., Zarogiannis, P., & Salado, R. (2003). *Assessment of the impact of the new chemicals policy on occupational health.* Final Report for the European Commission, Environment Directorate General, Risk Policy Analysts Ltd, Looden, Norfolk.

Projekt PragMaGuS. (Ed.). (2004a). *Regionales Netzwerken*, Dortmund. Electronically available at: http://www.pragmagus.de/main.html

Projekt PragMaGuS. (Ed.). (2004b). *Arbeitsverfahren, -mittel: Arbeitsstoffe*, Dortmund. Electronically available at:
http://www.pragmagus.de/gb/index.php?PHPSESSID=12c8bb97f6d9698478b94fb3a a1f4e2d&site=/module/unternehmer/u13/u130&status=unternehmer&modul=arbeits stoffe

Quinlan, M., Mayhew, C., & Bohle, P. (2001). The global expansion of precarious employment, work disorganisation and consequences for occupational health: A review of recent research. *International Journal of Health Services, 31*(2), 335-414.

Rebitzer, J. (1995). Job safety and contract workers in the petrochemicals industry. *Industrial Relations, 34*(1), 40-57.

Research International. (1997). *Industry's perception and use of occupational exposure limits.* HSE Contract Research Report. Sudbury, UK: HSE Books.

Rheker, R. (2005). Gefahrstoff-Informationssystem der Berufsgenossenschaft der Bauwirtschaft, Frankfurt/Main. Personal communication, 31.10.2005.

Rheinland-Pfalz (Ministerium für Umwelt und Forsten und Ministerium für Arbeit, Soziales, Familie und Gesundheit, Land Rheinland-Pfalz). (Ed.). (2000a). *Über das Projekt SGU. Vorwort.* Mainz. Electronically available at:
http://www.sgu-rlp.de/Ueber_das_Projekt_SGU/P0B80A443-536B-4844-81EB-278 2F772C70E.htm

Rheinland-Pfalz (Ministerium für Umwelt und Forsten und Ministerium für Arbeit, Soziales, Familie und Gesundheit, Land Rheinland-Pfalz). (Ed.). (2003a). *Neues aus der Fachkommission SGU.* Mainz. Electronically available at:
http://www.sgu.rlp.de/Neues_aus_der_Fachkommission/P744D348A-AB34-42BC-9 91B-78A4D0122389.php3

Rheinland-Pfalz (Ministerium für Umwelt und Forsten und Ministerium für Arbeit, Soziales, Familie und Gesundheit, Land Rheinland-Pfalz). (Ed.). (2003b). Download-Bereich. Mainz. Electronically available at:
http://www.sgu-rlp.de/Download/P4C9372F9-A468-4573-9727-7898318BBD2.php3

RIP 3.2.1 (REACH Implementation Project 3.2.1). (2005). *General Framework of Exposure Scenarios Scoping Study—Final report,* Service Contract Number 22551-2004-12FISPISPBE European Commission, Brussels.

RIP 3.5.1 (REACH Implementation Project 3.5.1). (2006). *Technical Guidance Document on Requirements for Down Stream Users. Preliminary Study. Final report.* Service Contract Number CCR.IHCP.C430321.XO, European Commission, Brussels.

Rogers, M. D. (2003). The European Commission's White Paper "Strategy for a Future Chemicals Policy": A review. *Risk Analysis, 23*(2), 381-388.

Rosén, G. (1999). *WISP. Workplace Improvement Strategy by PIMEX.* Final report to the European Commission; SAFE project no. 97 202356 05F05. Download-http://annhyg.oxfordjournals.org/cgi/content/full/49/3/201

Rosén, G., Andersson, I-M., Walsh, P. T., Clark, R. D. R., Säämänen, A., Heinonen, K., Riipinen, H., & Pääkkönen, R. (2005). A review of video exposure monitoring as an occupational hygiene tool. *Annals of Occupational Hygiene, 49,* 201-217.

Rousseau, D., & Libuser, C. (1997). Contingent workers in high risk environments. *California Management Review, 39*(2), 103-121.

Royal Society of Chemistry. (1996). *COSHH in laboratories* (2nd ed.). Cambridge, UK: RSC.

Rühl, R. (2004, January). *Das Nutzenpotential von REACH—Abschätzung für ein Teilsegment.* Unpublished manuscript of a presentation at the Workshop 'REACH . . .,' Loccum.

Russell, R., Maidment, S., Brooke, I., & Topping, M. (1998). Introduction to a UK scheme to help small firms control health risks from chemicals. *Annals of Occupational Hygiene, 42*(6), 367-376.

SACHSEN (Sächsisches Staatsministerium für Wirtschaft und Arbeit). (Ed.). (2002). *Arbeitsschutzmanagement.* CD-ROM. Dresden.

Schaapman, M. (2002). OHS discourse and implementation of the framework directive. In D. R. Walters (Ed.), *Regulating health and safety management in the European Union* (pp. 101-144). Brussels: Peter Lang.

Schmidt-Jung, I. (2005). Zentrum für Umwelt und Arbeitssicherheit der Handwerks-kammer Koblenz. Personal communication, 6.1.2005.

Schulte, A. (2004). Betriebsärztliche Betreuung von Handwerksbetrieben—Modelle und deren Bewertung. Schriftenreihe der BAuA—Forschung—Fb 1021. Dortmund/Berlin/Dresden, 307 pp.

Schulte-Hubbert, P. (2005a). Ministerium für Umwelt und Forsten Rheinland-Pfalz. Personal communication, 3.2.2005.

Schulte-Hubbert, P. (2005b). Ministerium für Umwelt und Forsten Rheinland-Pfalz. Personal communication, 12.10.2005.

Seiler, K. (2004). Das NRW-Landesprogramm 'Gefahrstoffe im Handwerk' (Stand 12/2004). Powerpoint presentation (unpublished). Düsseldorf.

Seiler, K. (2005). Landesanstalt für Arbeitsschutz Nordrhein-Westfalen. e-mail corre-spondence, 4.10.2005.

SGU (Ministerium für Umwelt und Forsten und Ministerium für Arbeit, Soziales, Familie und Gesundheit, Land Rheinland-Pfalz). (Ed.). (2000a). *Über das Projekt SGU. Aufbau des Leitfadens.* Mainz. Electronically available at:
http://www.sgu-rlp.de/Ueber_das_Projekt_SGU/PDE4D9ACA-0C22-474B-957D-6B8D30624C75.htm

SGU (Ministerium für Umwelt und Forsten und Ministerium für Arbeit, Soziales, Familie und Gesundheit, Land Rheinland-Pfalz). (Ed.). (2000b). *Über das Projekt SGU. Zahlen und Fakten.* Mainz. Electronically available at: http://www.sgu-rlp.de/Ueber_das_Projekt_SGU/P007FE5BD-F1E7-44B5-B53B-C4 0E3CAB09CA.htm

SGU (Ministerium für Umwelt und Forsten und Ministerium für Arbeit, Soziales, Familie und Gesundheit, Land Rheinland-Pfalz). (Ed.). (2000c). *Schnupperversion. Schnupperversion des Leitfadens Metall.* Mainz. Electronically available at: http://www.sgu-rlp.de/Schnupperversion/P8F479F33-13D5-4217-A8EE-C13B7C56 E8BE.htm

Shaw, N., & Turner, R. (2003). *The worker safety advisors pilot.* HSE Research Report 144. Sudbury, UK: HSE Books.

SMS (Steinbruchs Berufsgenossenschaften). (Ed.). (2005). *'Sicher mit System' Die Organisationshilfe für die Praxis.* Langenhagen o.J. Electronically available at: http://www.stbg.de/sms/

STAFA Aachen (Staatliches Amt für Arbeitsschutz Aachen). (Ed.). (2003). Sicherer Umgang mit gefährlichen Arbeitsstoffen im Handwerk. Praktische Hilfen per (Maus)Klick! Aachen o.J.

Steber, W. (1999). Branchenlösung Gefahrstoffhandbuch für das Kfz-Gewerbe—Wie gehe ich damit um? In Bundesanstalt für Arbeitsschutz und Arbeitsmedizin (BAuA) (Ed.), *Europäische Woche für Sicherheit und Gesundheit bei der Arbeit. Von der Werkstattplanung bis zur Führung des Betriebes. Informationstagung für das Kfz-Handwerk,* Schriftenreihe der BAuA—Forschungsanwendung—Fa 44. Dortmund/ Berlin, pp. 101-112.

Steber, W. (2005). Zentralverband Deutsches Kraftfahrzeuggewerbe, Bonn. Personal communication, 8.2.2005.

Sul, O. (2004). Volkswagen AG, Kassel. Personal communication, 15.12.2004.

Sul, O. (2005). Volkswagen AG, Kassel. Personal communication, 26.10.2005.

Swedish Chemicals Inspectorate. (2004). *Säkerhetsdatablad för arbetsplatsens behov. Myndighetssamverkan 2004—ett tillsynsprojekt om säkerhetsdatablad för avfettning* [Safety data sheets that meets the need of the workplaces.—Supervision of safety data sheets for degreasing agents]. PM 35.

Thebaud-Mony, A. (1999). Contracting and subcontracting by the French Nuclear Power Industry. *International Journal of Occupational and Environmental Health, 5*(4), 296-299.

Thebaud-Mony, A., Rondeau du Noyer, C., Huez, D., Brenier, F., Forest, H., Geraud, C., Haillot, M. J., Pillore, R., & Surribas, H. (1992). Contractors' employees working in nuclear power plants. *Documents de Medicine de Travail, 51,* 347-362 (in French).

Tickner, J., Friar, J., Creely, K. S. Cherrie, J., Pride, D. E., & Kingston, J. (2005). The development of the EASE model. *Annals of Occupational Hygiene, 49*(2), 103-110.

Tischer, M., Brendendiek-Kamper, S., & Poppek, U. (2003). Evaluation of the HSE COSHH Essentials Exposure Predictive Model on the basis of BauA field studies and existing substances exposure data. *Annals of Occupational Hygiene, 47*(5), 557-569.

Tijssen, S. & Links, I. (2002). *Ways for SMEs to assess and control risks from hazardous substances. Report of an international workshop held on 26 and 27 November 2001,* RR 014, TNO, HSE Books, ISBN 0 7176 2543 5.

Trägårdh, C. (2005). Presentation from the Swedish Work Environment Authority at the Swedish Associations of Occupational and Environmental Hygiene Conference April 28, 2005, Stockholm (unpublished).

UBA. (ed.). (undated). ECLIPS. *Europäisches Projekt zur Kontrolle der Einstufung und Kennzeichnung sowie der Sicherheitsdatenblätter von gefährlichen Zubereitungen. Österreich-Beilage. Zusammenfassung des Projektes und Auswertung der österreichischen Ergebnisse.* Vienna: Austrian Federal Environmental Agency. Download: www.umweltbundesamt.at/fileadmin/site/umweltthemen/chemikalien/ECLIPS_Oest erreich_Bericht.pdf.

Uberti-Bona, V., & Rodrigo, F. (in press). *Reflexiones sobre sistemas de inspección y sistemas de prevención.* Archivos de Prevención de Riesgos Laborales.

Van Heemskerk, F., van Blijswijk, M., Treur, H., Cobben, M., Wekema, E., & Verstappen, P. (2003, November). *Kleine bedrijven en arbo* [Small companies and OSH]. Report for the Ministry of Social Affairs and Employment by TNO and BMVS Management Consultants.

Van Niftrik, M. F. J, van Haandel, M., & en Goede, H. (2005). *Substitutie van kankerverwkkende en andere zeer gevaarlijke stoffen* [Substitution of carcinogenic and other dangerous substances. Progress report]. Voortgangsrapportage TNO Rapport V6716, Zeist.

Vickers, I., Baldock, R., Smallbone, D., James, P., Ekanem, I., & Bertotti, M. (2003). *Cultural influences on health and safety attitudes and behaviour in small firms.* HSE Research Report 150. Sudbury, UK: HSE Books.

Vincent, R., Dervilliers, J, Binstein, S. et al. (1996). *Evaluation of EASE 2.0 assessment of occupational exposures to chemicals.* INRS/CTIS, ECB.

Vogel, L. (1993). *Prevention at the workplace. An initial review of how the 1989 Community Framework Directive is being implemented.* Brussels: European Trade Union Bureau for Health and Safety.

Vogel, L. (1998). *Prevention at the workplace: The impact of Community Directives on preventive systems in Sweden, Finland, Norway, Austria and Switzerland.* Brussels: European Trade Union Technical Bureau for Health and Safety.

Voullaire, E., & Kliemt, G. (1995). Gefahrstoffe in Klein- und Mittelbetrieben; Neue Wege überbetrieblicher Unterstützung. Schriftenreihe der Bundesanstalt für Arbeitsschutz—Forschung—Fb 703. Dortmund, 205 pp.

VNCI. (2005). *Responsible Care report.* (VNCI—Vereniging van de Nederlandse Chemische Industrie—Association of the Dutch chemical industry).

Walters, D. R. (1987). Health and Safety and Trade Union Workplace Organisation: A case study in the printing industry. *Industrial Relations Journal, 18*(1), 40-49.

Walters, D. R. (2001). *Health and safety in small enterprises.* Brussels: Peter Lang.

Walters, D. R. (2002). *Working safely in small enterprises.* Brussels: ETUC.

Walters, D. R. (Ed). (2002). *Regulating health and safety management in the European Union.* Brussels: Peter Lang.

Walters, D. R. (2004). Worker representation and health and safety in small enterprises in Europe. *Industrial Relations Journal, 35*(2), 169-186.

Walters, D. R. (2005). The challenge of change for strategies on health and safety at work in the 21st century? *Policy and Practice in Health and Safety, 3*(2), 3-19.

Walters, D. R. (2006a, February). Rovers no more? *Health and Safety at Work*, pp. 21-22.

Walters, D. R. (2006b). One step forward, two steps back: Worker representation and health and safety in the United Kingdom. *International Journal of Health Services, 36*(1), 87-111.

Walters, D. R., & Grodzki, K. (2006). *Beyond limits? Dealing with chemical risks at work in Europe.* Oxford: Elsevier.

Walters, D. R.. Grodzki, K., & Walters, S. L. (2003). *The role of Occupational Exposure Limits in the health and safety systems of EU Member States.* HSE Research Report 172. Sudbury, UK: HSE Books.

Walters, D. R., & Kirby, P. (2002). *Training and action in health and safety.* London: TUC.

Walters, D. R., & Nichols, T. (2007). *Worker representation in workplace health and safety.* Basingstoke: Palgrave Macmillan.

Walters, D. R., Nichols, T., Connor, J., Tasiran, A. C., & Cam, S. (2005). *The role and effectiveness of safety representatives in influencing workplace health and safety*, HSE Research Report. Sudbury, UK: HSE Books.

Waterman, L. (2007). Occupational health in the UK: A personal view on the future for occupational health.

Westerholm, P., & Walters, D. R. (Eds). (2007). Supporting health at work: International perspectives on occupational health services, Leicester, IOSH, UK.

Wichtl, M., & Novak, H. (2002). Einsatz und praktische Anwendung des Pimexplus-Systems. In *Proceedings of the XVIIth World Congress on Safety and Health at Work*, Vienna 26-31 May 2002. Vienna: AUVA.

Wiseman, J., & Gilbert, F. (2002). *COSHH Essentials: Survey of firms purchasing this guidance.* Contract Research Report 434. Sudbury, UK: HSE Books.

Wright, M., Marsden, S., Antonelli, A., Norton, J., Norton Doyle, J., Genna, R., & Bendiq, M. (2005). *An evidence based evaluation of how best to secure compliance with health and safety law.* HSE Research Report 334. Sudbury, UK: HSE Books.

WSI (Wirtschafts- und Sozialwissenschaftliches Institut in der Hans-Böckler-Stiftung). (2004, July). Erste Ergebnisse einer WSI-Betriebsrätebefragung zu Gesundheitsbelastungen und Prävention am Arbeitsplatz. Download: http://www.boeckler.de/pdf/wsi_betriebsraetebefragung_gesundheit_07_2004.pdf

Zahm, S. H., & Blair, A. (2003). Occupational cancer among women: Where have we been and where are we going? *American Journal of Industrial Medicine, 44,* 565-575.

ZAI. (Ed.). (2004). *Die Arbeitsinspektion.* Vienna: Federal Ministry of Economics and Labour (Central Labour Inspectorate). Download: www.arbeitsinspektion.gv.at/AI/Arbeitsinspektion/

Zober, A. (2002). Information on occupational diseases due to chemical exposure in Germany. Personal communication. Quoted in: Risk & Policy Analysts Ltd.: *Assessment of the Impact of the New Chemicals Policy on Occupational Health,* prepared for European Commission, Environment Directorate-General. Final Report. Loddon (Norfolk), March 2003:101.

Index